# JOURNALISM: ETHICS AND CODES

# JOURNALISM:
## Ethics and Code

*(For PG Diploma & Degree Courses in Journalism & Mass Media)*

**Nayyar Shamsi**

**ANMOL PUBLICATIONS PVT. LTD.**
**NEW DELHI - 110 002 (INDIA)**

**ANMOL PUBLICATIONS PVT. LTD.**
4374/4B, Ansari Road, Daryaganj
New Delhi - 110 002
Ph.: 23261597, 23278000
Visit us at: www.anmolpublications.com

*Journalism: Ethics and Codes*



First Published, 2005



PRINTED IN INDIA

---

Published by J.L. Kumar for Anmol Publications Pvt. Ltd., New Delhi - 110 002 and Printed at Mehra Offset Press, Delhi.

# Contents

# Preface

In Modern world, Journalism is one discipline, which attracts people like any thing, but, it is equally challenging and drastic in cases. Particularly, under the new world order and in current global scenario, its value has increased manifold.

Apart from being a glorious profession, Journalism, today is a full-fledged subject, mastery of which leads one to a successful career and an all powerful status in society.

As a discipline, Journalism requires proper training and a comprehensive course, if possible. Although, there is no defined qualification for appointment as a journalist, in any capacity, in any media organisation, yet it is always better to be properly qualified and well-equipped with all essential knowledge.

Of course, there are books on Journalism but not in a great number. And, if one goes selective, then only a few books would rest in hand, as there is still a dearth for exclusive and exhaustive books on several streams of Journalism.

This series of books on Journalism is an effort to fill the abovesaid vaccum only. Here are books on all subjects and topics, related to Journalism. The undersigned is confident enough that this humble endeavour would prove to be worthy on the basis of its merits and receive a warm acceptance by students of journalism, scholars and the working journalists, as well.

**— Editor**

# 1

# Introduction

To the outsider, journalism and ethics are about as incongruous a mixture as you can get. Even to put the two words in the same sentence is to risk reducing the listener to helpless laughter.

To the insider on a mass-market tabloid, ethics are largely an irrelevance. Editors, pressured by intense competition for readers, demand that staff cut ethical corners; and competition among staff encourages some to respond. Lecturing these journalists about ethics is as pointless as advocating celibacy to sailors arriving in port after six months at sea.

To the insider working on a quality paper, where there is virtually unanimous agreement about basic professional morality, ethics are a code of principles to which all journalists should adhere, or at least feel guilty about if they do not. They are rarely, if ever, required to step outside this code.

Ethics, more than any other aspect of the job, are where personal circumstance produces experiences so that the different ethics employed are barely recognisable as the same thing. The reason is that ethics, as actually practised, are conditioned less by morals than by what is rewarded or punished in any given newspaper. On a British mass market tabloid (or agency serving one) journalists may be regarded, paid and promoted according to how many dramatic, possibly invasive, stories they produce. Not too many questions are asked about how they obtained them or what degree of exaggeration is involved. Indeed the news desk, or higher executives, often tell reporters what line they want, regardless of any reservations reporters have. Not much scope for Mr. or Ms. Proper here. At the other extreme - on a US paper enjoying a monopoly and sharing the same city as its sources and readers- reporters are judged and rewarded differently, with ethics playing a far greater part in their lives.

Ultimately the main factor in deciding what ethics are actually practised is competition. In monopoly situations, papers know that there is no rival paper to scoop them, and readers have no alternative to turn to-save for giving up papers altogether. This lack of competition gives the journalists the moral luxury of generally being able to apply far more idealised standards of professional ethics. In a mass market, highly competitive and with a macho culture, almost the only sanction on what papers will do to get a story, or publish once they have got it, is the prospect of upsetting readers, especially to the point where they will not buy the paper. Only then will word go out to the staff, and the little news agencies that feed them, that it is time to call a halt (perhaps only temporarily) to stealing pictures from the bereaved, invading hospitals where sick celebrities are being treated, publishing pictures of royal children in private moments, condemning a community for violence without sufficient evidence, or whatever. On tabloids especially, the periodic little eruptions of ethics that are sometimes seen nearly always come from proprietors acutely aware that readers can always, and maybe are about to, buy another paper. Or that the government is about to legislate.

But journalists have a sanction, too. We do not have to be mere creatures of the papers we work for; we have a choice. Just as readers can stop buying, so journalists can change jobs. We can decide that there are some things we will not do and leave the paper - either discreetly after having found another post, or publicly, in a blaze of righteous indignation. If more of us did that, and made clear our reasons for doing so, journalism would be better for it.

This element of moral choice, the distinction between how papers acting under commercial pressures expect us to behave and how we can choose to behave, explains why ethics have a daily purpose - or rather, two purposes. The first is to provide some kind of moral compass, telling us how far we are diverging from a desired route. So far as I know, the magnetic north in our trade is found in the clauses of an unwritten contract which should exist between all newspapers and their readers:

- Every story in the paper is a result of decisions made free of political, commercial or non-commercial pressure.
- None are there because of any favours or money exchanged.
- All stories are written and edited in a spirit of free enquiry, and chosen for publication entirely on their own merits, be they real or imagined.

Second, ethics provides a practical guide to the production of safe and credible journalism. Honestly, with plain dealing and with the removal of conflicts of interest are the best ways to do this job because they are the safest ways to do it. At the most base level, they keep you out of the courts and help you to sleep at nights. And, at the risk of shocking some of the more raunchy reporters, ethics are the most decent way to do the job, too, giving us attitudes to readers (and sources) that are based on some sensitivity, rather than mere sly commercial calculation.

## General Principles

Viewed like this, ethics are not some optional extra but are integral to every aspect of the job. This book therefore deals with them as they occur - in handling sources, asking questions, writing, etc. - and not in some moral parking lot tucked away from the main action. There are, however, some general principles and these have been gathered here.

***Journalists should Serve only their Papers and their Readers :*** If you want to be a propagandist, then go and work in public relations, or politics. Journalists should owe no loyalty to anyone or anything else; not a political party, source, commercial interest, non-commercial interest or particular cause, however worthy. Balanced journalism is difficult enough to achieve without such conflicts of interest. The Washington Post newspaper has a rule that its journalists cannot take part in any political activity. That includes marching on demonstrations. So when several Post reporters were spotted on an abortion rights demonstration, they were told they would not be allowed to cover anything touching on the abortion issue.

The dangers of allowing a missionary zeal for some cause to infect reporting are even more obvious. One of the more notorious examples is Walter Duranty, the New York Times correspondent in Moscow in the 1920s and 1930s. So taken was he by the ideology of the new Soviet Union that his reporting was often little more than propaganda. At the height of the famine in the Ukraine, for instance, largely engineered by Stalin to break local resistance to Soviet control, Duranty wrote of 'village markets overflowing with eggs, fruit, poultry, vegetables, milk and butter' at prices far lower than in Moscow. 'Anyone can see this is not famine, but abundance', he added; and a Pulitzer committee, knowing no better, gave him a prize. In fact, millions died, and Duranty knew this full well, telling colleagues in private that he thought the death toll was around ten million. Malcolm Muggeridge, the Manchester Guardian's reporter in Moscow at the time, called him 'the biggest liar of any journalist I have ever met.'

***Every Story should be an Honest Search for the Truth :*** Each story should be an open-minded attempt to find out what really happened, accompanied by a willingness to print that truth, however uncomfortable it may be to our own, or the paper's, cherished beliefs. Thus, journalists should not accept work which seeks to bolster a point of view in the face of evidence, or undertake reporting which aims to support a preconceived theory.

You would think this so self-evident that it would not need stating. But every day you can read reporting which stretches and strains the facts to fit a particular thesis. One of the worst examples in recent memory was committed by the Sun, Britain's biggest-selling daily. For reasons best known to himself, the then editor became convinced that Aids was a disease limited to drug addicts and homosexuals. On several occasions government statistics were wilfully manhandled to support this view. The most flagrant occasion was a story headlined 'Straight Sex Cannot Give You Aids —Official', which reported, among other absurdities, that the chances of getting Aids from heterosexual sex were 'statistically invisible. Anything else is homosexual propaganda.' Eventually, the volume of protests at this coverage produced an apology - which the paper ran at the bottom of page 28.

Here, and this is no isolated case, was reporting that deceived readers and possibly endangered them. Preconceived theories have no place in journalism. Newspapers should be at war with closed minds, not employing them.

***No Inducements to Publish should be Accepted :*** This means not only money and free gifts, but also the promise of advantage or preferment. It specifically means two things. The first is hidden advertising, where journalists or their papers take money for writing public relations pieces about firms or people which then appear in the editorial columns parading as normal stories. In recent years this has become a widespread practice in countries like Russia, and the temptation to write hidden advertising in places where pay is very poor is understandable. But that does not make it journalism. It is advertising, PR, puffs, whatever you call it, dressed up to look like journalism. It is a deception, and a damaging one. First, it breaks the basic contract with readers, with stories, purporting to be a normal editorial in print only because money has changed hands. Second, such deceptions destroy any trust that should exist between readers and papers. Third, the practice makes editors suspect their staff have taken bribes to write about a company when their story may be perfectly honest. Fourth, editors and publishers will, like hotel owners paying waiters low salaries because of tips, use hidden advertising as an excuse not to pay journalists properly. Fifth, it establishes that the journalists who do it have their pens and minds available for hire. What will they accept money for next? Writing favourable stories about criminal groups% Keeping stories about wrongdoing out of the paper: That is but a short step away from collecting information with a view to selling its destruction or suppression. In other words, blackmail.

(Lest anyone think this a good original money-making scheme, an American publisher called Robert Harrison got there first in the 1950s with a magazine called Confidential. It specialised in Hollywood scandal and, by paying large sums for tips and information, he and his investigators obtained decidedly intimate details of the stars' private lives. Each story was well-researched and Harrison's staff were not fussy about their methods, hiring prostitutes to trap victims, secretly taping and filming encounters and confessions. Sales of Confidential soared and eventually hit four million. But soon the temptation to sell the negatives, tapes and other evidence to wealthy stars proved too strong. The inevitable court case happened, a staff member killed herself, the editor shot his wife and himself in a New York taxicab, Harrison sold the magazine and both he and it went into a richly-deserved oblivion.)

Hidden advertising (which should be correctly labelled 'advertising' and typographically treated accordingly), is very rare in developed countries. Far more common is the acceptance by journalists of what they call 'freebies', that is, free trips with vacation companies, free meals from restaurants or free tickets from theatres, all given so that journalists can review them. The danger here is that the writer will feel obliged to write a favourable piece. This need not be so, and the dangers can be minimised and faith kept with the reader if it is made plain somewhere in the piece or in a footnote that the ticket/trip/meal or whatever was given free to the newspaper.

***Journalists should not Allow Advertisers to Influence, directly or indirectly, the Paper's Editorial Content :*** It is not unusual, especially on smaller, less profitable or local papers, for advertisers to try to use their commercial weight to bully the paper. This pressure should be resisted at all times. It normally comes from the paper's advertising department who will say to the editor that it would be helpful if this important client could have some 'good coverage'. A few years ago the Riverside Press-Enterprize, a paper in California, published a total of eleven news pieces and 22 photographs of a new department store called Nordstrom's in the six days before, during and immediately after its opening in the town. These 400 column inches appeared in the same week as 20 full pages of ads for the store. A coincidence? Unlikely.

More rarely, groups of advertisers act in concert to try to force the paper to change its coverage. When I took over as editor of a British provincial paper, one of the things I did was to stop the automatic reporting of all shop-lifting court cases because they were so common as to be boring. Within a week, all the department stores in the city approached the publisher and told him that unless reporting of all shop lifting cases was resumed they would withdraw their advertising, which was considerable. They said the coverage acted as a deterrent to wouldbe thieves. Luckily the publisher supported me. The advertisers' threat was not carried out.

The danger of giving in to advertisers' pressure, whether individual or collective, is that your content ceases to be freely chosen. You would also find that what is granted to one advertiser would soon be demanded by many. Give in once, and you would never be free of the pressure.

***Do not Use your Position to Threaten or Gain Advantage :*** A journalist has power. It should never be abused, either in the course of a story or in one's daily life. Prosecuting personal disputes with stores, neighbours, etc. by threatening exposure or reference to high-placed connections is bullying, and unsafe bullying at that. How could you ever write a future story about any person or organisation you have threatened in this way? How could you write about the connections you have used in your threat? You will be in their pocket for the favour you owe them.

Neither should you use your newspaper's headed notepaper to write a letter demanding preferential treatment, compensation for some alleged negligence or faulty service. It implies to the recipient that your paper exists as a sort of private protection racket for its staff.

***Do not Promise to Suppress Stories for Friendship or Favours:*** It sometimes happens that you are asked by someone to 'forget' a story, or part of it, in return for some favour, or even cash. It is clearly wrong to accept such an offer, for the same reasons as it is wrong to put in a story for favours. When friends are involved, refusal might be more delicately phrased, but just as swift and sure. So should it be with colleagues, as these two stories illustrate.

The first case comes from Oregon in the United States where a few years ago a local television station reported that the long-time chief of staff of the state's Republican senator had served for 2 5 years as director of a bank that collapsed and was bailed out at a cost to taxpayers of $100 million. It was suggested that the man's involvement with the bank may have influenced the senator's position on bank deregulation and the subsequent bailout. The story was picked up by the Associated Press and was the talk of the state, but the main newspaper in the state, the Oregonian, chose to ignore it. It also ignored allegations a week later that the chief of staff's official travel, at taxpayer's expense, had included 52 trips to New York, where he published an annual guidebook to the city that had earned him more than $1 million.

The paper's reluctance to write this story may have had something to do with the fact that the chief of staff wrote a weekly column for the paper. It eventually published parts of the story only after the Washington Post gave the revelations national exposure.

Contrast this with a paper called the Daily Item in Sudbury, Pennsylvania. Among the daily stories from the police in one issue was an uncensored account of charges filed against a town resident for driving at an unsafe speed under the influence of alcohol. The item included the man's name, age, address and occupation - editor of the Daily Item. Which paper would you trust most, the Item or the Oregonian?

***Do not Invent or Improve Information :*** Inventing information is obviously wrong and dangerous. So, too, is even a light doctoring of the facts, embellishment of the truth or temporary amnesia about certain details that inconvenience the main thrust of the story. Your report will be a cheat. This applies with equal force to photographers and the dishonest 'set-up' picture, where an event or situation is staged to imitate some alleged reality.

Some news photographers in Western Europe also have been known to carry around in their cars certain 'props' to insert into pictures. A well-known ploy used to be to have a child's shoe, or teddy bear available, so that photographers covering disasters like train or air crashes, could set this prop among the wreckage for a 'poignant' picture. Such pictures have now become a cliche. Besides, there was always the danger that the passenger list, when finally issued, would reveal that there were no children aboard. Deliberate fakes, or at least the detected ones, are very rare. Perhaps the most famous recent example was Janet Cooke's Pulitzer-winning story in the Washington Post. It was called 'Jimmy's World' and told the story of an eight-year-old heroin addict. Jimmy, however, did not exist. The story was an invention from beginning to end. When the fiction was revealed the Post saw that, with hindsight, there were many warning signs. Some staff, for instance, had harboured doubts about the story at the time, but had either thought it best to keep quiet, or thought the story 'too good to check'. This journalistically-lethal attitude was encouraged by Cooke's warnings that her (and Jimmy's) life would be endangered if checks were made. Nor did anyone think to check Cooke's own credentials. She said she was a graduate of Vassar, had a master's degree from Toledo, studied at the Sorbonne, was an accomplished pianist and spoke four languages. No editor thought this a tall order for someone aged just 25. Among these executives, ironically, was Watergate hero Bob Woodward.

***You should not Benefit Personally from Information you Acquire :*** Using information you have acquired in order to make a commercial gain before the story is published is a temptation most likely to be faced by business reporters. A few years ago a reporter for the Wall Street journal called R. Foster Whinans co-wrote a column based on information from sources that traded stocks. He decided to sell information to a stock-broker friend.

He was paid $31,000 to leak the contents of the column to several stock-brokers, enabling them to buy and sell shares in companies before this information became public and thus would affect the price of the stock. The brokers made about $690,000 from the leaked information. Whinans and the brokers were eventually caught and found guilty in court of violations of the Securities Exchange Act by misappropriating confidential information. Whinans was sentenced to 18 months in prison, five years' probation, 400 hours of community service and a $ 500 fine. Many Western papers now make their financial staff declare their investments and financial dealings.

## Complicated Matters

The above issues are clear-cut. But a lot of issues in reporting are more complicated. Hard and fast rules are difficult to design and apply. Take phoney by-lines, for example. Plainly wrong if used routinely to give the impression a paper's staff is several times what it is, the practice is a good deal less harmful when sports editors use it to disguise the identity of, say, staff reporters from a daily moonlighting to cover events for a Sunday. Since the story purports to be written by someone who does not in fact exist, I would still contend phoney by-lines are a deceit. It is particularly unsafe where the story may be challenged, or even end in a law suit. Who do you produce in court', An actor taking the name of the fictitious reporter?

***Privacy :*** There have been many attempts to be dogmatic about privacy, but none can be sustained beyond the most simplistic instances. We all agree that if a President fools around with a junior employee in his office, there is a legitimate story. If someone is asking for our votes (and our taxes to pay their wages), we have a right to know about them, their lives and how they impact on their duties. On the other hand, few would suggest writing a story about a second junior employee fooling around, in their own time, with a third. The sex lives of private citizens, however fascinating, are not regarded as a legitimate target for a story, unless the law is broken. But between these two extremes, in all the less clear-cut cases, is the gaping space where we argue about privacy.

The conventional, and largely sensible, guideline is that the person should be a public figure and the invasion of their privacy must have a legitimate justification based on the public interest, not merely tickling the public's curiosity. If a man standing for public office makes a great deal of public fuss about morality and the virtues of family life, but you can prove he has a string of mistresses, then it is right to publish a story. His double standards are clearly relevant to public life.

There are two problems with this conventional wisdom. First, if a paper thinks the story is sufficiently entertaining or salacious, almost any 'public interest' pretext can be dredged up. Second, justifications tend to be applied in a partisan way: papers defend the privacy of those they admire and invade the privacy of those they seek to destroy.

Part of the answer lies in that traditionally most unjournalistic of qualities: sensitivity. Journalists must have very good reasons for invading someone's privacy and should also be aware of the consequences of such reporting. A few years ago in Britain a policeman began an affair. His wife learnt about it and persuaded him to give up his mistress. The jealous lover then told a national paper and her account was printed under the headline, 'The Love Life of a Detective'. As a result, the couple's child was teased at school, the husband had to give up his job and the family had to move. Some may think that a fitting punishment for his original sin. I do not think so, and neither would I like to justify that reporting.

***Law-breaking :*** An issue which comes up less frequently is where journalists get involved in wrong-doing in order to investigate it. This is not a good idea. Breaking the law in pursuit of a story is both wrong and unsafe. It removes whatever moral legitimacy their reporting may otherwise have had.

Sometimes reporters investigating drug-dealing, crime or prostitution learn information that should be passed straight to the police. I think you should do that. Otherwise you are compromising your legitimacy, and may also be putting the lives of innocent citizens at risk. Only the police - not you - can judge that. (This condition about the safety of citizens also applies to the situation where journalists are accused of merely spectating in disaster or war situations and not doing anything to help those who are in danger. Our rule should be that if you can have any influence on the outcome of a situation you should follow your normal instincts and act to help.) : Never accept a free ticket from a theatre manager, a free ride from the chamber of commerce, or a favour from a politician.

# 2

# Ethical Codes

'Right to Privacy', is a rapidly developing concept. It was Thomas Cooley, the American scholar who, about a century back, named this, then extremely nebulous concept as privacy, defining it simply as 'a right to be let alone'. Since then, some aspects of the right of individual to be free from and protected against highly offensive publicity, have come to be recognised in several countries, including USA, France, Federal Republic of Germany, Canada, Denmark and the Netherlands.

## Right to Privacy

Right to Privacy has been recognised by the International Convention of Human Rights (1948), Article 12 of the Universal Declaration of Human Rights made by the Convention (which was ratified in 1978), states:

> No one shall be subjected to arbitrary interference with his privacy, family, home or correspondence, not to attacks upon his honour and reputation. Everyone has the right to the protection of the law against such interference or attacks.

Article 8 of the European Convention of Human Rights (1953) also makes a similar declaration.

Though privacy has not been mentioned anywhere in the Constitution of the United States, yet its Supreme Court has held that it is a fundamental personal right emanating from the totality of the constitutional scheme.

A general right of privacy as such does not find a place in any law of the country.

There is no provision in the Indian Constitution, or any statute specifically recognising a right to privacy, though some of its aspects such as defamation, nuisance, criminal trespass, criminal breach of trust, copyright, etc., are indirectly protected by law as actionable wrongs or even as offences with penal sanctions.

There is a school of thought which holds that this right is a fundamental right integral to 'personal liberty' guaranteed by Article 21 of the Constitution and also as a derivative of the freedom guaranteed by Article 19(1) (a).

In Kharak Singh vs. State of U.P., while holding that the domiciliary visit by the police to the petitioner's house was without the authority of law, Justice Subba Rao of the Supreme Court made the following observations:

> It is true that our Constitution does not expressly declare a right to privacy as a fundamental right, but the said right is an essential ingredient of personal liberty. Every democratic country sanctifies domestic life; it is expected to give him rest, physical happiness, peace of mind and security. In the last resort a person's house where he lives with his family is his 'castle'. It is his rampart against encroachments on his personal liberty.... Indeed, nothing is more deleterious to a man's physical happiness and health than a calculated interference with his privacy.

In Govind vs. state of M.P., the Supreme Court observed:

> Even assuming that the right to personal liberty...and the freedom of speech create an independent right of

> privacy as an emanation from them which one can characterise, a fundamental right, we do not think the right is absolute.

Several other scholars, including retired judges, are also inclined to favour the view expressed by Justice Subha Rao in Kharak Singh's case.

**Concept of Privacy**

The concept of privacy despite its growth in the post - World War I era, is a somewhat cloudy topic, the precise parameters of which are not clear. It is still not capable of a precise, all-embracing and satisfactory legal definition. Various attempts made in the past to devise an exact and comprehensive definition of this right have not succeeded. The Younger Committee on Privacy in UK (1972) found that the old seminal formulation of privacy being, 'the right to be let alone', was unrealistic and means different things to different people and changes significantly over relatively short periods. Judgements in the past, in the committee's view, would be an unreliable guide for the courts to any current evaluation of 'privacy'.

The U.K. Calcutt Committee on privacy and related matters in its report (June 1990), accepted that there is little possibility of producing a precise or exhaustive definition of 'privacy'.

Despite the difficulty of formulating a satisfactory and exhaustive legal definition of privacy, popular demands for protecting this right, at any rate some aspects of it, with statutory sanctions against unwarranted invasions of privacy and unauthorised intrusions by unscrupulous media men, detectives and others upon the private lives of the people, have been made with increasing stridency after the Second World War.

The developments which provided justification for these demands have been neatly summed up by the Second Press Commission (1982) as below:

The concept of privacy has been widely discussed in recent years mainly because of two developments:

(1) the growth of the modern state into a powerful administrative body capable of governing every aspect of the life of its citizens, and

(2) the technological revolution which has thrown up devices with which it is possible to fantastically pry into a man's house even without his knowledge. Microphones reduced to the size of a matchhead can pick up sound waves and transmit the same to eavesdroppers. Infrared light techniques enable a room to be watched and photographed from an adjoining room even through opaque walls.

Sophisticated photographic equipments enable photographs being taken from very long distances. Man's house is no longer sacrosanct and inviolate.

The emergence of devices for wiretapping, eavesdropping and bugging and the growth of computers, it is said, has allowed vast masses of information to be collected in centralised and easily accessible locations and freely and rapidly disseminated to other persons with a specific interest in the particular information. It is further said that a situation has come about in which a person may find himself threatened and uncertain in a kind of psychological prison fashioned by a complex technology not knowing when and by whom he is being watched or overheard. An individual may find himself manipulated and overseen by those who have control of a mass of computerised data relating to him which lays bare everything he has done and which may also distort truth by recording false, inaccurate or incomplete information about him.

Thus, an individual is said to have become more vulnerable in regard to his personal, private and emotional feelings on account of adverse publicity, scandal mongering, vulgar curiosity and sensationalism. It is stressed that there is dire need to protect persons from consequent emotional disturbances, anxieties, humiliation and embarrassment.

**Law Commission Report**

The Law Commission of India, in its 42nd Report (1971), Chapter 23, while observing that it is not advisable to have comprehensive legislation to deal with all aspects of invasion of privacy—a subject which was still in a rudimentary state—suggested that to begin with, those invasions of privacy be made penal offences which would amount to eavesdropping and unauthorised photography.

Pursuant to these recommendations of the Law Commission, the Indian Penal Code (Amendment) Bill, 1978 was passed by the Rajya Sabha on March 23, 1978. However, owing to the dissolution of the Lok Sabha, this Bill lapsed. The Bill proposed to insert in the Indian Penal Code, three sections:

(1) Section 490 sought to make eavesdropping as also publication of information obtained through the use of artificial listening or recording apparatus, offences punishable with imprisonment or with fine or with both;

(2) Section 491 would make the taking of an unauthorised photograph, intended or likely to cause annoyance to any person, elsewhere than in a public place, an offence punishable with imprisonment or fine or with both;

(3) Section 492 would exempt from the operation of the preceding Section 430 and 491, certain public servants and persons acting under their directions, in good faith, in the interest of the security of the state, prevention, detection or investigation of offences, the administration of justice or the maintenance of public order.

These recommendations were endorsed by the Second Press Commission in 1982. After examining the question of privacy in the context of the Press, the Commission concluded:

> We are of the view that the Press should not be unduly inhibited in performing its important function of giving news in the public interest as distinct from news that may ponder to prurient or morbid curiosity. But a correct balance has to be struck between the citizen's claims to privacy and the public's right to information. We recommend that the Press Council should be interested with the responsibility of looking

into complaints of invasion of privacy and of monitoring the performance of the Press in this regard. To this end, Section 13(2) of the Press Council Act, 1978 may be suitably amended.

**Press Council Act**

It is submitted that even under the Press Council Act, 1978 as it stands at present, the Council is competent to hear and determine a complaint alleging invasion by a newspaper journalist of the personal privacy of the complainant, where such invasion offends against the canons of journalistic ethics, decency or public good taste. In the past, complaints of invasion of privacy by the Press made to the Council were not many. The Council had a few occasions only to enunciate through its adjudications, norms to regulate the conduct of the Press vis-a-vis some aspects of privacy. Nevertheless, violations of personal privacy seem to be on the increase.

***Investigative Journalism :*** Investigative journalism, world over—India not excepted—is becoming evermore aggressive, often intruding deep into the preserves of personal privacy, where no public interest is involved. It is, therefore, high time to lay down norms of conduct for journalists fishing for information in grey areas where the line between 'public interest' and 'personal privacy' is blurred. Such a course would also conduce to the fulfilment of India's international commitment under Article 12 of the Universal Declaration of Human Rights (1948). In performing this task, the Council can legitimately adopt, by analogy, principles of law and ethics evolved for protection of personal privacy in certain other democratic countries.

In India scandalous and defamatory news is published by some district newspapers and magazines which thrive on blackmail. Here we are mentioning of a news item published by a district newspaper with a headline, 'Tehsildar Ke Kale Karname' (Bad deeds of Tehsildar) with a pointer that details would be published in the next issue. The details were never published. There could be a compromise after consideration.

***Western Law*** : In some western countries, like USA and Australia, there are deterrent laws on publication of news which intrude into the private life of the individuals unless it is in the public interest to do so. The administration of justice is quick to redress the grievances of the aggrieved. Such heavy penalties are imposed on the erring parties that they would think twice before publishing defamatory news.

In Sweden, for instance, the publication of the identity of a suspect or even a convicted person in the Press is considered unethical as this could hamper his rehabilitation in society, besides causing considerable trouble for his family.

According to Dr. Thorston Cars, the Swedish Press Ombudsman, this might seem astonishing, but the Swedish Press is not allowed to disclose the names in such cases without public interest.

But if the story involved a politician, bureaucrat or a trade union leader with power in society, he could be identified to highlight that 'he is not the right man for such a position.'

But otherwise the Press could not disclose the person's identity though the crime itself could be reported as well as the investigation.

In fact, in the assassination case of Swedish Prime Minister Olof Palme, Thortson along with the Press Council of Sweden had to rebuke some newspapers for having published the name and picture of a youngman who was arrested as a suspect in that case. Ironically, just a day after the publication of his name and photograph in the newspapers he was released, but his reputation was totally ruined.

The young man complained to Dr. Cars. The three of the 150 odd newspapers which had published his name and photograph argued that many foreign newspapers had done so. But Dr. Cars pointed out that this was a very 'bad exercise' as the provision in their code of ethics was to protect a person from getting his reputation ruined in his own country. He also wanted to know of what legitimate interest this matter was to the Swedish public as the youngman had not been prosecuted or convicted.

The person concerned sued the largest of the three newspapers for one million rupees. It is rare that an appeal is filed against the decision of the Ombudsman.

**Scene in India**

In India we print what we like, secure in the knowledge that people hardly ever sue. There is little respect for the privacy of others.

In addition to district newspapers, the film magazines are galore with scandalous love stories with no fear of libel suits. In the USA they would have to pay a million dollars in damages for such stories.

The tendency to inject an element of sensation in the national Press is noticeable, facts are not checked before publishing them. This is eroding the credibility of the Press. Public curiosity must not be allowed to replace public interest.

***Pamella's Care :*** During 1989, the Pamella Bordes affair rocked Britain and India. The British and the Indian newspapers carried stories about her love affair on the front page. The Indian Press did not even spare her mother and family. Stories on Bordes could be justified in public interest, but it was totally unjustified to drag her mother in this affair.

One national daily carried the following news item which was objectionable and defamatory.

Head line: Pamella's mother too has defence links

> New Delhi: Mr. Pratap Singh, chairman of the Haryana State Small Industries & Export Corporation Ltd., demanded repatriation of Ms Pamella Bordes, who, he claimed, had access to India's defence secrets because of her mother's alleged intimacy with the former defence Minister, Mr. Bansi Lal. Talking to newsmen here, Mr. Pratap Singh, who is Mr. Devi Lal's second son, alleged that Pamella's mother, Mrs. Shakuntala Chaudhury, had a meteoric rise in her life

> after she lost her husband in the Indo-Chinese war in 1962, 'only because of her intimacy with Mr. Bansi Lal'.

Mr. Pratap Singh demanded an inquiry by the Central and the state government into the 'scandals' of Pamella and her mother 'so that people occupying high positions within India are exposed'. He refused to name the other who, he said, had relations with Pamella. 'I will wait for some more time before naming the other VIPs who had links with Pamella. Many heads will roll in India also he added.

He said he was shocked to know through Press reports that Mrs. Chaudhury had disowned her daughter after Pamella became Miss India in 1982 and took to modelling. 'Official records will prove that she took earned leave from the Haryana government between May 5, and July 31, 1987, then extended it till August 4, 1987, and again extended it till December 25, 1987, when she went to the US and the UK for her son's treatment. At that time, she did mention in her leave application that she would stay at her daughter's house in the UK and the US.'

'All this happened due to her influence on Mr. Bansi Lal and some other high officials' he said. The government must dig out her past to know how she and her daughter were used by an international spy ring to ferret out India's defence secrets,' he added.

To support his allegation, Mr. Pratap Singh said that Mrs. Chaudhury was a 'mere matriculate' when she was nominated to the Haryana Civil Service (HCS) in 1972. Earlier, he claimed Mrs. Chaudhury was given the post of a 'matron' in a women's hostel in Chandigarh when Mr. Bansi Lal was a member of the Rajya Sabha.

He claimed that Mr. Bansi Lal got her 12.5 acres of land in Hissar from the war widow's quota. He also got her a gas agency from the same quota.

He said Mrs. Chaudhury was not what she had been projected through the Press.

It is interesting' to know about the love affairs of Pamella Bordes and the public men involved in it.

Pamella Bordes, nee Singh, was born in New Delhi on April 18, 1962, is not even referred to by her real name anymore. The tabloids have rechristened her with several names.

The 20-year-old girl who flew out of her nest in 1982 after winning the Miss India competition is now flowingly referred to as 'Sauch Pamella', 'Stunna Pamella', 'Sex Siren Pamella Bordes', 'Sultry Sex Bomb Pamella', or something just as 'Stunning West minister call girl', or simply 'High Society Hooker'. It seems the Fleet Street hacks worked overtime on all the double meaning adjectives starting with the letter'S' and the result is that this girl at the centre of the storm may never again be called what she was when she left India. Pamella's fortunes took a turn in 1982 when she was crowned Miss India, bagging numerous advertising assignments and the nomination to the Miss Universe competition in Peru. She was not successful in Peru but instead of returning home, she apparently had a rather longish stay in New York where, according to published reports, she had affairs with American men and a Libyan arms dealer. Since then, she has only returned to India on holidays, reportedly in the company of rich Arabs and looking every bit expensive.

She later met a French record producer, Dominique Jacques Bordes, in Paris, and married him within a few months. The marriage was an attempt to get around the European immigration laws and shed the last trace of her Indianness.

She changed her name from Pamella Singh to Pamella Bordes and abandoned her husband just three months after the marriage, crossing the channel to London looking for greener pastures.

Dominique, according to the tabloids, accepts that she has used him but does not grudge it. Like a typical Frenchman, he says: It was worth it...she was great sexually.

But in the long list of her alleged lovers in London, not a single one has had the guts or the decency to say a few nice things about her ever since the News of the World, dubbed 'The News of the Screws' by the satirical fortnightly *Private Eye,* led their weekly issue of March 12 with the banner headline: 'Call girl works in Commons.' The *Now* story alleges that Pamella Bordes, who worked as a Research Assistant on £3000 for Tory MP David Shaw on the issue of scrapping the fixed prices for books, was doubling as a high society prostitute.

The *Now* hacks had actually laboured on the story very seriously, sending, one of their colleagues as a customer pretending to be a Hong Kong film producer. Once the story was out, causing embarrassment to the fellow tabloid rags, Pamella Bordes went underground and out-popped her numerous lovers with lurid details of their affairs.

According to various reports, Pamella Bordes, after her arrival in London befriended a certain Tony Le Ray Cook restaurant Critic of *2 Boardroom,* a magazine distributed free exclusively to a very rich clientele. It is difficult and pointless to figure out the actual order of her friendship.

The published accounts and society pictures show in great detail that she moved into the very exclusive circuit of the rich and powerful which included the Sports Minister, Colin Moyniham a man of less than average looks.

The fact that her charmed circle included only Conservative politicians were greatly exploited by the opposition Labour MPs. The following Monday after the story appeared in the *Now,* Labour MPs were vigorously flaunting copies of the tabloid, which in normal circumstances they love to hate because of its virulently anti Labour political stance.

Since then Labour politicians have been demanding a full investigation into the scandal because of its alleged security repercussions.

Apart from Tory politicians, Pamella's name has been linked with Andrew Neil, editor of *The Sunday Times* and the Chairman of the recently launched Sky Satellite television company both owned by media magnet Rupert Murdoch; Charles Daniels of Pearl and Deen Company, Bungalow Hill Wiggins, the former lover of soap opera star, Joan Collins, and various other show biz personalities.

One man who has taken exception to his name being associated with Pamella Bordes is Donald Trelford, the editor of *The Liberal Observer* Sunday newspaper.

In January 1992, Pamella Bordes came to Bombay on an assignment from *The Sunday Mail* to take photographs for an article on the Indian film industry. After an interview she gave to Rahul Singh of *The Times of India,* this is how the latter described her.

'She has lovely hair, a beautiful complexion and there is that famous generous mouth below the high cheekbones. She is taller than I expected and very trim-looking in her denim jeans and black T. Shirt. But her eyes are easily her best feature—expressive and animated. She has a confidence which belies her 30 years and she turns out to be extremely articulate, choosing her words like a veteran politician. I had promised that I would let her tell her story, so here goes.'

Here are some of the excerpts from Rahul Singh's interview with Pamella Bordes:

What have you been doing in the past three years since the scandal:

I have been healing myself.

From what ?

From the unmitigated disaster that befell me three years ago. I'm trying to reconstruct my life. I had a nervous break-down which lasted two years. I lost 30 pounds, all my hair fell on. It was a very frightening experience. Before I did anything, I had to get my mind in order. Some people can be very sensitive and fragile and if you disturb that equilibrium it takes a long time to repair things. I spent the first year being with nature, by the trees, painting and drawing. Then I took up photography very seriously as a form of therapy and it has worked very well.

Is that what you do for a living ?

Yeah. You have to work a lot, you have to syndicate, take stock pictures, come put with stories, do a lot of research and then you have to try and go on good assignments, that pay well.

It's not easy. But that's all I do with my life. My work is my life from morning to night. I do nothing else, my whole energy goes into it.

Is that what you're doing now in India ?

"Yes, I'm taking photos for an article on the Indian film industry which has been commissioned by the *Mail* on Sunday. Mihir Bose is writing the article. I have also worked for the *Independent* on Sunday and the *Sunday Telegraph* and done portraiture—I am very strong on portraiture. I am a very visual person.

Is photography a good livelihood ?

Well, I don't own a house, or a car and take public transport. I don't even have one piece of jewellery. But I break even.

Going back a little, tell me about your upbringing ?

My father, who was a Major in the Indian Army was killed in the 1962 war with China. He was a war hero. I went to boarding school in Sanawar when I was just five years old then, when I was 13 or 14,1 was sent to the Maharani Gayatri Devi school in Jaipur. I used to read a lot, my father's books. By the time I was 12 or 13, I had read books which were for grown-ups. I grew up very quickly and I was aching to get up and see the world. It was a very lonely period for me. I felt constricted.

Did you go to College ?

Very briefly. I did some modelling and then won the Miss India contest.

You went to Lima, Peru for the Miss Universe contest and then disappeared. Why ?

I did not really want to come back to India and thought this was a brilliant opportunity to escape, to do all the things I had wanted to. I had my dreams. I didn't want to come back to an arranged marriage. I did not want to be intellectually stunted. I'm too much of a free spirit. I don't want to stay at home and knit. I don't want to knit sock for the rest of my life.

What about your family ?

My relationship with my family had not really jelled. My brother is a very reclusive character and I could not live up to my mother's idealism. So the umbilical cord was cut a long time ago.

You were in the U.S. for some time, then went to Paris and got married and divorced there and then landed up in England. What happened there? Did you start moving in high society ?

No it didn't happen like that. I had a boyfriend who was a bit of a lad and he was a very social person and I met a lot of people through him. Andrew Neil, the editor of the Sunday Times—he still is the editor—came much later.

Then you became a researcher for the House of Commons Didn't you?

Well after my affair with Andrew Neil was over, I didn't know what I wanted to do. I even went to cooking school to Cordon Bleu, and started a catering business. But there was no intellectual stimulation in that, in organising lunch parties. Satellite T.V. stations were coming up and I wanted to become a presenter for one of them. Then a Conservative MP who was a friend suggested that while I was waiting why not work in the House of Commons. That's how the House of Commons job came along. But I must make it clear that I was not really working there. I was not getting a salary. I was just helping out with research, with writing speeches. That House of Commons pass which they made such a big fuss about—security threat and all that—was no big deal. It only allowed me to go where tourists could go as well.

How did the story become such a big one that the British papers started talking about the government falling and why did you become such a focus of attention and media hype ?

Well, that's when the film scandal on the Profumo affair came out. The same ingredients were there but actually nothing was happening. How could I bring down the government, when I don't know the Thatcher government? Absolute rubbish and sensationalism. If I didn't know these Fleet Street editors the story would have died. Andrew Neil is not very popular with his staff, he's not much liked by people and I also know the editor of The Observer. It was a set up and I had no protection. Everybody abandoned me. One veteran Indian photographer even made £ 70,000 from the photos he had taken of me earlier.

What do you mean set-up ? Was it some kind of a conspiracy against you?

Yes, I think so. And now after three years, I know who set me up and who the culprits were but there's nothing I can do about it. I shall write about it in my memoirs not now. I am too young, but may be 20 years later.

Why didn't you sue for libel or take the matter up with the British Press Council ?

The Press Council is useless and to sue costs a lot of money. Just to write a legal letter costs a thousand pounds. I did not have that kind of money.

Yet after such a terrible and traumatic experience, why have you decided to base yourself in England?

For work reasons. It's very good place to do research from. But eight or nine months of the year I spend out of England. I am only going back there in July.

You must have had film offers—does India figure in your future plans?

I have already started getting film offers, but it's all so surreal. I am firmly on the other side of the camera now. I want to be taken seriously in my work. I'm coming into my prime. If s a great age for me. Yes, I want to work in India, cover Punjab, Nagaland. A lot of people here have written to me, saying. 'How can we help you?'

The interview—the first one she has ever given in India, she tells me—has lasted for an hour. We are both drained. But she stays at my place for another couple of hours, sipping soda (she does not drink alcohol) and having pot luck while picking tips from the photographer.

She has that haunting quality that so many talented, beautiful and complex women have. I don't really know what to make of her. Is she an Indian tragedy or an Indian triumph? I don't think she knows herself.

***Sharif's Care :*** In the issue of November 24-30, 1991, The Sunday Observer, a newspaper belonging to Reliance group, front paged a story on the romantic affair between the Pakistan Prime Minister, Mr. Nawaz Sharif, and an Indian citizen Dilshad Sheikh, sister of movie stars, Feroz Khan, Sanjay and Akbar Khan.

The story in The Sunday Observer ran as follows:

***'Nawaz Sharif's Indian Friend'***

New Delhi, Nov. 23 (1991): A few whispered words crooned over the telephone in soft memory of a brief but torrid encounter last summer, today threatens a government's survival.

The romantic peccadillo would hardly have been news were it not that the man was Pakistani Prime Minister Nawaz Sharif and his mysterious lady love with an Indian socialite, the auburn haired sister of the filmi Khan clan, Dilshad.

The controversy, limited initially to the tabloid Press of Pakistan, has snowballed into major scandal in both countries today. The mounting opposition to Sharif—who is backed by the conservative Mullahs and the Jamaat-i-Islam—has pounced on it insisting that the Pakistani High Commissioner in New Delhi Abdus Sattar had warned Islamabad that the Bangalore based beauty was a Research and Analysis Wing (RAW) agent.

On this side of the border, ministerial circles are *abuzz* with talk of audio recordings of Sharif's crooning of sweet-nothings and snatches of popular Hindi film songs over the telephone to Dilshad. The RAW, it is believed, has been asked to 'keep an eye' on the beautiful widow of a Kashmiri businessman Javed Sheikh.

As for Dilshad, the sister of Feroz, Sanjay and Akbar, she has denied any romantic liaison with the Pakistani Premier. She reportedly told a friend, 'I may be no angel, but I'm not involved with him. The vivacious Dilshad had gone to Pakistan for a wedding last May. She became the toast of the Pakistani jet-set during that whirlwind visit. Feted as 'the subcontinent's most beautiful woman' by the publishers of the fashion magazine *Liboss*, she met Sharif at a party thrown by the Saigols, textile magnates of Pakistan. If the tabloid Press is to be believed, assignations at the hill station, Murree, followed soon.

But for all Dilshad's disclaimers about the 'dangerous liaison' with the married Sharif, the allegation has stuck.

Even her plans to visit relatives in Kashmir have had to be shelved for the militants there have placed her on their hit list for embroiling their supporter Sharif in a controversy.

Mean while, the Pakistani High Commission here claims that it has been more than six months since they last issued a visa to Dilshad.

The affair was first unveiled by *Sunday Times*, London. A one-para item last month called it 'the Romeo and Juliet story of the subcontinent'. It, however, did not identify Dilshad. Sharif is the second Pakistani Premier to be involved in such a controversy. In the 1960s Islamabad had been rocked by President Ayub Khan's alleged love affair with a London call girl Christine Keeler.

Expressing acute distress at this news item, Akbar Khan, Dilshad's brother issued the following statement: 'We are a family that lives for our honour. We even die for our honour.'

The blot on his family's reputation became apparent when he returned after a hard days work to find his home was no longer a castle. It was, instead, surrounded by a horde of journalists, trying to get an interview with Ms Sheikh, who is a widow with three children.

Akbar Khan said: 'This vile reporting has even reached the school where my sister's daughter is studying.' According to him the family first heard of the whole thing when a Pakistani tabloid published these accusations. But he was surprised and shocked to see the article in *The Sunday Observer*. 'It was vile and degrading whoever wrote it has no respect whatsoever for women.'

In an emotional letter to the editor-in-chief of *The Observer* group of publications, Dilshad claimed that the news item has exposed her family to 'unjustified contempt, prejudice, public hatred and the ultimate peril of threat to life' (J&K militants).

Emphasising that the report was false and baseless, Ms Sheikh added: 'your paper has shown a cynical disregard for truth and published a grossly libellous story, which all right thinking people would regard as imputing certain conduct and qualities to me....'

She said the paper did not bother to check facts before publishing the articles, clearly indicating that it was 'bent upon' publishing a defamatory canard.

'The truth is that I have never met Nawaz Sharif anywhere, I have never seen him in person at any stage of my life. I have never talked to him or communicated with him in any matter whatsoever.'

*The Sunday Observer* report had alleged that Dilshad had gone to Pakistan to attend a wedding last May. She is reported to have met Sharif at a party thrown by the Saigols, a top industrialist family there.

M's Sheikh contended that the article had compounded the libel by claiming she was a Research and Analysis Wing (RAW) agent. *The Observer* report had mentioned opposition members in Pakistan 'insisting' that the Pakistan High Commissioner in New Delhi, Mr. Abdus Sattar had warned Islamabad that Ms Sheikh was a RAW agent.

A letter dated November 26 from Mr. Sattar to Mr. Akbar Khan, brother of Ms Sheikh was given to *The Times of India*. It reads: 'I am distressed to read in *The Sunday Observer* of November 24, 1991 reference to a baseless allegation that I had warned Islamabad' to the effect that your sister was a RAW Agent. 'The allegation is a transparent issue of lies, transparent because no newspaper has access to what I report to my government and its because I had made no such statement about your sister.'

Ms Sheikh asked *The Sunday Observer* to publish an apology on the front page of all the editions as a first banner story, with her photograph with equal prominence like the original story was published.

She added. 'I call upon you *(Sunday Observer)* to confirm in writing, within the next 48 hours, that you will do so. You will also confirm that you will not publish any more libellous stories or statements about me. In case you choose not to confirm in writing that you will not do as requested, I will take all necessary legal actions against you at your cost and risk.'

The Editor-in-Chief of the *Observer* group of publications, Mr. Pritish Nandy, was arrested and later released by the Bombay police for publishing this story.

The arrest was a result of Rs 1 crore defamation case filed by Dilshad Begum in a city court of Srinagar.

On December 20,1991, the Supreme Court stayed till January 10 the prosecution pending in a Srinagar court against the Editor-in-Chief of *The Sunday Observer* Mr. Pritish Nandy and two others for a write up alleging intimate relations between Ms Dilshad Sheikh and the Prime Minister of Pakistan, Mr. Nawaz Sharif.

Chief Justice M.H. Kania, before whom the matter was mentioned in the morning, also stayed the execution of the warrant of arrest issued against Mr. Nandy, the editor Mr. Chandan Mitra, and the printer and publisher of the weekly, Mr. Baljit Kapoor. The accused were directed by the city magistrate (Srinag), Ms Gousia-ul-Nissa Jeelani, to appear before her on January 2.

Counsel for the petitioners/ Mr. Harish Salve, sought stay of the proceedings and exemption from the personal appearance saying that the proceeding by Ms Sheikh the widow sister of cine star Sanjay Khan and Feroz Khan, was aimed at harassing them.

However, Ms Sheikh's counsel, Mr. M.H. Beg, argued that the petitioner could not seek transfer of the matter outside the state as

Section 406 of the Court of Criminal Procedure was not applicable. Ms Sheikh had filed a private criminal complaint seeking damages from the Weekly and its editors for publishing 'a grossly libellous and baseless' report alleging dangerous liaison between her and the Prime Minister of Pakistan.

Mr. Beg also pointed out that the petitioners could not seek transfer of the case outside the state as it was a private criminal complaint. He said the provisions of Indian Penal Code were not applicable in Jammu and Kashmir where instead of IPC, Ranbir Penal Code, named after the former Maharaja of Kashmir is enforceable.

On this Mr. Salve submitted that Ms Sheikh chose to file the complaint in Srinagar to harass the editor, printer and publisher of the weekly. He said Ms Sheikh lives in Bombay and sometime in Delhi. She had sent the notice asking the paper to apologise for the report from New Delhi. Ms Sheikh rarely visits Srinagar which however, was her in-laws home. Moreover, the Weekly is not dispatched to Srinagar, the petition said.

The petitioners invoked Article 32 of the Constitution for transfer of the proceedings from the Srinagar court on the ground that they could not resort to Section 406 of Cr. P.C. since the case was pending in Jammu and Kashmir. Therefore, they had no other efficacious remedy but to invoke writ jurisdiction to vindicate their fundamental rights including Article 32.

Saying that the news story titled 'Nawaz Sharif's Indian Friend' (November 24) was published in exercise of the editor's fundamental right under Article 19 (1) (A) and its contents had been verified, the petition pointed out that it was never an objective to make libellous insinuations against Ms Sheikh. It was neither an 'exercise of yellow journalism', the petition added.

The petitioners maintained that it was 'objective reporting and had no mala fide intentions behind it'. Therefore, the petitioners said, they neither withdrew the allegations nor published an unconditional apology as was sought by Ms Sheikh.

The petitioners also apprehended criminal intimidation and unfair trial in Srinagar.

A prominent journalist Khushwant Singh in his column 'With Malice towards One and All. . . .' in *The Hindustan Times* dated December 7, 1991 offered the following comments on the Dilshad issue:

> 'I am inclined to agree with Haqqam's verdict on the new breed of Pressmen who establish their reputations as scoop-mongers. The unfortunate aspect of the scenario is that they get published in papers with large circulations and enjoy a certain amount of prestige. The recent example is the story of Dilshad and her visits to Pakistan. Dilshad is an extraordinarily good looking rich widow; a sitting duck for scandal mongers. Her sister is married to a rich Pakistani.'

'She has also three grown-up daughters studying in Indian schools. From the word go, whatever has been published against her in Indian papers and in Pakistan was a farrago of falsehood. The tragedy is that no matter how strongly a court of law or the Press Council censures this kind of reckless and criminal disregard of people's right to privacy and unsullied reputations, a certain amount of mud will stick and blight the lives of the likes of Dilshad and their kindred. On behalf of my fraternity I tender apologies to them.'

***Nuns Murder Case :*** A complaint was filed by Sr. Cyrilla—Superior Franciscans of St. Mary of the Angels 'Snehasadan' and Father Flacino Fonseca, Director 'Snehasadan' Andheri, Bombay, against four Bombay papers, namely, *Indian Express, Free Press Journal, Times of India* and *Samna.*

***Facts of the Case :*** Two Christian Catholic nuns, Sister Sylvia D 'Souza and Sister Priya Joseph belonging to the Snehasadan, Bombay, were brutally murdered on November 16, 1990. On November 18, the respondent newspapers published the impugned stories. The gist of their portions objected to by the complainants, are extracted as below:

*Indian Express, Bombay* edition, dated 18.11.1990

In the impugned, story captioned : '2 held for nuns murder 7, it was alleged 'The sensational killings, took a shocking turn today with. . .the post-mortem reports revealing that they were used to frequent sexual intercourse. Moreover, one of them was suspected to have been infected with venereal disease.'

*The Times of India,* Bombay edition, dated 18.11.90

In the impugned news item captioned : 'Nuns murder case : 2 held', it was alleged the post mortem examination today revealed that the women are used to sexual intercourse and that one of them even had a sexually transmitted disease.'

*Free Press Journal,* Bombay edition, dated 18.11.1990

Splashed the impugned story on the front page as a four column boxed item under the heading; 'Sex, nuns and venereal disease' about the gruesome murder of two nuns, Sister Sylvia and Sister Priya Joseph at Jogeshwari on November 16, 1990. Alleging that 'Police sources confirmed the findings of the post-mortem report which stated that both the sisters had regular sexual intercourse', it also stated that one of the two nuns was also suspected to be suffering from venereal disease.

*Samna,* a Marathi Newspaper

In the impugned news item captioned—'The Jogeshwari murder—two persons arrested', it was alleged. . .Ashok Makasura (20) and Sunil Naik residing at MICD orphanage were arrested by the police. After checking rooms of the nuns they found several love letters written by Sunil Naik to Sylvia D 'Souza and of Ashok Makasura to Sr. Priya Joseph. All this proves that they had a sexual relationship and before the murder they had intercourse. All this had been proved by the post-mortem report. It also proved that Sylvia was suffering from venereal disease.

It was submitted by the complainants that the above quoted impugned reports were 'irresponsible, distorted and vulgar and defamatory' and 'apart from cruelly maligning the two innocent women dedicated to the service of the destitute children, the obnoxious report had hurt and unsettled the disadvantaged children under the care of the killed nuns and "seriously affected...the working of our institution".'

The complainants had further submitted as follows: 'We have with us at present, about 300 boys and girls in the houses. We interact with hundreds more through personal contacts in situ, with the children or their own referred centres.'

During the night of November 15-16, 1990 two of our nuns (Sister Sylvia and Sister Priya aged 40 and 25 years) were brutally murdered in the three-room cottage in which they lived along with their 26 wards and our distress was further aggravated when leading local and national newspapers published the baseless, vulgar and defamatory stories that the murdered nuns used to have sexual intercourse and one of them even had sexually transmitted disease.

The source of information was stated to be the police. On making inquiries at the Coroner's, we learnt that the preliminary post-mortem report had reported absence of hymen in both the nuns. But the absence of hymen could be due to variety of reasons. The Police, who were quoted as a source by some reporters, denied that they had communicated the misinterpretation of the post-mortem report to the Press.

'The reporters had made no independent inquiries in or around the institution and even after publication of police denial, the Press did not contradict the police refutation. The editors had deliberately abandoned their responsibilities. The publication of the impugned reports were reprehensible and condemnable, particularly as not only two dead women, but a faith and religious order, institution and disadvantaged children in their case, were all affected by the calumny, and it was all the more unethical as the dead women were unable to defend themselves.'

The complainants furnished the forensic and histopathological reports. These according to complainants, had been carefully analysed and scrutinised by the experts in the medical field and it was their unanimous conclusion that the reports did not give any indication whatsoever to arrive at a finding that the murdered nuns were used to sexual intercourse. It further submitted that various organisations through Mr. Mahem Babu, Advocate, had called on the newspapers (except Samna) to publish retraction and apologise for the scandalous report, but only Indian Express responded.

Editor, Free Press Journal, in his written statement, stated that the impugned news item was based on information provided by official sources who did not want to be identified and that as the source was reliable, they carried the said item.

Resident Editor, Indian Express, Bombay in his written statement stated as under:

1. We were of the firm opinion that the complainant had not only misconstrued our report but misinterpreted the same.
2. We had, in our reports, never mentioned that 'one of them even had a venereal disease', as alleged by the complainants. Our report published on November 18, 1990, clearly stated: 'One of them was suspected to have been injected with a venereal disease. The viscera had been sent to chemical analysis.
3. Our report right from the day of murder on November 16 had been unbiased and without any prejudice. The first report discussed all possible motives behind the murder. The second day's report was based on the findings of the post-mortem and its interpretation. The third day we not only carried the reactions of Christian organisations (nuns autopsy report sparks protests November 19) but we also carried a report highlighting the humanitarian work of Snehasadan for the last 30 years (Haven for homeless kids, November 19). On November 20 the police denial was carried in full detail. The report clearly showed that we had no prejudice against the nuns, Snehasadan or Christianity.'
4. On November 21, we published not only the follow up of the case by the police but also the news about the demonstration by an organisation and their memorandum which was submitted to the Jogeshwari Police.

Our report dated November 18 was based on the findings of the post-mortem report which revealed:

(a) Sister Priya:

(i) Hymen absent.

(ii) Vagina patulous.

(iii) Warts +++(on both sides)—here the word venereal was struck off.

(iv) Reddish discolouration on lower vagina, (v) Whitish thick discharge+++ (vi) No sign of struggle.

(b) Sister Sylvia:

(i) Hymen absent.

(ii) Vagina patulous.

(iii) Reddish discolouration on lower vagina.

(iv) Whitish thick discharge+++.

(v) No sign of struggle.

6. The complainants themselves stated 'this was an issue of a technical report and its interpretation by experts or professionals.' The interpretation of the post-mortem findings mentioned in number four above indicated :

(a) Hymen

(i) The principal signs of virginity may thus be summarized as :

(1) an intact hymen (2) a normal condition of the fourchette and posterior commissure, and (3) a narrow vagina with runose walls' (Dr. C.K. Parikh : Parikh's Textbook of Medical Jurisprudence and Toxicology (PTMJT), CBS Publisher and Distributors, Bombay, 1990, Page 415.)

(ii) Certain signs in the breast and the genitals particularly the intactness of the hymen was always held to signify the physical virginity of a woman. But in reality it is seen that this particular anatomical structure had limited value since it happened that a single coitus was not necessarily sufficient to rupture the membrane.' (Modi's Medical Jurisprudence and Toxicology (MMJT) ed. Dr. C.A. Franklin, retd. Police surgeon, ex- professor and head of the department of Forensic Medicine, Grant Medical College and examiner in Forensic Medicine in All India Institute of Medical Sciences, N.M. Tripathi Pvt. Ltd. Bombay, 1988 (21st edition, pp. 356).

(iii) 'With frequent intercourse the opening of the hymen is enlarged and after the birth of a child the hymen is completely lost....' (MMJT, pp. 415).

(iv) The hymen is always present in some form or the other in a virgo intact but rarely it may be congenitally absent. The hymen may be intact but this does not prove virginity' (MMJT, p. 416) 'It is said that the hymen may be congenitally absent, but no authentic case has so far been recorded.' (MMJT, pp. 354).

(v) 'Such cases where sexual connection had taken place without rupture of the hymen were known as false virgins. If (a) the labia majora are fleshy and do not completely close the vaginal orifice (b) the labia minora are cutaneous and not covered by the labia majora (c) the clitoris is enlarged (d) the vagina is roomy there is no doubt about the case being a false virgin in spite of an intact hymen' (PTMJT, pp. 416).

(vi) Vagina patulous : 'The external os is enlarged, irregular and patulous so as to admit the tip of the finger and the internal os is not so well defined as in the virgin or nulliparrous woman' (MMJT: Signs of remote delivery in the dead, pp. 367).

(vii) Warts : Majority of the warts or papules in the genitals are due to venereal disease. The scratching of the word venereal has not been explained by anybody. Generally the sign of cross indicates 'Plus' e.g. to indicate heavy bleeding in a patient the doctor would write'+++'.

(viii) The sexual activity suggested by the clinical picture could be of any type heterosexual/lesbian/autoarotic.

7. While reporting any murder the antecedents of the victim as well of the accused is important and all aspects are looked into including the circumstances under which the incident takes place. This is reported irrespective of the social standing of the victim or the accused. The circumstances under which the two women were murdered are:

   (a) The dogs in Snehasadan did not bark at the intruders';

   (b) None of the inmates heard any screams or scuffles;

   (c) The latch of the room of the victims was intact.

8. Taking into consideration the circumstances, the investigating authorities were working on the theory that some insider or some person known to the women was involved in crime. Subsequently, the police also seized some letters from the expelled inmate who was taken into custody and also interrogated.

It is the duty of every reporter to convey to the reading public various theories on which the investigating agencies work at a particular time. The particular report is not for the scientific community but for the day reader who is interested in knowing the cause of a particular murder. In case of murder of a woman, sexual motive is one of the prominent hypothesis and police have to eliminate that hypothesis before going to the other probable hypothesis. When the press report was published sexual activity was a respectable hypothesis both for police investigation and for medical jurisprudence. To conceal this hypothesis from the reading public merely because it would offend some hypersensitive people, would have been unprofessional and an act of intellectual dishonesty. The question is whether there was any ground for doubting the report. A glance at the post-mortem would convince anyone without having any bias that the reporter has the strongest ground for such hypothesis.

9. From the above statements you could clearly see that we had no bias whatsoever while reporting the murder of the

two women. Also the interpretations of the post-mortem findings were based on standard medical jurisprudence text books in circulation on the subject used in the courtrooms and medical circles.

In the light of these facts, we would request you to dismiss the complaint. If this request of ours does not find favour with you, we would make an alternate request to allow our representative to cross-examine the complainant and witnesses and also to lend evidence in our support.

Resident Editor *TOI,* in his written statement, submitted as follows:

1. The story, which was published simultaneously by at least three major dailies was based on official sources.
2. According to at least two other city newspapers *(Daily* May 2, 1991 and *Mid Day,* May 6, 1991), the Director General of Police, Mr. V.K. Saraf, had submitted a report to the Bombay High Court on who had revealed the information regarding the alleged sexual behaviour of the nuns to the Press. A medical official in the Additional Coroner's Court in Juhu was cited as the person who had divulged this information.
3. It was quite clear this newspaper relied on such information because it came from official sources. In our opinion, the alleged sexual behaviour of the nuns was material to the story because it could possibly throw some light on the motives for the murder.
4. The fact that till today no one had been apprehended for committing the crime only confirmed our contention (published in subsequent articles on the case) that there was considerable confusion not only as to who committed the murders but the motives.
5. Several reports, including subsequent ones in our newspaper, had pointed to the obstructive tactics used by some church persons in not allowing the authorities to proceed with a thorough, investigation. The subsequent

involvement of CROSS a Christian revivalist organisation, only communalised the issue and further compounded the confusion. The call by CROSS for the closure of Catholic schools over the incident was sufficient indication of the charged atmosphere at the time.

6. Our reporter merely cited the bare details given to him from authentic sources and this was published in a sober form in the Sunday *Times of India* of November 18, 1990. The details about the post-mortem findings were buried in the copy in one sentence and there was no attempt whatsoever to sensationalise these details or incite people in any manner.

7. It would not be at all correct to say that our reporter did damage to all living sisters, 'cast aspersions on the life style of Catholic religious women' or that religious women in general, Snehasadan institution and hundreds of disadvantaged children in our care were affected by the calumny.' This was reading into the report intentions which were totally unsubstantiated.

8. It was also alleged immediately after the post-mortem reports were published that the reports were not based on any authentic document and that the reports were speculative, scandalous, motivated and calculated to assail religious sentiments of the Christian community which is a minority community. CROSS went further and alleged that the post-mortem findings were doctored to cast aspersions on the nuns and demanded Rs 10 lakh from the Prime Minister as ex-gratia payment as a 'token of respect'. It was clear that such statements and threats went a long way in vitiating the atmosphere.

9. It would be pertinent to point out that a newsletter published by the National Catholic Convention with its registered address as Archbishop's House, Bombay, had stated in no uncertain terms that 'the thief was inside the ship' and that 'if the case was pursued, it would tarnish the reputation of a section in the church.'

10. It would thus seem that the petition to the Press Council was premature. The church itself was not questioning the post-mortem findings but their interpretation. The petitioners should not treat these findings as an attack on the whole church or body of nuns. On the contrary, *The Times of India* had conducted itself with utmost restraint and dignity in keeping with its traditions of objectivity and fair play. To accuse this newspaper of any other bias in this case was to draw completely untenable conclusions.

This matter was considered by the Inquiry Committee of the Press Council on 4 June, 1991.

As far as *Samna* was concerned, its editor had not sent any response with reference to the show-cause notice in spite of a reminder. Nor was there any response from him with reference to the notice for the hearing before the Inquiry Committee of the Press Council.

***Complainant's Case :*** Ms Sheela Barse argued the case on behalf of the complainants. She made the following submissions.

*The Indian Express* : The impugned publication in the issue of the newspaper, dated 18.11.90 did not reveal any source of the information, excepting the post-mortem report. It only said that, 'The sensational killings. . .took a shocking turn today with...the post-mortem reports revealing that they (the two nuns who had been murdered) were used to frequent sexual intercourse. Moreover, one of them was suspected to have been infected with a venereal disease.' In the post-mortem reports there was no foundation of what was mentioned in the impugned story. If the statements in question were assumed to be an interpretation or an opinion of the newspapers and the court they were not competent to do so. It was a matter for the forensic experts and the court. As regards the two boys (Sunil Naik and Ashok Makasare) who had beers picked up by the police as being suspects, they were ex-inmates of the Snehasadan. They had no such relations with the two murdered sisters. They only kept in touch with 'mothers' in Snehasadan.

*The Indian Express* in their letter dated 16.5.91 were claiming some interpretation from the book by Dr. C.K. Parikh, titled 'Parikh's

Text Book of Medical Jurisprudence and Toxicology' and Modi's Medical Jurisprudence and Toxicology ed. Dr. C.A. Franklin. In this letter, their defence before the Press Council of India was mischievous because the book of Dr. Parikh did not give that interpretation; *The Indian Express* had quoted portions torn out of context.

In this connection Ms Sheela Barse submitted a photo copy of a letter dated 1.6.91 from Dr. C.K. Parikh, addressed to her. With this letter, was attached a five page note signed by Dr. C.K. Parikh dated 1.6.1991 on the subject of post-mortem reports, on the bodies of Priya and Sylvia. The copies of the letter and the note have been taken on record. In regard to the post-mortem report of the body on Priya, Dr. Parikh said that laboratory reports said that neither semen nor gram negative diplococi were detected in the smear and swab. No semen was detected on pubic hair. Histology of Sylvia showed normal histology. There was no evidence of venereal disease. Histology of warts showed no evidence of any pathology but only normal epidermis and dermis. In regard to the post-mortem examination report on the body of Sylvia, Dr. Parikh said that 'laboratory reports find neither semen nor gram negative diplococi were detected on vaginal swab or smear. No semen was detected on pubic hair.

In the note, Dr. Parikh had made general comments on post-mortem report. He also said that he had been asked to review the post-mortem reports and the findings of Forensic Science Laboratory, and to state (a) if the genital organs were in a virgin condition and (b) if there was any evidence of venereal disease. He said that he had carefully gone through the post-mortem reports as well as the findings of the Forensic Science Laboratory. He had them extensively quoted from Dr. Parikh's Textbook of Medical Jurisprudence and Toxicology for Classrooms and Courtrooms. In regard to signs of virginity, the books say that such signs in a healthy woman are seen in the genitals and breasts. At the end of his note, Dr. Parikh had given his conclusions which are reproduced below:

(1) The post-mortem had been done very carelessly without realising the responsibility it entails on the doctor

performing it. A number of vital observations were not made and some observations had been just mentioned without clarifying the significance (Early decomposition started).

(2) There were several factors to determine virginity, such as hymen, labia minora, labia majora, fourchette, posterior commissure, clitoria, rugosity of vaginal walls, and intriotus. He had made only very few observations, viz. hymen, patulous, vagina redness at lower vagina and thick vaginal discharge, and in the case of Priya the presence of warts.

As explained above, the observation on hymen is probably incorrect. Patulousness of vagina is probably a wrong interpretation as it is likely to be due to early decomposition changes. Redness of lower vagina may be due to post-mortem lividity, an observation which the doctor did not make or due to irritation from thick vaginal discharge.

The Forensic Science Laboratory had not been able to find sperms either on pubic hair or vaginal smear and swabs. It had not been able to find any evidence of venereal disease. And, in the case of Priya, the laboratory reports the warts as having normal skin structure, meaning thereby that they were tags of skin and not warts as wrongly interpreted by the doctor.

In view of the above, and lack of many observations on diagnostic signs of virginity, it was not possible to believe that any of the two deceased were either not virgins or they suffered from venereal disease which had been ruled out by laboratory examination, and in view of all this, the question of frequent intercourse or in fact any intercourse could not arise.

Ms Barse, continuing her arguments, said that *The Indian Express* had published the impugned news item without a sense of responsibility. Investigations into the murder were still going on and the case had not yet been filed in court. How far was it in accord with professional propriety for the Press to arrogate to itself the functions of the investigating police and court asked Ms Barse? She further pointed out that according to the impugned report in *The Indian Express* the post-mortem reports were the source of the report in question, but they did not have post-mortem reports with them at the time of publication of the impugned story.

The inferences drawn by *The Indian Express* from the post-mortem reports, said Ms Barse, were not there in the post-mortem report at all. She further submitted that the inferences drawn from the correspondence between Sunil and Sister Sylvia were also wrong, and in fact, the two boys had been let off by the police. Despite that, *The Indian Express* vide its Resident Editor's letter dated 16.5.91, had tried to defend the impugned publications and further submitted that the newspaper continued to promote theories which had no foundation in the post-mortem but were the coinage of the reporter's brain.

Regarding *The Times of India,* she said that the impugned report in this paper's Bombay edition dated 18.11.90 was even worse than that which appeared in *The Indian Express.* Whereas *The Indian Express* report said, 'Moreover, one of them was suspected to have been infected with a venereal disease', *The Times of India* report outdid it by saying that'.. .one of them even had a sexually transmitted disease.' By his letter dated 8.5.91. Ms Barse contended, the Resident Editor of *The Times of India,* Bombay, had tried to make the confusion worse confounded and had compounded the wrong done by it by distorting facts. She maintained that the respondent-paper had quoted the organisation, CROSS, out of context to justify the irresponsible comments and inferences of defamatory character in the impugned report.

Regarding *Free Press Journal,* she said that the headline of the news item published in this newspaper's Bombay edition, dated 18.11.90: 'Sex, nuns and Venereal disease'—was very vulgar. She pointed out that this newspaper had attributed the impugned news item not only to post-mortem report but also to police sources as confirming what was mentioned in the post-mortem report; and these recitals had been shown to be wrong: firstly, there was no mention or interpretation of these sisters being used to sexual intercourse or one of the nuns being suspected to be suffering from venereal disease in the post-mortem reports.

Secondly, the police had also got published a denial through a Press release. Ms Barse further pointed out that some individuals had brought out a booklet after meeting the editors (She gave a copy of the booklet which was taken on record). She also informed the committee that this was discussed in a Press Conference in Bombay.

Regarding *Samna,* she submitted that the respondent had neither sent any reply nor cared to appear before the Inquiry Committee, to answer the charges in the complaints.

Summing up her arguments, she said that the impact of all these news reports had been very deleterious which the Press Council must assess. Since 18.11.90, the discussion in newspapers was, whether the murdered nuns had been indulging in sexual activity etc. Nobody had realised that 300 children were staying in cottage of Snehasadan. Nobody thought of the traumatic effect on the boys. Many boys ran away from Snehasadan because of the horror by the murders and the impugned publications. She expected that the concerned newspapers should apologise for publishing these scurrilous reports, which offend against all canons of decency and ethics of journalism. She urged the Press Council to pass strictures against the respondent newspapers for the gross unethical conduct.

On being asked she replied that Snehasadan had not gone to the Bombay High Court. It was some other Christian organisation which had moved the High Court. She submitted that many Christian organisations were agitated over this irresponsible reporting by the newspapers, particularly when the dead nuns were unable to defend the defamatory stories injurious to their reputation and personal privacy.

***Press Council Judgement :*** The Press Council in its judgement on Press reports about the autopsies on the murdered nuns, ruled that four Bombay newspapers erred in failing to distinguish comment and fact and that they passed on conjectures or comments which did not find mention in the post-mortem reports.

'Even assuming that the reporters had heard from some sources that the autopsy report revealed what they published, then also, as a matter of professional caution, they should not have published them, it being a sensitive matter touching the chastity and privacy of the murdered women', the Press Council stated.

It directed the papers to publish a gist of its decision with an expression of regret.

The decision against *The Times of India, Indian Express, Free Press Journal* and *Samna* was arrived at by the Council following hearings on July 8 and 9, 1991. A request from *The Times of India* for extra time of 10 days to submit expert opinions on the post-mortem reports was refused on the ground that enough time had already been given.

Instead, the Committee in its report lent heavily on a letter from Dr. C.K. Parikh to Ms Barse who argued the case on behalf of the complainants.

***Careless Post-mortem :*** Dr. Parikh, who is the author of a textbook on medical jurisprudence and toxicology, said in a letter with a five page note attached to it that the post-mortem was done carelessly without realising the responsibility it entails on the doctor performing it. 'A number of vital observations have been just mentioned without clarifying the significance.'

Affirming that the range of journalistic ethics is broader than that of law, the Press Council said that reporters who were laymen were not competent to spell out their own opinions or hypotheses on the basis of inconclusive data mentioned in the post-mortem reports'.

The Council said that opinions of forensic experts only were admissible to aid a court in reaching a finding on a matter relating to forensic science—'Even the experts opinion may not conclude the issue. Such opinion has to be listed by the Court in the light of other evidence on record.'

'It seems in publishing their opinion/comment with such abandon and alacrity at a stage when the investigation had just commenced, the reporters' investigative zeal, spared by a not very healthy curiosity, outran their discretion and they arrogated to themselves the functions of the investigation police and the forensic expert and of the court, which alone was competent to give a judicial finding on such controversial technical issues, if and when the accused would be put for trial,' the Council observed.

'Publication of the impugned story at that stage of the investigation did not serve any overriding public interest', the Council further observed. 'On the contrary, it could harm and prejudice a fair and unbiased police investigation.'

The unethicality of the publication had to be viewed in the context that 'the dead women were unable to defend themselves against these voluminous imputations' whose publication was 'bound to cause distress to their kin, surviving associates and all those belonging to the Catholic faith engaged in running the Snehasadan institution.'

***No Fair Comment :*** The publication of the reports could not be justified as fair comment published in good faith as the reporters did not act with due care and caution, notwithstanding that the reporters had no malicious motive or deliberate intention to malign the deceased or the institution.

'Even assuming that the newspapers published the story on the information divulged by the police or a medical officer in the Coroner's team or other judicial source, it would not justify infringing the personal privacy of the murdered women,' the Council ruled.

At best, this would show that the official informants also willingly or unwillingly contributed to the impugned publication which were the product of an overwhelming curiosity, rather than an overriding public interest.

# 3

# Principles of Morality

"Journalism requires a discipline of mind. It requires a sympathetic understanding of mankind and also a cold objective analysis of how mankind meets the problem of this age"-as laid down by Wes Gallgher, the former correspondent of Associated Press of America. "Facts are sacred, comment is free. Facts must not be tampered with. News must be reported with complete objectivity, without any distortion. A journalist shouldn't mix news and views and must be careful enough to clearly distinguish between the two"-as said by the editor of The Manchester Guardian.

Maintenance of high professional standards is certainly a major responsibility of the publisher and the editor. On the one hand journalists ought to be vigilant to safeguard the freedom of the press and on the other they must see that this freedom is used and not misused, that they always act with a great sense of responsibility.

*Role of Journalists*—According to Prof. John Hohenberg, a journalist should stick to the following four ideals-

(a) He should imbibe a never-ending search for the truth

(b) He should be able to meet needs of the changing times.

(c) He should be able to perform services of some consequences and significance to mankind.

(d) He should maintain a steadfast independence.

A journalist is an important unit of the democratic system in our country. He is supposed to gather facts, organize them and disseminate them to the masses. A journalist must be cool, detached, even skeptical as he approaches his material, and should have high degree of skill in organising material and in using the language.

***Responsibilities of Journalists***—The press is no doubt an industry, a business, but with a difference. Journalists have a social obligation, they must act with a profound sense of responsibility towards the society. The responsibilities of a journalist are many and varied which are discussed below-

***Social***—The social responsibility of journalists is of paramount importance. "Journalism is the mirror of society". He must, therefore, provide a truthful, comprehensive, and intelligent account of the events in a context that gives meaning. The press must serve as a forum for the exchange of comments and criticism.

***Legal***—Publication of baseless, graceless and manipulated material should be avoided at all costs in order to safeguard yourself and your organization from the legal clutches. 'Defamation' is always a 'live wire' on which a sensible journalist dreads to tread. He must be well aware of the various laws relating to the press.

***Professional***—Journalists have certain professional obligations to honour. His basic responsibility is to disseminate information in all circumstances. The information provided helps the readers to make up their minds on vital issues and thus shaping their attitudes. He is expected to have his commitment to his profession and thus must strictly adhere to the accepted professional norms. He has to know the limits within which to operate and must keep his biases at bay. Let news not be distorted or suppressed. One of the most important responsibilities of a professional journalist is to ensure that in hurry and haste, accuracy in the language is not sacrificed.

***Editor's Responsibilities***—The editor has to assume responsibility for all matter published in the newspaper. Editor's Charter adopted by All India Newspaper Editor's Conference in 1953, is still valid. It is-

(a) The Editor shall enjoy complete freedom in respect of the implementation of the editorial policy and the staffing and the conduct of the paper.

(b) The annual budget of editorial expenses is prepared in consultation with the Editor.

(c) His decision is final in all matters concerning the editorial staff and the contents of the paper.

(d) He has direct access to the Board for the discussion of matters relating to his department.

(e) He shall have the power to grant special increments in recognition of the special merit of a worker.

(f) As far as the editorial side of the newspaper is concerned, the editor vis-a-vis the government and the proprietor is to be left free, in the discharge of his responsibility.

## Concept of Morality

'Ethics' implies the norms which a journalist must uphold and cherish in order to keep the integrity and the sanctity of the profession intact. Journalists, like other citizens, are governed by all the laws of the land. In order to carry his message effectively, and to maintain the credibility of his newspaper, a journalist has to disseminate news and views in accordance with established norms and traditions of the society. Some of the well accepted ethical norms are as follows-

*Accuracy and Fairness*—A journalist must inform and comment on matters of public interest, in a fair, accurate, unbiased and decent manner.

***Prepublication Verification***—Verification and checking of news before publication is all the more necessary, where its publication can create complications.

***Caution against Defamatory Writings***—Newspapers should not publish anything, which is libellous against any individual or organisation, unless they have sufficient reason to believe that it is true and that its publication will be for public good.

***Privacy***—Intrusion on the privacy of individuals is not permissible unless out-weighed by genuine overriding public interest.

***Eschew Suggestive Guilt***—Newspapers should eschew suggestive guilt by association. They shouldn't name or identify the family or associates of a person convicted or accused of a crime when they are totally innocent.

***Corrections***—When any factual error is confirmed, the newspaper should publish the correction promptly, with due prominence and with an apology in a case of serious lapse.

***Communal Reports***—Proper verification must be done before publishing reports regarding communal clashes. The report should not vitiate the situation.

***Sensational Headings***—Sensational headings should be avoided. Headlines should conform to the contents of news stories. They should be clear, unambiguous and authentic.

***Eschew Vulgarity and Obscenity***—Obscene and vulgar items should be done away with as these offend the public's good taste. Also, never violence.

***Avoid Caste, Religion or Community Disclosures***—In general, a newspaper should not identify a person with his caste, religion or community. It may be derogatory to his caste, religion or community.

***Respect Confidence***—If information is received from a source confidentially, the confidence should be respected.

***Codes of Ethics in India***—It would not be possible in code of ethics, to detail all the probable incidents which could come up for discussion on ethical grounds. To formulate a comprehensive, rigid code of ethics for a journalist is neither feasible nor prudent. The society keeps on changing with time. And to formulate cast-iron rules is a futile exercise.

Several codes have been formulated from time to time, to guide journalists in their work. In 1968, the All-India Newspaper Editors' Conference formulated a code of ethics. Other codes such as the Parliamentary Code (1976) and the International Code (1991) were also proposed to give direction to the press. Although, Press Council is against cast-iron rules, it has formulated guidelines from time to time.

***All India Newspaper Editor's Conference Code (1968)***—In 1968, AINEC adopted a code of ethics for the press. It is a useful effort which retains its significance even in present times. It is as follows-

(1) A free press can flourish only in a free society.

(2) The press has a vital role to play in consummation of the fundamental objectives enshrined in our constitution. To this end the press should adhere to the following guidelines in reporting—

(a) Generalised allegations casting doubts and aspersions on the patriotism and loyalty of any community should be eschewed.

(b) Truth should not be suppressed.

(c) Generalised charges and allegations against any community must be eschewed.

(d) The source from which casualty figures are obtained should always be indicated.

(e) No facts or figures should be published without the fullest possible verification.

(f) Items of news calculated to make for peace and harmony and help in the restoration and maintenance of law and order should be given prominence over other news.

(g) Names of communities should not be mentioned and the terms 'majority' and 'minority' communities be ordinarily used in the course of reports.

***Press Council Guidelines***

(a) Provocative and sensational headlines should be avoided.

(b) Headings must reflect and justify the matter under them.

(c) Headlines containing allegations made in statements should either identify the person making allegations.

(d) Comments and value judgements should not be motivated or guided by partisan feelings.

(e) Language employed in writing the news should be temperate.

(f) Corrections should be promptly published with due prominence and regrets expressed in serious cases.

*International Code of Ethics*—In 1991, at the Stockholm Symposium, an International Code of Ethics was drafted and adopted. It is not a legal document.

(a) The fundamental objective of a journalist is a fair, accurate and unbiased story.

(b) Unnamed sources should not be used unless the pursuit of truth will best be served by not naming the source.

(c) Corrections or clarifications should be published for errors of fact promptly.

(d) Journalists should identify themselves, except in some exceptional cases.

(e) The use of obscene language should be limited to quoted material.

(f) Journalists should avoid paying for information unless public interest is involved.

(g) Plagiarism, i.e., using someone's work without attribution, is a serious ethical breach and should be avoided.

(h) Journalists should distinguish between comments, conjectures and facts clearly.

(i) Journalists should judge no one unheard.

(j) Journalists should maintain highest professional and ethical standards.

(k) Acts of violence should not be glorified.

***Ombudsman***—"Ombudsman" is an institution which took its birth in Sweden. Its function is to establish and maintain smooth relations between the press and the people, between the press and the governments, various associations and political parties, public bodies, court and the parliament.

***Professional Organizations and Statutory Bodies :*** Mass media have been recognised as powerful instruments to mould public opinion, therefore, various interests have tried to control them. The clash of interests always leads to tremendous pressure on the media and the media men. Interests of media consumers may also clash with the interests of media owners and practitioners. This has led to the establishment of some statutory bodies and formation of several associations and councils.

***The First Press Commission***—On May 16, 1952, Dr. Rajendra Prasad, the then President, told Parliament that the Government hoped to appoint a Commission to consider various matters connected with the Press. Mr Justice H.S. Rajadhyaksha was appointed the Chairman. The Commission started its work on October 11, 1952 and submitted its report on July 17, 1954. The Press Commission was asked "to inquire into the slate of the Press in India, its present and future line of development and in particular, to examine—

(a) the control, management and ownership and financial structure of newspapers, large and small, the periodical press and news agencies.

(b) the working of monopolies and chains and their effect on the presentation of accurate news.

(c) freedom of the press and repeal or amendment of laws not in consonance with it, and to make recommendations thereon.

(d) the adequacy of newsprint supplies and its distribution among all classes of newspapers.

(e) the effect of holding companies, distribution of advertisements and such other forms of external influence as may have a bearing on the development of healthy journalism.

The Commission did a work of lasting value and presented a clear picture of this important means of mass communication. The Commission discussed the principles relating to the Press and the prevailing practices of the time, they considered whether any law required repeal or amendment. The Commission suggested new enactments for—

(a) establishing a Press Council,

(b) printing into existence a State Trading Corporation for dealing in newsprint and for furnishing finances for the operation of the Press Council,

(c) establishing a Public Corporation to take over the Press Trust of India,

(d) defining the powers, privileges and immunities of legislatures.

***Registrar of Newspaper for India***—The office of RNI was established in July 1956 on the recommendation of 1st Press Commission. The functions of RNI are two-fold-statutory and non-statutory. Statutory functions include-maintenance of the register containing particulars of all newspapers published in India, issuance of registration certificates in respect of newspapers and watch the regularity of newspapers, scrutiny of annual statements sent by publishers of newspapers, and verification and checking of circulation claims of newspapers.

*The Non-statutory Functions Include*—To work out and authorize newsprint entitlement to individual newspapers, to advice the State Trading Corporation of India and Newsprint. Advisory Committee regarding the quantity of newsprint to be imported, to examine and certify the essentiality of printing, composing and allied machinery required by the newspapers/periodicals.

***Press Council***—On the recommendation of the first Press Commission and the National Integration Council, the Press

Council Act was passed by Parliament in 1965 and it was set up on July 4, 1966. The Press Council Act was however repealed in 1976. But, a fresh legislation providing for the establishment of a Press council was enacted by the Press Council Act, 1978. The Act came into force on March 1, 1979. Under Section 5 of the Press Council Act, 1978, the council shall comprise of 28 members, apart from the chairman who is nominated by a committee consisting of the chairman of the Rajya Sabha, the speaker of the Lok Sabha and a person elected by the members of the council.

To preserve the freedom of the Press and to maintain and improve the standards of newspapers and news agencies, are the main objectives of the Press Council of India. The important tasks of the council are-

(1) To build up a code of conduct for newspapers, news agencies, and journalists in accordance with high professional standards.

(2) To help newspapers and news agencies to maintain their independence.

(3) To ensure maintenance of high standards of public taste on the part of newspapers, news agencies and journalists.

(4) To encourage the growth of a sense of responsibility and public service among all those engaged in journalism.

(5) To concern itself with developments such as concentration or other aspects of ownership of newspapers and news agencies which may affect the independence of the Press.

(6) To keep under review cases of assistance received by any newspaper or news agency in India from any foreign source.

***Second Press Commission***—There was no major enquiry into the working of the Indian Press since the First Press Commission. The Janata government in 1977 felt that a comprehensive enquiry was needed. The second Press Commission was appointed under justice P.K. Goswami. However, Justice Goswami and his colleagues resigned in 1979 when Janata government went out of office but was again asked to carry on when Charan Singh's government was formed. However, they again resigned in 1980 with the formation of a new government. The commission was reconstituted with Justice Mathew as the Chairman with fresh terms of reference.

The conclusion that emerges from the report of the 2nd Press Commission is that the Indian Press has grown considerably since the first commission reported but is still not adequate for the needs of the people. The recommendations made by the commission to reform the structure of the press are mainly the establishment of a Newspaper Development Commission. The commission repeated the recommendation of the First Press Commission, that every newspaper, independent or a unit of a chain or group, should be constituted as a separate unit. It also recommended a measure of delinking and has found it to be constitutionally unobjectionable. The commission also recommended amendments to the law of defamation and suggested changes in several other laws so that the area of freedom can be enlarged.

***Broadcasting Council***—The Prasar Bharati Act, 1990 provided for the establishment of a Broadcasting Council. It shall consist of:-

(a) a president and ten other members to be appointed by the President of India.

(b) 4 members of Parliament (2 from House of People nominated by speaker and 2 from Council of States nominated by the Chairman).

The Broadcasting council shall receive and consider complaints from: (1) any person or group of persons alleging that a certain programme or the functioning of the corporation in specific cases or in general is not in accordance with the objectives for which the corporation is established. (2) any person (other than an officer or employee of the corporation) claiming himself to have been treated unjustly or unfairly in any manner in connection with any programme broadcast by the corporation.

***Audit Bureau of Circulation Ltd.***—The ABC was registered in 1948 as a non-profit making company with no share capital and limited liability by guarantee. Its affairs are controlled by a council of management.

**Trade Bodies**

There were two main bodies related to media in pre-Independence days. Indian and Eastern Newspaper Society and the All India Newspaper Editor's Conference (AINEC). But after Independence such bodies increased.

***Indian Newspaper Society***—The INS is a representative body of newspapers and periodicals, founded in 1939 as IENS. Since 1940, the IENS (which became INS in 1988) is publishing an annual Handbook containing advertisement rates, circulation and other data for all member publications and relevant information about the accredited agencies. In 1974 it set up a Research and Publication Divisions.

***Indian Languages Newspapers Association***—ILNA was founded in 1941, to serve special interests of language newspapers. Any newspaper or periodical published in any of the Indian languages or an organization or society of newspapers is eligible for membership. Language Press Bulletin is an official organ of the Association and is published monthly in English.

***All India Newspaper Editors Conference***—AINEC is an organisation of newspapers and periodicals as represented by their editors. It was founded in 1940. Any newspaper or periodical published in India qualifies for membership.

***Indian Federation of Working Journalists***—The All India Connection of Journalists held in New Delhi in 1950, clinched the issue in favour of journalists forming a trade union, thus laying the foundation for the establishment of the Indian Federation of Working Journalists in October, 1950. When the IFWJ was formed in 1950, it was intended to be an organisation not only for fighting for better working conditions for journalists, but also for safeguarding their professional interests and the freedom of the press.

***National Union of Journalists***—The NUJ was born on January 23, 1972.

***Indian Journalists Union***—Bogus membership charges were hurled at each other by the two factions of IFWJ before another split in December 1990. The new organization that came up at Ranchi is called Indian Journalists Union.

### *Training Institutions*

***Press Institute of India (PTI)***—It is a professional body of Indian Newspapers and Journals, set up in 1963. It holds professional seminars, workshops, awards fellowships, conducts research into press problems, organizes selection of Indian Journalists. It also publishes books relating to mass media, a bi-monthly media journal Vidura, a weekly archive of developmental information about India-Data-India. There is no individual membership.

***Indian Institute of Mass Communication***—IIMC is the centre for advanced training and research in communication. It is an autonomous society, with main focus on conducting orientation courses for officers of the Indian Information Service, conducting training programmes and communication research, holding seminars and workshops.

# 4

# Traditional Conventions

Decline of ethical values, in public life as in personal, is at the root of the corruption on an increasing scale among sections of politicians, business men, public servants in the civil and defence services—even the judiciary—and others. The ascendancy of consumerism and eroticism in the mass media, specially TV, is part of this syndrome.

What accounts for the post-independence weakening of the moral fibre of Indian society and the Indian State ?

A major reason, in the view of competent observers, is the secularisation of education ordained by Article 28 of the republican Constitution which came into force on 26th January 1950. It reads : "No religious instruction shall be provided in any educational institution wholly maintained out of State funds." In a poor country like ours, the overwhelming majority of young people who are privileged to go to school instead of entering the child labour market go precisely to schools, and the luckier among them to colleges, that are run by the State—from the panchayat and municipal board to city corporation and the State and Central governments.

## No Religious Values

This banishment of religion from formal education has had far-reaching consequences because the prime source of ethical values has been, through human history, religion. This is not to say that religious institutions, or men wearing religion on their sleeves, have been free of corruption—whether in the traditional god-based religions or in the new, godless religion of Marxism which arose in the 19th century and spread over a large part of the globe. There have been in India greedy and lecherous rogues wearing saffron robes; the English word 'nepotism' has its origin in Popes, vowed to celibacy, granting undue favour through appointments to their illegitimate sons whom they called nephews; and a powerful attraction offered by Islamic *Jihad* to the successful warrior professing the true faith is the wealth and the women of the conquered group. The post-Enlightenment religion of Marxism proved to be no more immune to human failing. Corruption was rampant in Stalinist U.S.S.R., as it continues to be in Communist China whose president, Jiang Zemin, in the course of a speech in September 1995 expressed distress at the cropping up of 'money worship' and 'pleasure seeking' and a resurgence of 'corrupt and ugly phenomena'.

There is, however, no gainsaying the fact that godbased religion and humanist ideology have been potent carriers of the values of human fellowship, compassion and sharing, calling for self-restraint and frugality.

The best insights of modem science, too, confirm those of traditional religion and of non-theological humanism. As the Indian space scientist Yash Pal put it while speaking at a South Asian seminar convened in 1980 by the Indian Institute of Mass Communication : "It has become clear from science that myself, all my cells, all my constituents and those in this match-box or in this table, or in a piece of stone—that all this material at some time past was cooked together in the same star. Does not this have any implications for questions like our essential relatedness, about ecology? And does it at all conflict with the very beautiful, holistic inspiration of all the great religious teachers ?"

## Non-religious Values

Jawaharlal Nehru, moulder of independent India for nearly two decades, as Mahatma Gandhi had been of a whole generation of fighters for freedom, strove to reconcile in his own mind religion and science, tradition and modernity. But Nehru, for the greater part of his life, was more conscious of the negative features of religious tradition than of the positive, and was much attracted by modem technology. His close friend and colleague Maulana Azad, whom he chose as free India's first Education Minister, was unashamed of humanity's religious heritage though he was not opposed to technology (Azad held the portfolio also of natural Resources and Scientific Research).

## Human Aspects

Like Mahatma Gandhi, Maulana Azad was in favour of instructing children in the humanist values which are common to all religions at their best. Writing a decade before independence, Gandhi said in 'Harijan' in response to a correspondent's query on the place of religious instruction in his Wardha Scheme of Basic Education : "I regard it as fatal to the growth of a friendly spirit among children belonging to the different faiths if they are taught that their religion is superior to every other, or that it is the only true religion. Fundamental principles of ethics are common to all religions. These should be taught to the children."

Speaking in similar strain in February 1947, a month after assuming the Education portfolio in the Interim Government, Maulana Azad said : "The religious instruction imparted in India in private institutions is of a kind which, instead of broadening the outlook and inculcating a spirit of toleration and goodwill towards all men, produces exactly the opposite results. The aim of all religious teaching should be to make men more tolerant and broad-minded. And it is my opinion that this can be more effectively done if the State takes charge of the question than if it is left to private initiative."

In advocating instruction in the essence of all religions as part of the curriculum, Maulana Azad was at one not only with Mahatma Gandhi, the great experimenter with the practice of religion, but with Dr. Kadhakrishnan, the renowned exponent of the philosophy of religion.

The Commission on University Education headed by Dr. Radhakrishnan expressed itself, in the report it drew up in 1949, in the same terms as Maulana Azad. Religious instruction in the universities was one of the issues remitted to the Commission, which included distinguished scholars and scientists. The report of the Commission referred to the Constitution of free India that was then being drawn up, and said : There is no State religion. The State must not be partial to any one religion. Each one is at liberty to approach the unseen as it suits his capacity and inclination. If this is the basis of our Secular State, to be secular is not to be religiously illiterate. It is to be deeply spiritual."

However, the Constitution that came into force in January 1950 contained provisions relating to religious instruction that were contrary to the advice of Mahatma Gandhi, Maulana Azad and RadhaKrishnan. Section (1) of Article 28 expressly prohibits religious instruction in any educational institution wholly maintained out of State funds. But, strangely, it is permitted in privately run institutions even if they receive aid out of State funds. And Article 30 reads :

> "All minorities, whether based on religion or language, shall have the right to establish and administer educational institutions of their choice."
>
> "The State shall not, in granting aid to educational institutions, discriminate against any educational institution on the ground that it is under the management of a minority, whether based on religion or language."

Here is a case of unilateral secularism. The majority of Indian students (necessarily Hindus) were to be denied religious instruction; but students belonging to the minority religions—of which Islam and Christianity are the largest—are allowed to be indoctrinated in their respective monotheistic faiths according to which there is no salvation except through the teaching of Jesus Christ and Prophet Mohammad respectively.

The prohibition of religious instruction in State-run schools and its permission in those run by religious minorities runs counter to other Articles of the Constitution which guarantee non-discimination between citizens on the ground of religion. The unilateralism is reminiscent of the Khilafat years, in the early part of the century, when Gandhiji called upon Hindus to support their Muslim fellow-countrymen's Fight to preserve the territorial empire and the spiritual suzerainty of the Sultan of Turkey over Muslims world-wide, but refused to ask for a quid pro quo from Indian Muslims. M. Asaf Ali, nationalist Muslim leader of Delhi, made a visit to Deoband, a centre of Muslim theological learning, to persuade the teachers and students there that Muslims in India would do well to reduce or eschew cow slaughter voluntarily, as a mark of respect for Hindu sentiment and a reciprocal gesture for Hindu support to Khilafat. But Gandhi was against anything smacking of a bargain. He wanted Hindu support for the Muslim cause of Khilafat to be unconditional. It is another matter that his hopes of enduring Hindu-Muslim unity being forged thereby went awry. India was partitioned in August 1947 to constitute Muslim-majority areas into a separate State of Pakistan.

Maulana Azad returned to the subject of moral instruction in the course of an address to the Central Advisory Board of Education in February 1948. He said : "It was at first considered that religious instruction would stand in the way of the free intellectual development of a child, but now it has been admitted that religious education cannot altogether be dispensed with. If national education was devoid of this element, there would be no appreciation of moral values or moulding of character on humane lines."

***Hedonism and Fanaticism :*** Maulana Azad's warning has proved only too true. In the case of the majority of India's younger generation comprising those who are Hindu by the accident of birth, secular education has nurtured the pursuit of money and of pleasure, never mind the ethics of how they are secured. Jawaharlal Nehru was able to sense this danger by 1959 when, during the Azad Memorial Lecture, he said that 'the passion for riches, for acquisition, for more and more wealth tends to corrupt" and cautioned against the tendency to criminality and eroticism.

On the part of many members of the Muslim community, the constitutional sanction of indoctrination in a single religion in educational institutions run by religious minorities has kept alive and intensified the separatist mentality that resulted in the partition of India in 1947. Among the factors that have nurtured secessionist sentiment in Kashmir over the decades since the State acceded to India in 1947 is the continuous indoctrination of Muslim children in a fanatical version of Islam in madarsas run by the Jamaat-e-Islami.

This is grim proof of the soundness of the warning sounded by Maulana Azad in January 1948 : "What will be the consequence if the Government undertakes to impart purely secular education? Naturally, people will try to provide religious education to their children through private sources. How these private sources are working today or are likely to work in future is known to you. I know something about it and can say that not only in villages, but even in cities the imparting of religious education is entrusted to teachers who, though literate, are not educated. To them religion means nothing but bigotry."

***Inter-religious Ecumenism :*** Ecumenism is a term used by Christians for unity of the whole Christian world, transcending differences between Christian sects. A higher vision, that of a vast inter-religious ecumenism, inspired Gandhi, Azad and Radhakrishnan. Jawaharlal Nehru came to accept this when he said in the course of the Azad Memorial Lecture delivered by him in November 1959, less than five years before his death : Two great religions have influenced India—two emerging from her own thought, Hinduism and Buddhism, and two coming from abroad but establishing themselves firmly in India : Christianity and Islam. Science today challenges the old concept of religion. But if religion deals not with dogmas and ceremonials, but rather with the higher things of life, there should be no conflict with science or *inter se* between religions, it might be the high privilege of India to help in bringing about this synthesis."

While Nehru thus finally arrived at the truth perceived earlier by Maulana Azad among others, it did not impel him to call for a reconsideration of the provisions in the Constitution relating to religious instruction in schools and colleges which run flatly counter to inter-religious ecumenism: these provisions, as we have seen, banish religious instruction from State-run schools but permit fanatical indoctrination in a single religion in private schools run by religious minorities—including those that are recognised by and given financial aid by the Indian State.

What Jawaharlal Nehru came to see in 1959 is being gradually recognised by Nehruites. G. Parthasarathi, a protege of Nehru who distinguished himself in the fields of diplomacy and education after initial grounding in journalism, said in the course of his convocation address at the University of Hyderabad in March 1987 : "Now that the concept of a core national curriculum has been accepted, it seems to me that consideration might be given to the inclusion in it of a course covering the development of human values the world over, and with special reference to India. Such a course would cover the contributions made to the development of a humanistic outlook by the various religions, by outstanding thinkers, by Marxism and the different schools of socialist thought, as well as by modem science many of whose findings are supportive of the concepts of humankind's oneness and of the ecological relatedness of all life on earth."

Another Nehruite, Aruna Asaf Ali, approvingly quoted the above passage in the course of the Azad Memorial Lecture she delivered in 1989. She went further and called for a review and amendment of the Constitutional provisions pertaining to religious instruction in schools so as to promote the inter-religious ecumenism which the best Indian minds have commended through the ages, and of which recent advocates include Gandhi, Azad, Radhakrishnan and the later Jawaharlal Nehru.

***Clarifying Secularism Failure :*** Among the paradoxes of free India is that the noble concept of inter-religious ecumenism has come to be equated with and referred to as 'secularism'. This is a violation of the English language. As the Concise Oxford Dictionary tells us, secularism stands for, 'concerned with the affairs of this world; not sacred or monastic or ecclesiastical; sceptical of religious truth or opposed to religious education'.

Like much else in post-independence India, the confusion of thought about secularism has its origin in the development of Jawaharlal Nehru's ideas. Beginnings as a Marxist and an agnostic, he matured over the years to the advocacy, cited earlier, of inter-religious ecumenism. In between, for long years, he popularised the term 'secularism' to stand for his own vision of the good society. In a letter to Chief Ministers of States in 1956, he wrote : "We call our State a secular one. The word 'secular' perhaps is not a very happy one. And yet, for want of a better, we have used it. What exactly does it mean ? It does not obviously mean a state where religion as such is discouraged. It means freedom of religion and conscience, including freedom for those who may have no religion. The word 'secular", however, conveys something much more to me, although that might not be its dictionary meaning. It conveys the idea of social and political equality. Thus, a caste-ridden society is not properly secular."

It is a pity that, along with Nehru, the Indian Press by and large failed to see the absurdity of constitutional provisions some of which ordain equal treatment of citizens irrespective of their religion, and Articles 28 and 30 which treat citizens differently precisely on the ground of religion. The Ramakrishna Mission seeking the status of a religious minority in order to avoid State interference in the educational institutions run by the Mission, and securing legal recognition as such in 1985 through a judgment of the Calcutta High Court, was a reduction ad absurdum of Article 30. The Press hardly said a word about the case. Nor has there been much notice taken of the Supreme Court's reversal, in the second half of 1995, of the Calcutta High Court's judgment in the Ramakrishna Mission case.

Nehru, again, saw no violation of secularism in his confining to Hindus the reform of marriage and family laws in the 1950s. As a result, it became an offence for a Hindu to practise bigamy or polygamy, while Muslims remained free to practise bigamy or polygamy. No wonder that the Muslim vote bank, virtually controlled by the community's fanatical and male-chauvinist leaders, remained available to the Congress party for decades.

It is not only the Congress that has followed the policy of placating Muslim sentiment, while professing secularism, with an eye on the Muslim vote. On 7th June, 1969, the Community Party of India (Marxist), then ruling the State of Kerala in coalition with the Muslim League, announced that it would carve out a Muslim-majority district of Malappuram, on the eve of a by-eiection there. Other secularists did not criticise the politically opportunist decision aimed at securing the Muslim vote. It was left to Kelappan, an aged Gandhian, to lead an unsuccessful protest.

Many Muslims in northern India became alienated from the Congress during the emergency regime of 1975-76 because of the strong-arm methods employed by Prime Minister Indira Gandhi's second son, Sanjay Gandhi, to promote family planning through sterilisation. This was among the factors leading to Congress defeat in the Lok Sabha elections of early 1977. The post-emergency Janata Party government soon fell, due to internal squabbles for power. After returning to power in 1980, Indira Gandhi issued instructions for implementation of a 15-point programme for upliftment of the religious minorities (meaning Muslims since the second largest religious minority, the Christians, are neither educationally nor economically backward compared to the generality of the population). The special programme, which has continued to be implemented by successive governments to this day, is reminiscent of the days of British rule when the alien regime showed solicitude for the minorities in an effort to keep them away from the national movement. The Press, by and large, found nothing wrong in special favour being shown to certain citizens on the basis of their religion.

***Opportunism, no Monopoly :*** Opportunism is no monopoly of political groups professing secularism. The Bharatiya Janata Party, which accuses others of appeasing Muslims and exploiting caste feelings, has not dared to question the concept of reservation in admission to colleges and in recruitment to government services and public sector undertakings for persons—irrespective of his or her merit—belonging to a particular caste (Scheduled or 'Other Backward') or tribe. The BJP obviously values the OBC vote bank as much as every other political party does. It has been left to the judiciary to come to the rescue of a polity plagued by caste-based vote-bank politics, by placing a limit on such reservations and insisting on a means test by calling for exclusion of the 'creamy layer' which is to be found in every caste.

The Press neither noticed the BJP's call in 1989 for a system of proportional representation which will more truly reflect popular opinion in the legislatures, nor BJP's subsequent abandonment of this important item of electoral reform. Till the elections to the ninth Lok Sabha, the BJP had been securing fewer seats in the State Assemblies and the Lok Sabha than its share of the popular vote warranted. Thereafter, it became in many states a beneficiary of the prevailing electoral system of first-past-the-post.

When the Rajiv Gandhi government sponsored the disgraceful Muslim Women's Act following a howl of protest by Muslim male chauvinists against a Supreme Court judgment of 1985 which held that Muslims were as much bound as other citizens of India to provide maintenance to a divorced and needy wife, there was criticism of the opportunist legislation by a wide section of the Press. But thereafter the newspapers lost interest in the subject. The Press, by and large, did not criticise the call by the Muslim League, emboldened by the Rajiv Gandhi government's retreat, for repeal of the Directive Principle of the Constitution which calls for enactment of a uniform civil code for all citizens. In 1995, when a Supreme Court bench reminded the government of the subject and asked what the government was doing about it. Prime Minister Narasimha Rao trivialised the issue by speaking of the difficulties of enacting a uniform marriage law when there were different practices in different communities, and different parts of the country, in the matter of marriage between cousins.

Few commentators told the Prime Minister that the issue is not about marriage between cousins, but whether bigamy should be legitimate for some citizens of India and a crime for others, depending on their religion; and that equal treatment of all citizens irrespective of their religion is what secularism—which Narasimha Rao frequently swears by—is all about.

On 16th March 1995, the Press Information Bureau of the Central Government put out a news item that the Finance Corporation for Minorities, which the Narasimha Rao government established after conferring statutory status on the Minorities Commission, would extend aid on concessional terms to members of minority religious communities whose household income is twice the poverty level as defined by the Planning Commission from time to time. Here was a virtual laying down of two poverty line definitions, one for the Hindu majority and the other for religious minorities. There can be no more blatant violation of secularism, yet the Press has hardly taken notice of it. True, the PIB's daily output is largely of publicity puffs, but it is surely the duty of the national news agencies which supply the staple of news to newspapers of varying political persuasion, and of the special correspondents of individual newspapers, to retrieve the few needles of significant information from the haystack of PIB's output. In respect of these parodies of secularism, it was not to be expected that A.I.R. and Doordarhan, tightly controlled by the Government, would attempt critical discussion.

The failure of the Press in the cases—illustrative, not exhaustive—cited above perhaps arises from the fact that the intellegentsia manning the Press—belonging as they do to the same social, economic and educational background as the middle and higher levels of the teaching profession and the judiciary—share the general confusion of thought about secularism. Another reason could be that journalists, like academics, have been well looked after by successive governments—-through Wage Boards in the case of the Press, as by the University Grants Commission in the case of the higher class of the teaching profession.

In any case, it is remarkable that the Press took hardly any notice when intellectuals sustained in comfort by the Establishment through such government-funded bodies as the Indian Council for Social Science Research, the Institute for Advanced Studies and the Indian Institute of Mass Communication, adopted a resolution at a gathering at Shimla in April 1987 which said : "Secular values should be actively promoted by judges, teachers and religious teachers." This extraordinary proposition would have been laughed to scorn anywhere except in India. Not surprisingly, intellectuals of that age, as well as the Indian Press by and large, have been in a state of amnesia about Prof. Mushirul Hasan who was expelled by Islamic mobs from Jamia Millia (a central university funded by the Government) in 1992. Me was thus punished for suggesting that reasoned discussion is a better way of countering the views expressed in a book (in this case 'The Satanic Verses' by Salman Rushdie) than banning it. Mushirul Hasan continues to be holed up in the campus of Jawaharlal Nehru University where his wife teaches.

So devoid of meaning has the term secularism become that (the then) President Shanker Dayal Sharma has described Guru

Teg Bahadur, who put his religion above his life, as a 'secularist'. According to a Press release of the PIB on 17th December, 1993, Dr. Sharma said in the course of his statement on the anniversary of the Guru's martyrdom : "May his shining example of service and secularism and the glory of his sacrifice inspire each one of us to work for national unity." Earlier, Prime Minister Narasimha Rao said in the course of his convocation address on 22nd November, 1991 at the Sathya Sai Institute of Higher Learning that the Sai Baba's "emphasis on five universal values of Sathya, Dharma, Shanti, Prema and Ahimsa is truly Secular in character, and these constitute the major bedrock of all the religons of the world."

*Confused Thinking* : No wonder that, in this climate of totally confused thinking on what secularism means, the Press did not report at any length, nor studied and discussed, the judgment delivered by the Supreme Court on 11th March 1994, upholding the dissolution of the popularly elected legislatures in four States following the demolition of the Babri Masjid in December 1992, on the ground that the Bharatiya Janata Party that ran the governments there was not committed to secularism.

In a medley of judgments that concurred on this central point. Justice A.M. Ahmadi (now Chief Justice) said in the course of his order : The term 'Secular' (in the Preamble to the Constitution) has advisedly not been defined, pre-sumably because it is a very elastic term not capable of a precise definition, and perhaps best left undefined." (SUPREME COURT CASES, 1994, Vol. III, page 77). Another Judge on the nine-member bench that decided the case. Justice B.P. Jeevan Reddy, remarked in the course of his order : "Both the expressions—'socialist' and 'secular'—by themselves are not capable of precise definition."

Our newspapers have hardly noticed the implications of the remarks of the two learned Judges quoted above, who held along with seven of their brother Judges that Secularism, though it is undefinable, is a basic feature of India's Constitution. Failure of the media to demand, and themselves to attempt, clarification of the concept of secularism has detracted from their social role as agencies of non-formal education.

The media and the general public will do well to ponder the advice given on this subject by Aruna Asaf Ali, heroine of the freedom struggle and a lifelong fighter for women's equality and economic justice. Pointing out that the Muslim League and the Bharatiya Janata Party claim to be secular, as do the Congress and the Left parties, she said in the course of an article in *'National Herald'*, Delhi, of 2nd October, 1993 : "Considering that all political parties have made a mockery of the concept of secularism, is it not time to drop the term from the vocabulary of our political discourse ? If what we want to advocate is equal goodwill on the part of the State towards all citizens of India irrespective of their religion, and civilised and humane treatment of each other by the citizens themselves, I would suggest that we find another word. Perhaps it could be humanism."

***Humanist Education :*** A document that has not received the public attention it deserves, since the media have taken hardly any notice of it, is the report of a Core Group on Value Orientation of Education, set up by the Planning Commission. The group, which was headed by Dr. D. Swaminathan, member of the Planning Commission, was formed as the result of the notice taken of the subject by the Commission while formulating the Eighth five Year Flan (1992-97). The Plan document said, in the chapter on education : "The significance of value education has been highlighted by several committees and commissions on education. The Planning Commission has recently constituted a core group on value orientation in education. The recommendations of the group will be considered for implementation in consultation with the Ministry of Human Resource Development, University Grants Commission, Association of Indian Universities and National Council for Educational Research and Training."

The core group's report, submitted in October 1992, says in the Introduction : "In post-independence India, in the name of secularism which was not correctly understood, hardly any serious efforts were made to promote value orientation of education." (para 2.06). This was a surprisingly daring statement to be found in a document emanating from the Congress establishment, even if the report abounds elsewhere in instances of equating—though it is linguistically absurd to do so—secularism with religious values. It is also of interest that most of the institutions where instruction is imparted in moral values, whose work is surveyed approvingly in the lengthy annexures to the core group's report, are associated with traditional religion, not secularism. They include : Sri Sathya Sai Institute of Higher Learning, Prasanthi Nilayarn; the Banasthali Vidyapeeth, where the students recite 'Sarva Dharma Prarthana' on the lines advocated by Mahatma Gandhi; the Dayalbagh Educational Institute which was founded by the fifth guru of the Radhaswami faith, which seeks to promote an understanding of various beliefs so that students may develop an attitude of tolerance; and the Ramakrishna Institute of Moral and Spiritual Education, Mysore, whose B. Ed. course includes compulsory study of the major religions of the world.

Much of the report of the Planning Commission's core group consists of a recital of what earlier committees and commissions said on the subject. Of special interest is the following extract from the report of the Committee on Religious and Moral Education set up by the Union Ministry of Education in 1959, with Sri Prakasa as chairman : "Many ills that our world of education and our society as a whole is suffering today, resulting in widespread disturbance and dislocation of life, are mainly due to the gradual disappearance of the hold of basic principles of religion on the hearts of the people. The only cure, it seems to us, is in deliberate inculcation of moral and spiritual values from the earliest years of our lives."

Again, the Education Commission headed by Dr. D.S. Kothari said in its report (1966) : "Modernisation does not mean, least of all in our national situation, a refusal to recognise the importance of, or to inculcate, necessary moral and spiritual values and self-discipline. While a combination of ignorance with goodness may be futile, that of knowledge with a lack of essential values may be dangerous." The weakening of social and moral values in the younger generation is creating many serious social and ethical conflicts in western societies, and there is already a desire among great Western thinkers to balance the knowledge and skills which science and technology bring, with the values and insights associated with ethics and religion at its best."

Two questions arise. Will politicians, engaged in a ceaseless battle for survival in, or capture of, power find time to implement the recommendations made by the Planning Commission's core group on value orientation in education ?

The recommendations amount to what we have described as the promotion of an inter-religious ecumenism. This raises the second question. Will the leaders of the two largest religious minority communities agree to compulsory instruction in the values common to all religions ? This will amount to an admission that Islam and Christianity are not the only true religions.

The Sufis of Islam cheerfully accepted the oneness of all religions. Thus saint Sarmad of Delhi, who hailed from west Asia, said that he had passed from Jewish faith into Islam and had wandered from Islam "into the garden of Sri Rama and Laxman". Sarmad's friend and follower, Dara Shikoh, translated some of the Upanishads into Persian. But Dara's younger brother Aurangzeb, a fanatic, caused both Sarmad and Dara to be put to death. And the dominant influence on the minds of Indian Muslims has continued to be the Shariat, and not Sufi teaching. Similarly, in the deeply humanist teaching of Jesus Christ himself there is no sectarian dogmatism, but Pauline churchianity has been a different matter. As for India's principal religion, while the history of Hinduism is not free of instances of sectarian pride and intolerance—as for instance on the part of the fanatical among Saivites and Vaishnavltes—Hindu polytheism has served to make intelligible at the popular level, and thereby to sustain, such humanist insights as that truth is one though the learned call it by different names, and that different faiths are only different paths that lead to the same goal. It is this catholic strain in Hinduism that has made it possible for the people of India, most of whom are Hindus, to accept the democratic and egalitarian foundations of the Constitution which—aberrations like Articles 28 and 30 apart—treats all citizens alike.

The teaching of inter-religious ecumenism as a compulsory part of education will be as difficult to achieve, and for the same reasons, as a common civil code. But both are equally necessary for building a just and agalitarian society. The media can do a great deal, through sustained education of public opinion, to make this possible.

## Heritage and Culture

The hope of the mass media drawing on the best elements in each of India's religious traditions is considerably dimmed by their present performance, which Is subversive of our cultural heritage.

The threat to culture posed by the mass media was ably summed-up by the Parliamentary Standing Committee on Human Resource Development, in its twelfth report presented on 25th August, 1994. After considering the approach paper on a Rational Policy on Culture prepared by the Ministry of HRD, the committee said it was "deeply disturbed at the virtual absence of any reference in the Approach Paper to the impact of the mass media on cultural development, nothing in the recent past has had such dramatic and deleterious impact on our cultural traditions as the invasion of the mass media, both indigenous and foreign." An important objective of the NPC is to evolve a creative response to this new challenge which alone will enable us to preserve our cultural continuity with the past, while rejecting the baneful and integrating the desirable in the influences which are entering our country through the new electronic technology. Should we fail to evolve a sufficiently creative response to this challenge, there is every danger of India succumbing to an imitative culture and losing its indigenous creative genius. It will avail us nothing if we attain material progress but lose our soul in the bargain.

> "There is no way in which we can shut ourselves off from the consequences of satellite technology. Retracting into a shell is not the answer. At the same time, passively succumbing to the invasion is not the answer either. Even while emphasising the need for a creative response to this invasion, the NPC must see how we can avail ourselves of this technology to promote an understanding of our cultural heritage among the masses of our people at large, as well as take the message of India to the outside world."

> "On the domestic front, this will require the conscious and deliberate use of the electronic media for the dissemination of our many rich regional cultural and linguistic traditions within the region and in the country at large. It will also call for the deployment of numerous local T.V., Video and Radio Production centres, especially in remote and rural areas, for local communities to actively participate in Radio and T.V. programmes of their own making, instead of being reduced, as at present, to merely passive recipients of programmes produced, broadcast and telecast from elsewhere, many of which have little relevance to their lives. Such production centres, with responsibility delegated to grassroot bodies, would be the ultimate answer to the dangers of consumerism, commercialism, heedless Westernisation, and imitative cultural modes. This will also counteract the tokenism which now represents the media attitude towards both folk and classical culture. A few small slots in a crowd of commercial entertainment respect neither the artistes nor their public. The proliferation of channels on Doordarshan must be utilised to encourage both

> tradition and experiment in rural and urban art forms."
>
> "At the same time, global satellite technology offers us an unprecedented opportunity of disseminating our culture to the world at large; it is a challenge to which our electronic media must rise, in concert, with the Department of Culture, whose duty it is to ensure that Indian global T.V. does not become a pale imitation of existing Western-dominated networks."
>
> "The Committee recommends that the NFC should explore measures to make the mass media an effective instrument for the dissemination of culture. The emphasis should be on the production of serials, documentaries and films relating to important personalities, places, festivals, literature and the arts. The mass media should not promote superstitious and magical belief systems. Doordarshan should use innovative methods to attract attention to the classical arts. Children should be exposed to the diversity of India's cultural and linguistic traditions through translations into their mother tongues of the poetry and the songs of great patriots and poets."

The Committee expresses its serious concern over the ever increasing and reckless exhibition of violence, antisocial activities and obscenity through the cinema, the worst sufferers of which are the younger generation whose finer sensibilities are being coarsened and creative faculties dulled. The Committee, therefore, recommends that the NPC should address these issues and discourage these trends.

***Sensitive Awareness :*** Among the glories of India's cultural heritage is the sensitive awareness of our forbears to the relationship between human wellbeing and the environment, exemplified by veneration of the *pancha bhoota* of air, water, earth, fire and the sky. It is tragic that the mass media did not bring out, over the decades of the heedless pursuit of industrialism and of profit for contractors and industrialists, the social cost in terms of the pollution of our rivers and denudation of our forests. Environment has begun to be discussed by the media only after the subject became a fashion in the industrially developed countries of the west. This is one of the many instances of the imitativeness of western culture on the part of most of our media practitioners, arising from their ignorance of and consequent lack of pride in our own cultural heritage.

5

# The Guidelines

## Press Guidelines

In an annexure, listing guidelines on the right to privacy, the Council pointed out that the Indian Constitution does not expressly declare any right to privacy unlike certain global instruments to which India is a signatory, like the human rights charter. Even so, there is a school of thought which holds the view that the right to privacy is a fundamental right emanating from Article 21.

According to the Press Council, the law of defamation covers certain limited aspects of privacy. Certain countries have, therefore, enacted privacy laws which go beyond the range of defamation or reputation to protect personal interest, grief and the personality or psyche of the individual.

*Litmus Test :* The guidelines laid down by the Council specify that for journalists writing about people in terms of human interest, the litmus test must be in public interest—the person being public person by some reasonable definition (politician, sportsman, scientist or anyone in the public eye by virtue of his position, achievements or notoriety) and a person whose actions fall within the domain of public interest, as an example or warning to others. Even then, the publication must be justified by the legitimate public interest, not a prurient or morbid curiosity.

The personal and family or social life of a public figure or one who adopts a position of moral leadership can legitimately be open to public scrutiny where the private conduct can adversely affect or influence the proper discharge of his/her public functions and he/she may be setting a bad example where seen as a role model by others.

Any private activity liable to result in the commission, of a crime or result in evasion of criminal liability or in seriously antisocial conduct may also be legitimately exposed in the public interest.

***Added Protection :*** While all individuals are equal, certain vulnerable categories like children, women, the aged, the mentally retarded or handicapped and the sick require added protection.

Rapes and molestation of women, sexual abuse of children etc. are fit cases where privacy should be respected and the identity, photographs or sordid details of the offence should not be publicised to those unconcerned with law enforcement or with administrative jurisdiction in the matter.

A discharged convict has a right to a fresh start in building his/her life anew. It would be an invasion of privacy to recall his/her earlier crime to damn a redeemed criminal in the absence of any public interest consideration.

It would also be an invasion of privacy to name the family or associates of a wrongdoer when they are totally innocent of the crime and no public interest is involved. Suggestive guilt by association would be unfair to the privacy of others.

Even in cases where the reports are legitimate and proper, but the means by which the information has been gained entails an unwarranted intrusion into the privacy of an individual, such reporting is to be eschewed. Such intrusive reporting may be by gate-crashing into a home or hospital room unnoticed to write about an accident or illness, or publishing casual conversation overheard or something told in confidence or in a privileged gathering.

Interception of mail, phone tapping, bugging, photographing people in their homes without their consent or by using telephoto lenses would be invasion of privacy. Breach of fair practice by one journal would not justify publication by another.

*The Times of India* published the regret on September 27,1991 with the following note from the Editor :

> 'The Press Council has directed this paper to publish the gist of its decision of how the murder of the two nuns in Bombay in November 1990 was reported and has asked us to express our regret, which we now are doing. We are deeply sorry if our report has hurt the sentiments of a section of our readers. However, in the light of the Press Council's findings, we will now review several issues of journalistic ethics which this case has given rise to — Editor.

***J.B. Patnaik Case and Illustrated Weekly :*** The Illustrated Weekly of India in its issue dated May 18, 1986, carried an article by its correspondent S.M. Abdi entitled, 'Shocking: The strange escapades of J.B. Patnaik' (Orissa Chief Minister). It dealt with deviant sexual life of the Chief Minister.

This article was followed by another captioned: 'Why is J.B. being allowed to gag the Press? The second supported the first.

The first article carried photostats of FIR of complaints against Patnaik. Soon after it was published, Patnaik filed a suit for damages of Rs 1 crore against The Illustrated Weekly of India.

In the suit filed in the Orissa High-Court, Patnaik asked for details about the documents, source of information from the writer of the article and the editor and publisher of the Weekly.

Even as the case was pending in the High Court, the editor and the publisher moved the Supreme Court against the order of the lower court arguing that the application for better particulars etc. amounted to seek disclosure of evidence which was not permissible under Order 6 of the Civil Procedure Code and no journalist could be forced to disclose his source of information.

Advocates for the petitioners also submitted that what was before the court was a libel suit and if anyone of the objection raised was proved, the suit would be decreed.

It is strange that this landmark in journalism should be attributed to The Illustrated Weekly of India. Magazine journalism came of age in India primarily due to this journal. Under Khushwant Singh's editorship in early seventies, the Weekly gained unprecedented heights. Magazine reports had never before been taken so seriously. Also the magazine had never sold so well. The seeds of the magazine revolution, which swept India in the late seventies and the early eighties, were sown in the offices of the Weekly.

It was the Weekly success story which led to the launching of Sunday and India Today in mid-seventies.

It was the first magazine to send its young reporters for field assignments. Investigative reports and human interest stories became the byword for magazine journalism.

As described earlier, the events of 1977 and the subsequent developments saw magazines emerge as a dominant force on the Indian media scene. Indepth reports and investigative stories became the preserve of the magazine. The dominance of the magazines over newspapers continued till mid-80s.

By mid-80s, the newspapers had begun to overtake the magazines in the field of indepth and investigative reporting. Sunday editor M.J. Akbar, who emerged on top of the scene after starting as a brilliant reporter for the Weekly under Khushwant Singh, started concentrating on daily newspapers. Slowly the glamour days of the magazines faded out.

With the sole exception of India Today, which showed a steady upward trend in its circulation figures, magazines by and large suffered considerable loss in circulation. It is said the Weekly story on Patnaik came at this juncture. It started publishing a number of sensational stories, each accompanied with a mark of exclamation.

Soon after the story about Patnaik appeared, Patnaik brought the full force of his office to harass and humiliate Pritish Nandy. He was arrested and interrogated. He was made to appear before the courts time and again and barring a brave but solitary exception, even senior lawyers of the state were reluctant to come to Nandy's help. All those who had filed affidavits against Patnaik retracted.

The Weekly maintained the posture that it had committed no wrong, in fact, done public service by exposing a chief minister who had been using his office for purposes other than administration.

After three years of legal battle, The Weekly's will wilted. It agreed before the Supreme Court to tender an apology to the chief minister. The text of the apology was filed before the apex court, and sealed till it was published by The Weekly.

The apology was published by The Weekly in its issue dated August 27 - September 2,1989. It ran as follows:

*Apology :* We Bennett, Coleman and Company Ltd., Pritish Nandy, Editor of The Illustrated Weekly and S.N.M. Abdi, special correspondent of The Illustrated Weekly, had published two articles under the captions, 'The strange escapades of JB Patnaik' and 'Why is J.B. Patnaik being allowed to gag the Press,' in the issues dated 18-24 May 1986 and 3-9 August 1986 respectively, based on information available to us. Subsequently, we found that the information on the basis of which these articles were written was not true and was politically motivated. We regret the damage done to Mr. Patnaik s reputation and offer our apologies to him.

Commenting on the Weekly-Patnaik episodes, Khushwant Singh said that he would never have published this kind of an article. He said he had the same kind of material sent to him, when he was the editor of the Weekly, by a senior member of the IAS. It was accompanied with documentary proof as well as a confidential report of the services tribunal which had recommended his dismissal. But he refused to publish it.

He said his view was that a person's private life should be his own. A public figure's private life could only be exposed if there was a clear evidence of misuse of power.

An eminent freelance journalist Nikhil Chakravarty said that an apology did not add to the credit of any newspaper or journalist. Therefore, before writing a story, we should exercise a sense of responsibility not only in relation to the question of privacy but on any other issue. He said 'my point about this particular case is that it should not have dragged on for three years. When the case was launched then if those who were responsible for the story found that it could not be substantiated, then they should immediately have moved up and issued a contradiction. The question of code of conduct has been hanging fire for decades. If you want to have a code of conduct for journalists you cannot have it in isolation from the code of conduct for politicians or public life as a whole. Even if one were to have a code of conduct it will be very difficult to enforce.' *Navbharat Times* Editor Rajendra Mathur said that first it was difficult to prove a case like this when the allegations were made against the chief minister in his home state. Second, there was the question of expenses because the case could go on and on and Bennett and Coleman could not fight these cases in a very pedestrian way.

He thought what could have been awarded as damages if Patnaik had won, half of it or perhaps two-thirds would have been spent in litigating the case. All this might have influenced the decision to apologise.

Inderjit, editor, INFA said: 'When a publication like *The Illustrated Weekly* carried a cover story on Patnaik, I was little shocked. Having been associated with *The Times of India* group for almost ten years, these are not the kind of cover stories one normally carried. I felt that the editor of the paper would have good reason and solid facts to back up the story. Now that he has agreed to apologise I do think that the facts could not back up the story. Therefore, I am a little distressed by this development. It was not in keeping with the character of *The Times* Group. It was scurrilous and highly defamatory.

It is possible as some people suggested that it was not easy to get the required evidence, it was also suggested that people in Orissa were afraid of the consequences, it was also suggested that people who had given sworn affidavits had resiled, but these are the hazards of our profession and all these factors should have been taken into consideration before publishing the story.....'

*The Times of India* Editor Dilip Padgaonkar offered the following comments:

> '. . .I would say, as a rule, a public official had a right to privacy, but if that privacy is explored without malice for public good, the Press should be allowed to do so. In this particular case, the article is not the kind I would have published in *The Times of India,* but if the editor thought it necessary to expose certain aspects of private life of the public official concerned I would have given him the benefit of doubt because the person in power and authority has a far greater room for manoeuvre to get things done to bring subtle or harsh pressures to promote his interests.

I may not agree with the decision of the editor to offer to apologise, but I understand why it was done. If you are going to enter into a very hazy legalistic area and if at the end of it all there would be no victors of any kind then why go into it? This can be one line of argument. I have known people who have filed suits because of intrusion into their privacy and then they find that if they submit themselves to interrogation, then there will be worse defamation.. .not many people want to subject themselves to this.

. . .principles are involved and my hope was that certain professional bodies such as the Editors Guild would take up this matter. I certainly intend to do so because if this becomes a precedent—an out-of-court settlement of this kind—then I am afraid that sooner or later—sooner rather than later—we might end up by curtailing an important area of Press freedom.'

It is worthwhile comparing what happened in Goa in September 1989. Goa Legislative Assembly Speaker Dayanand Ganesh Narvekar, allegedly molested a clerk, Sumita Holdankar. The matter leaked out. Credence was given to it by a political opponent, the leader of the Maharashtra Gomantak Party, Mr. Ramakant Khalap. The latter insisted that the story of molestation was true and that if it was proved to be false, he would quit politics.

The matter was taken up by Goa's English paper, *Gomantak Times.* The paper demanded the resignation of Narvekar. The daily reflected popular sentiment for soon the cry was taken up by others as well.

It is not that efforts were not made by interested parties to silence Sumita. *Gomantak Times* published stories of how attempts were made to buy Sumita Holdankar's silence. Someone, apparently, gave her Rs 11,000 to buy jewellery. *Gomantak Times* published photostats of bills. Sumita still has to explain how she was bribed.

Demands for Narvekar's resignation gathered momentum. The Gomantak Kshatriya Marathis Samaj, which comprises people belonging to the Kharvi and Pagi communities and of which Dayanand Ganesh Narvekar is a member, launched a strong attack on him. Over 6,000 young people from all over Goa converged on Panaji, the capital, to demand Narvekar's resignation.

The protest rally convened by the Students Action Front was addressed by Sumita who braved the wrath of the Speaker. Subsequently, Narvekar resigned.

But in the case of *The Illustrated Weekly* none among the journalist's community came out openly to support it. The key witness disappeared or refused to give evidence against Patnaik. The lawyers in Orissa, with the sole exception of one Ranjit

Mohanty were not prepared to take up this case because of the fear of retribution from the Chief Minister.

There might be few politicians whose personal lives are completely above board. The U.K. Prime Minister Harold Macmillan's life was in a mess with his wife Dorothy carrying on for years with another man; so was Lloyd George, US President Franklin Delano Roosevelt, had an affair with a friend of his wife, Eleanor.

S. Gopal, son of India's President S. Radhakrishnan, has written about his father's liaisons and the affair of Jawaharial Nehru with Lady Mountbatten has been talked about for years now with everyone from Mountbatten's official biographer Phillip Ziegly down to others less knowledgeable trying to put a kind face on the subject. Only Nehru's personal secretary, late M.O. Mathai, had the temerity to suggest that the emperor had no clothes. But the important thing about these happenings i& that they never arose during the life time of these individuals.

The scandal involving Christine Keeler (U.K. Society girl) and former UK Minister John Profumo is an extreme case. John Profumo had to resign not because he was carrying on with Christine Keeler, but because Keeler also had a Soviet Official as a friend to whom it was suspected, she might' have passed on secrets. Profumo had to quit in public interest.

It is doubtless that the life style of a public official has a tremendous bearing on the administration, but this can be exposed only if it is in public interest to do so.

It is also true that in India, unlike in the West, the public officials do not lead a distinct private and public life. It is invariably mixed up. This, perhaps, requires a close tab on them.

Taking into account the increasing tendency to publish defamatory news in the newspapers and magazines there is a need to strengthen defamation laws in the country. The Press Council indictment of newspapers publishing defamatory news is not a sufficient deterrent to prevent such publications. The Editors

Guild and other Press associations should ponder over this problem and suggest steps for self- regulation.

But the move on the part of the Rajiv government to pass Defamation Bill was to gag the Press and stop it from exposing misdeeds of public men.

**Bill of Defamation**

The idea to enact the Defamation Bill was conceived by the government sometimes in early 1987. It was around this time that media exposures on Bofors, Reliance Industries, and Ajitabh Bachchan's alleged purchase of flat in Switzerland surfaced. The immediate provocation was the revelations involving Lalit Suri allegedly getting a Rupees Six Crore commission from a Japanese firm on a pipeline deal. This story was carried by *The Statesman.*

On August 29, 1988, the Lok Sabha passed the Defamation Bill putting unprecedented curbs on the freedom of the Press in the post-Independence era, barring the Emergency period. The Bill sought to bring the following changes in the old law.

*Old Law*

(1) Prima facie onus of proving defamation with the complainant.

(2) Defamation cases to be tried in the judicial magistrate's court.

(3) No deadline for clearing the case.

(4) No minimum imprisonment.

(5) Matters termed grossly indecent, scurrilous and intended for blackmail not covered by law.

(6) No penalty for criminal imputation.

(7) Ten grounds to prove innocence including publication in good faith.

(8) Government departments treated on par with others.

(9) No pretrial penalty.

(10) Specific exemption from personal appearance.

(11) No provision for summary trial.

*New Law*

(1) Entire onus of proving innocence on the accused. The prosecution would have the right to lead evidence in rebuttal.

(2) The cases to go directly to the second stage Sessions Court.

(3) 90-day limit for the final judgement.

(4) Minimum imprisonment of one month on first offence, three months to five for subsequent offence. The imprisonment could be up to five years for subsequent offences.

(5) All these terms ware included in the Bill without specific definitions, making it possible to twist their meanings to support trumped up charges. The bill created a new offence of publication of grossly indecent or scurrilous matter intended for blackmailing. The terms grossly indecent or scurrilous were not defined. The bill explained that it was not scurrilous to make true imputations against any person provided it was for the public good, but the fact that it was good for the public had to be proved by the accused.

(6) Criminal imputation was made an offence.

(7) No ground to prove innocence in the case of criminal imputation.

(8) No exemption at all. The editor, printer and publisher to be personally present at every hearing of the case which would proceed on a day-to-day basis.

(9) Provision for summary trial and the proceedings to be held in camera.

The bill was rushed through and passed in a matter of nine-hour acrimonious debate in the Lok Sabha which resulted in the opposition walkout. The government did not bother to consult any professional body of the journalists during the time of the formulation of the bill.

The Home Ministry proposed a policy paper on the Defamation Bill. The then Home Minister Chidambaram played an active role in its drafting and instead of sending the paper to the Cabinet for approval, it was directly sent to legislative wing of the Law Ministry. In mid 1987 when the furore over defence scandals such as Bofors and HDW deals was at its peak, the Home Ministry approached the Cabinet with a comprehensive Bill.

The Cabinet appointed an 8-member group of ministers including P. Shiv Shankar, Vasant Sathe, H.K.L. Bhagat, Chidambaram and H.R. Bhardwaj, with Home Minister Buta Singh as its Chairman. The group met at least 20 times to finalise the bill. The final approval was given on August 8,1988.

The Bill evoked angry reaction from the journalists, constitutional experts and lawyers. It soon snowballed into a nationwide agitation.

On September 5, 1988 in an unprecedented show of unity, various sections of the Press from all over the country came together at a rally in Delhi against the proposed Defamation Bill. The journalists were joined in the rally by proprietors, freelancers and press workers. The 800-strong protestors marched down India Gate to Boat Club carrying placards.

Among the prominent personalities present at the rally were Ram Nath Goenka, Proprietor of *Indian Express,* Mr. Rajaji Rao, editor and proprietor of *Eenadu* (A.P.), Mr. Girilal Jain, former Editor, *The Times of India,* Mr. C.R. Irani, Managing Director, *The Statesman,* Mr. Arun Shourie, editor, *The Indian Express,* Mr. N. Ram, Associate Editor, *The Hindu,* Mr. Prem Bhatia former editor, *The Tribune,* Mr. M.J. Akbar, editor, *The Telegraph,* Mr. Aroon Purie, editor and proprietor *India Today,* Mr. Khushwant Singh, Mr. Kuldip Nayar, Ms Amita Malik, Mr. Gour Kishore Ghose, veteran journalist from Calcutta and winner of Magsaysay award, Mr. S. Nihal Singh, former editor of *The Indian Post* and *The Statesman.*

Mr. Ramkrishana Hegde and Mr. Biju Patnaik, also put in an appearance to express solidarity with the journalists.

With the exception of the English daily, *The National Herald* and its Urdu counterpart *Qaumi Awaj* all newspapers and news agencies observed a day's token strike on September 6 as part of the protest at the proposed Defamation Bill. On September 11, seven thousand lawyers practicing in various courts in Delhi, except the Supreme Court abstained from work against the Defamation Bill.

While expressing their solidarity with the agitated journalists, lawyers also warned the government against undue delay in withdrawing, what they said, the draconian Bill which was said to be the worst statutory aggression and onslaught on the freedom of speech and expression.

In pursuit of their struggle against the Defamation Bill, newsmen on September 7 walked out of a Press Conference being addressed by Union Minister for Information and Broadcasting and Parliamentary Affairs H.K.L. Bhagat.

Bhagat's plea that the government was prepared to reconsider all aspects of the Bill could not satisfy the journalists who maintained that they could not offer any cooperation on the issue with the sword of Damocles hanging over their heads.

On September 8, the entire Pune Press and the correspondents of Bombay newspapers boycotted the felicitation of Congress Secretary and barrister V. N. Gadgil. The latter was to be felicitated by Maharashtra Chief Minister Sharad Pawar on his first visit to the city after becoming Congress (I) General Secretary.

To meet out this threat from the journalists, the government worked out a strategy. Meetings were arranged with senior journalists known to be pro-Rajiv, but most of these journalists advised the government against the enactment of the Bill. Rajiv's media managers then tried to create rift among journalists by inviting some of them on the television.

Later, Bhagat wrote personal letters to journalists, inviting them for a dialogue with a 7-member committee constituted by the

Prime Minister. But to the government's surprise, all the organisations, except three which are pronouncedly pro-Congress-I rejected the invitation.

Faced with this situation, Prime Minister Rajiv Gandhi and his advisers desperately tried to evolve a face-saving formula.

Shortly after his return from Punjab on September 21, 1988, Rajiv Gandhi summoned the ministerial group for a discussion at his residence. The meeting lasted for over three hours and Rajiv decided to withdraw the Bill.

On September 22, 1988, Rajiv Gandhi announced the Defamation Bill's withdrawal with the following statement.

The Defamation Bill, 1988 was brought forward to protect the individual from defamatory speeches, writings and actions and to provide adequate and timely redress to the aggrieved. The Bill seeks to codify the existing law on the subject and to take it forward in some areas.

Defamation as defined in the Bill is not an issue between government and the Press but an issue between individual and individual, between a person aggrieved and a person accused. The Bill attempts to reconcile the rights of an individual with the right to freedom of expression of another.

A free Press is an integral part of the inner strength and dynamism of our democracy. Without a free Press, there can be no democracy. The imperishable values of our freedom struggle have gone into the making of the Press in India. We uphold this legacy. We shall continue to do so. Our commitment to this freedom of the Press is total. We have no intention of curbing in any way, the freedom of the Press.

The freedom and rights of the individual are equally sacred. It is this that makes the issue of defamation a serious issue.

The bill seeks to resolve the issue in accordance with the basic principles of our Constitution and the laws. It has, however, aroused misapprehensions and misgivings. The Press and section of the public have expressed their concern.

We are alive to these concerns. We draw inspiration from Mahatma Gandhi, Jawaharlal Nehru and Indira Gandhi, who always responded to democratic expression of opinion. We, therefore, offered an unconditional dialogue on the subject. Some organisations and individuals have responded to this offer.

We feel, however, that there should be wider and fuller national debate in keeping with our heritage and traditions.

The issue of defamation remains. It is our earnest hope that the concerned citizens, jurists and media will participate in the national debate on the issue of defamation. In course of time, government may, if necessary, make suitable forum to carry forward the dialogue in a spirit of understanding and cooperation. A solution based on national consensus will strengthen the institutions of our public.

The Central Government has made every effort to manage the Press after managing the other two organs of the government successfully—the Parliament and the judiciary. The Press by and large in India is pro-establishment. Even then the government is not satisfied and wants to choke a few discordant voices in the Press. The passage of this Bill would have scared the Press to do whatever little investigative reporting they are doing. In fact, there was no need to enact such laws if the Press Council in India is adequate to deal with defamation cases.

It is worthwhile examining the laws pertaining to the freedom of the Press and the right to privacy.

The mechanisms that have been evolved in truly democratic countries for achieving the above objectives are generally twofold. One is to make defamation a crime punishable with imprisonment or fine or both. The other is an action in the courts of law for the Tort of defamation in which damages can be awarded.

It is well known that in countries that have followed the civil law system, like France, have favoured the system of subjecting the defendant or respondent to penal punishment.

In those countries where the Anglo-Saxon system of jurisprudence prevails, like the United Kingdom, the USA, Australia and India, there are provisions for imposing penal punishment and/or claiming damages in civil courts.

Although criminal action can be taken in Britain, this is done in very few cases. In the UK there was some thinking whether the law of criminal libel should be drastically reformed and whether a new statutory offence of criminal defamation should replace the old offence.

It was proposed that the offence should be triable only on indictment and the penalty should not exceed two years imprisonment or a fine or both.

In fact, the British Law Commission had made it clear in its report that the offence which it had in mind is the character assassination type. When the Faulk Committee in England considered defamation in 1971, the British Press Council was of the view that criminal libel would have no relevance so far as the Press was concerned.

In the US one hardly comes across any instances where penal punishment has been awarded in defamation cases. But in civil actions the damages that are granted are so heavy that every newspaper has to think twice before publishing a libellous article.

Any student of the law of defamation has to understand its basic object and aim. The question immediately arises as to when interference with an individual liberty can be allowed.

The answer given is that such interference would be permissible when the individual actions cause harm to other members of the society. What kind of harm should the law then punish. As defamation deals with harm, it is necessary for the person who has published a defamation matter to justify the publication by invoking the fundamental right of freedom of expression which would include freedom of the Press as guaranteed by Article 19 (a) of our Constitution.

This raised the point that if something has been done for public good or in public interest or its truthfulness established, the harm to reputation of the person defamed should not attract any such consequences as may be penal or may involve payment of damages.

These as regarded as some of the basis of the defamation laws.

In the US, the decision of the US Supreme Court in *The New York Times*—Sullivan case (1964) has brought about revolutionary changes, especially in cases of action against public officials. In Sullivan case, the court ruled that even erroneous statements about public officials were protected by the constitutional mandate unless a libellous statement had been published with full knowledge of falsity or reckless disregard or its truthfulness.

In Australia, the position seems to be similar to that in the US where if one is wise one would make sure that all assets are in somebody else's name. For if one wants to discuss anything which is even slightly controversial, however small one is, one will be sued for defamation and one will be out of business or bankrupt within months.

Indeed it would not be wrong to say that criminal libel is becoming outmoded in defamation laws even in those developed countries where freedom and privacy of the individual are zealously guarded and highly prized rights.

In most of the countries the right of an individual to privacy has been recognised and it has close connection with defamation. Although privacy has been defined in the US, the best definition appears to be the one given by Thomas Colley. Privacy has not been recognised as a Tort either in India or Britain.

The Second Press Commission in India did not recommend any legislation on the subject. The Commission considered that Section 13 (l) (c) of the Press Council Act, 1978 should be amended by adding the words 'including respect for privacy.'

In our country, any law of defamation has in the first place to pass the test of constitutionality. Article 19 (1) of the Constitution confers on every citizen the fundamental right to freedom of speech and expression.

The Supreme Court has left no one in doubt that freedom of the Press is included in the above provision. The ambit and the scope of the provision is no less wide than what has been conferred by the First amendment to the American Constitution.

Clause 2 of Article 19 indicates the parameters of the right guaranteed under clause (1) (1). Thus, existing or future laws can be made imposing reasonable restrictions on the exercise of the right in the interest set in clause (2) which includes defamation.

One of the most important steps taken for the purpose of preserving the freedom of the Press and of maintaining and improving the standards of newspapers and news agencies was the establishment of the Press Council in 1966 by an Act of Parliament. The Act was repealed in 1976 and there was no Press Council in existence till the end of March 1979.

Our Press Council being a statutory body derives its powers from an Act of Parliament. It has 28 members and a chairman. It is completely independent and the manner in which its chairman and members are nominated is such that no executive or outside interference is possible.

## Scene in Foreign Lands

*France :* In France the law relating to privacy has been developed largely through interpretation of Article 1382 of the Civil Code of 1859 by the courts on case-by-case basis. There was a spurt in this process during the fifth and sixth decades of the twentieth century as a response to the increasing invasions of personal privacy by the Press. The principles thus evolved, by courts, were embodied in the Law of July 17, 1970. Article 9 of this codified law provides that 'each person has the right to have his privacy respected'.

The law of 1970 does not provide a general definition of 'privacy'. This has been left to be spelled out by the courts. In general, family, personal, and sexual matters are all covered by the right of privacy. 'Public interest', 'good faith', and 'truth' do not in themselves, furnish a good defence in an action for violation of privacy.

***Germany :*** In Germany, the Penal Code punishes, as criminal offences, certain grosser invasions of privacy, namely:

(a) trespassing into another person's home, and in certain other private places;

(b) recording private conversation without permission;

(c) eavesdropping using bugging devices;

(d) obtaining certain private information (such as medical records) without permission, and

(e) obtaining any private information which is stored in a computer.

To the above, there are certain exceptions, e.g., pictures within the scope of contemporary history; pictures of public processions, and pictures created for genuinely artistic purposes.

German Civil Courts have, through an interpretation of the Constitution, devised the concept of the 'right of human personality'. Pursuant to this concept, the courts provide a civil remedy in actions for defamation and invasion of privacy in a number of situations, which include:

(i) Where a newspaper publishes inaccurate personal infirmation about a person and then refuses to correct it;

(ii) Where one person makes use of another's picture without his consent in order to advertise the products; and

(iii) Where someone publishes the past misdeeds of an ex-offender, where it is not in the public interest to do so.

***Netherlands :*** Like Denmark, in the Netherlands, apart from defamation, a number of invasions of privacy are criminal offences. These include: trespass into another person's home, to eavesdrop on private conversations, and to take photographs of people on private property, without their consent; publication of such photographs is also an offence.

***Canada :*** Several provinces of the Canadian Federation have enacted torts of privacy. The British Columbia Privacy Act has much in common with the laws on the subject enacted by the other Provinces. This Act of 1979 provides that it is a tort, actionable without proof of damage, for a person wilfully and without claim of right, to violate the privacy of another.

Eavesdropping and surveillance are specifically but not exclusively, cited as means by which privacy may be violated. However, it is not a violation of privacy to publish material that is of public interest or (in) fair comment on a matter of 'public interest'. Unauthorised use of a person's name or portrait is also a tort under the Act.

A similar approach to the subject of privacy has been adopted by the Saskatchewan Privacy Act, 1979.

The Canadian Federal legislation on privacy (relating to information about individuals, held by public bodies) provides by contrast an exhaustive definition comprising 18 paragraphs, of private information. It also includes a general public interest provision to cover matters falling outside the specific criteria. This definition has been widely criticised as too long and confusing.

***United States :*** Professors Philip Meyer and Ruth Walden of the University of North Carolina, Chapel Hill, have conducted research in ethics of journalism. They find that the laws governing the Press in United States of America are frequently confusing and subjective, particularly in the area of privacy law. Walden notes that with a few minor exceptions, there is no federal law governing invasions of privacy by the media. Essentially, every state has its own law. There are 50 different privacy laws as they relate to the media. Nevertheless, since Warren and Brandeis article of 1890, intrusion upon an individual privacy has gradually come to be recognised as a tort throughout most of the United States, even though its definition and application vary from state to state. According to experts, the tort appears to cover the following four kinds of invasion of privacy, though they are considered distinct rights having little in common:

(a) intrusion into an individual's physical solitude;

(b) publication of private matter violating the ordinary decencies;

(c) putting someone in false light; and

(d) appropriation of an individual's name or likeness (normally for commercial purposes).

It is proposed to elaborate these categories a little.

*Intrusion* : Intrusion upon the solitude and private life of an individual is prohibited as an actionable wrong. Unauthorised wiretapping, telephone tapping, room bugging, snooping, making illegal searches and breaking into private records of an individual and like acts, without the consent of the individual concerned, are considered torts falling in this category. This legal wrong is committed as soon as the intrusion takes place whether or not the private facts gathered are published. Intruders are liable for this tort regardless of what use is made of the purloined material. This was so held by a California Court in Dietemann Vs Time-Life Magazine Inc, (1971).

However, the whole area of the law relating to intrusion upon privacy has not yet come out of the grey zone. Some kinds of intrusions through new sophisticated devices are hard to define. For committing this tort, it is not necessary for the intruder to enter upon private property. He may commit intrusion from outside, remaining at a distance, with the use of some snooper aids as telephoto lens, hidden microphones etc.

'While the public interest', noted Don R. Pember, 'Is the key to defending most privacy suits, it has very little to do with intrusion'. It seems that in U.S.A. public interest defence, normally, does not avail against intrusion.

*Publication of Private Information* : This category has been defined as 'the disclosure of private, embarrassing, non-newsworthy facts about an individual'.

This may take the form of deceptive or illegal means of obtaining information such as trespassing or unauthorised use of cameras.

'Gossip substances of private conversation, and details of private tragedy or illness', particularly when their publication is repugnant to good taste and sense, are legal wrongs of this category. Truthfulness of the information published is no defence to a suit when this tort constitutes the cause of action.

An example of lapses in ethical standards, akin to this type of infringement of personal privacy, is furnished by the publication of a story in *The New York Times.* In the second week of April, 1991, in which not only the alleged Palm Beach rape victim, who has accused a member of the Kennedy family of the criminal act, was blamed, but also the details of the woman's past, including her alleged 'wild break' in high school, her mother's divorce, and her 17 tickets for speeding and careless driving, were given. *The New York Times* further reported, 'She gave birth to a daughter by a local man she did not marry. In 1989 she had a brief affair with the son of a once prosperous family He was the father of the child, friends say. . . .' Another acquaintance, Nathaniel Read said: 'She liked to drink and have fun with the never-do-wells in cafe society.'

The publication of this story is reported to have brought *The New York Times* into the centre of an embarrassing public debate of its unusual foray into tabloid journalism. The editors of the paper had to face sharp protest from members of its own staff. One woman employee said that 'we don't understand why you have got *New York Times* reports peeping in windows'. Another staffer said the paper had 'crucified' the woman.

*The Times* editor also faced criticism over the publication on the front page of the newspaper recently, on Kitty Kelley's biography of Nancy Reagan, which contained unsavoury and fallacious allegations against the former First Lady. The Executive Editor of *The New York Times* was reported to have admitted that Kelley piece was a 'mistake' and that 'the story did not live up to our standards'.

The primary defence to an action for this kind of invasion of privacy, is that the published material is newsworthy, that is to say, it is of wide public or general interest. A Newsworthy formula has been devised by American Courts for this purpose. According to this formula, the nature of the story, the status of the subjects, the intimacy of the revelations, and the degree of embarrassment to the plaintiff are all weighed against each other. Publication of information about public officials or public figures, such as Ministers, legislators, entertainers, labour leaders, sport personalities, even "some editors, journalists and broadcasters, normally qualify as newsworthy. But publication of the same kind of information about private persons who are not public figures might not so qualify.

*Putting Someone in False Light* : The kind of invasion of privacy, according to some scholars, is an outgrowth of category (d) Appropriation. For constituting a tort under this category, it is not necessary that the published material should be defamatory or has been presented in a derogatory manner.

It is sufficient if the representation of the published material gives a false impression, even though the impression is not unfavourable, of the plantiff. Photographs, rather than stories are the common source of 'false light' actions in tort. Truth of the report is a valid defence to such an action. The defendant can also use the First Amendment as a defence and maintain that the plantiff has failed to prove that the material /story was published by the defendant with actual malice knowing it to be false, or in publishing it the defendant exhibited reckless disregard for the truth of the story.

*Appropriation* : This includes the unauthorised use of individual's name or likeness for trade or advertising purposes. Appropriation is the least ambiguous and the oldest of these four kinds of torts, stated above. The law relating to all the above categories of invasion of privacy, in the USA, is being still developed by their Supreme Court through its adjudications in a manner which seeks to strike a proper balance between the right to freedom of speech and freedom of the Press on the one hand, and the right to individual privacy, on the other. The overall position in USA has been summed up by Calcutt Committee (UK), thus:

> 'Generally speaking, the Press is free to publish almost any true material about public figures on the basis that virtually all human activity reveals the character of the person concerned. In some states, however, the publication of truthful but embarrassing information about individuals who are not public figures, can give rise to a cause of action. The Supreme Court has yet to rule on the constitutionality of this. Where the material published is untrue, some states provide redress on the grounds of false light. Cases on such grounds have been upheld by the Supreme Court.'

***United Kingdom :*** Although the English Common Law does not recognise the invasion of privacy as a tort in all cases in which the courts in USA do, yet the development of the law in USA had its impact on British scholars and jurists. Salmond in his Law of Torts, 15th Edition, adopted the view of Dean Prosser, one of the outstanding exponents of this concept. Salmond identifies four distinct kinds of torts recognised by American Courts.

No general right of privacy has been recognised under Common Law of the United Kingdom. However, as invasions of privacy by the media, particularly by the tabloid Press, increased, complaints against these intrusive forays were voiced by several sections of the British public. At the advent of the 7th decade of the Century, Younger Committee on Privacy was set up to study the problem and suggest remedial measures. In its Report rendered in July 1972, the committee recommended, by a majority, against statutory right of privacy for the reason that there was before it no compelling evidence, of a substantial wrong to be tackled.

It noted that since in complaints of invasion of privacy there may be a conflict of interest between the need of the public to be informed and the need to respect the individual's privacy, the balancing of these interests in each case should be left to the judgement of the Press Council. It recommended that the Council should insist that its adjudications be published with equal prominence to the original item. It further recommended that the

Council should explore the possibility of codifying its adjudications on privacy to give readier guidance to busy practising journalists and to the interested public and to keep the codification up-to-date. Consequent upon this, the Council began codifying its general adjudications but remained opposed to the publication of a formal code of practice.

In 1976, U.K. Press Council issued the following declaration of principles on privacy, setting out the rules for guidance of editors in deciding when to publish stories about people's private lives:

(i) The publication of information about the private lives or concerns of individuals without their consent is only acceptable if there is a legitimate public interest overriding the right of privacy.

(ii) It is the responsibility of editors to ensure that inquiries into matters affecting the private life or concern of individuals are only undertaken when in the editor's opinion at the time a legitimate public interest in such matters may rise. The right to privacy is, however, not involved if the individuals concerned have freely and clearly consented to the pursuit of inquiries and publications.

(iii) The public interest relied on as the justification for publication or inquiries which conflict with a claim to privacy must be a legitimate and proper public interest and not only a prurient or morbid curiosity. 'Of interest to the public' is not synonymous with 'in the public interest'. It should be recognised that entry into public life does not disqualify an individual from his right to privacy about his private affairs, save when the circumstances relating to the private life of an individual occupying a particular public position may be likely to affect the performance of his duties or public confidence in him or his office.

(iv) Invasion of privacy by deception, eavesdropping or technological methods which are not in themselves unlawful can, however, only be justified when it is in pursuit of information which ought to be published in the public interest and there is no other reasonably practicable method of obtaining or confirming it.

(v) The Council expects the obtaining of news or pictures to be carried out with sympathy and discretion. Reporters and photographers should do nothing to cause harm or humiliation to bereaved or distressed people unless it is clear that the publication of the news or pictures will serve a legitimate public interest and there is no other reasonably practicable means of obtaining the material.

(vi) Editors are responsible for the actions of those employed by their newspapers and have a duty to ensure that all concerned are aware of the importance of respecting the legitimate claims to personal privacy.

The Third Royal Commission on the Press headed by Lord McGregor, in its report of July 1977, adopted an approach similar to that of the Younger Committee. In the Commission's view also, legislation was not necessary because the Press Council could be its appropriate substitute. It, however, recommended that the Press Council should formulate a comprehensive code of conduct for the Press.

During 1988 and 1989 there occurred a number of glaring invasions of personal privacy by a section of the 'British Press, particularly the tabloid Press. As a result, the Press came under severe criticism for intruding upon accident victims and other patients in hospitals, for using stolen private photographs or correspondence and for publishing scurrilous details of individuals' private lives. Matters reached a climax when a million pound out-of-court libel settlement was made following stories in *The Sun* about Eltson John's private life. In the course of discussions in the 1988-89 session of Parliament, on two private Members' Bills, one introduced by John Brown, MP, and the other by Tony Worthington, MP, on protection of Privacy and Right of Reply, respectively a number of cases of such unethical practices indulged in by the Press were cited.

This led to the appointment by the government of the Committee under the Chairmanship of Sir David Calcutt to consider what measures (whether legislative or otherwise) are needed to give further protection to individual privacy from the activities of the Press and improve recourse against the Press for the individual citizen, taking account of existing remedies, including the law of defamation and breach of confidence, and to make recommendations.

Following the appointment of the Calcutt Committee, there were two major developments. In November 1989 Newspaper Publishers Association, formulated and declared a code of practice. Thereafter, on March 13, 1990 the Press Council in U.K. adopted a revised code after discussion with the interested parties, including Newspaper Publishers Association (NPA).

Para 5 directs Newspapers and journalists serving them to use 'straightforward means to obtain information or pictures. The use of subterfuge can be justified only to obtain material which ought to be published in the public interest and could not be obtained by other means.'

As per para 7, newspapers and journalists serving them were required to avoid intrusion into personal grief and to carry out inquiries with sympathy and discretion.

Para 10 provides that save in exceptional circumstances newspapers should not, even where the law permits it, identify children under the age of 16 as victims, witnesses or defendants involved in cases concerning sexual offences.

Para 11 forbids newspapers to identify victims of rape, or publish material likely to contribute to such identification.

Para 12 provides that newspapers should refrain from publishing pictures which needlessly exacerbate grief or cause distress.

Para 15 directs journalists making inquiries at hospitals or similar institutions, to identify themselves to a responsible official before entering except in very rare cases where information which ought to be disclosed could not otherwise be obtained.

**Calcutt Committee**

The Calcutt Committee accepted that there is little possibility of producing a precise or exhaustive definition of privacy or for that matter public interest. It felt that working definition of privacy, however, is nevertheless needed as a yardstick against which to measure complaints and solutions. It, therefore, adopted the following working definition:

> Privacy could be regarded as the antithesis of what is public hence everything concerning an individual's home, family, religion, health, sexuality, personal legal and personal financial affairs. The formulation 'the right to be let alone' is too simplistic. There is a mismatch between what an individual might regard as private and what might be regarded as such by his neighbours, including the Press....
>
> ...our formulation is the right of individual to be protected against intrusion into his personal life or affairs, or those of his family, by direct physical means or by publication of information.

The Committee emphasised that individual privacy is not to be considered in isolation. It must be weighed alongside freedom of speech and expression. In balancing these two factors, the Committee preferred to be guided in its approach by what the European Court of Human Rights, when interpreting Article 10 of the Convention, in its judgement in *The Sunday Times* vs United Kingdom (1979-80) 2 EHRR 245: (the Thalidomide case) emphasised that it was faced not with a choice between two conflicting principles but with a principle of freedom of expression that is subject to a number of exceptions which must be narrowly interpreted. 'Thus, the Committee professedly started from a position that freedom of expression is preeminent. Certain exceptions protecting individual privacy may then prove to be necessary.

*Public Interest :* The Committee conceded that it is not possible to devise a simple criterion of what constitutes a justifiable intrusion into an individual's privacy, it may have to be recognised that not all people are entitled to expect the same degree of privacy. A distinction may have to be drawn between what is justified in respect of public figures and what is justified for other people. Nevertheless, a public figure should not be required to surrender his right to privacy over every aspect of his life when he takes up public office or pursues a career which brings him into the public eye.

The committee emphasised that 'Public interest' in bald terms is not helpful in determining whether an intrusion is or is not justified.

*Unwarranted Intrusion :* In general terms, the Committee accepted that any conduct which impinges upon the public, might reasonably be made public. An individual who publicly claims to practice certain special or religious principle or adopts a position of moral leadership, can reasonably be subject to greater public scrutiny than his fellow citizens.

The committee opined that (generally) the revelation about the private life of a public figure are justified only—

(a) to protect the health or safety of the public, or

(b) to expose crime or seriously antisocial conduct, or

(c) in his behaviour if his private life adversely affects his public duties or is so hypocritical that the public is likely to be seriously misled.

The Committee concluded that just as it is impossible to define privacy other than in terms of a series of general values, so what constitutes an unwarranted intrusion into an individual's privacy can only be set out in terms relative to that person's status and conduct in the context of what is socially acceptable at the time.

It is inevitable that decisions will be based on a series of value judgements. 'We consider', said the Committee, 'that every code of practice likely to be of practical use in newspaper offices must take account of these complexities.'

A number of witnesses urged that the Calcutt Committee to recommend the introduction of a statutory tort of infringement of privacy. There was also a suggestion that the civil law might be evolved in relation to privacy by courts on case-by-case basis. In this context, the Committee observed:

> 'A Common Law right to privacy could possibly develop in Scotland, where there is more general concept of Culpa (wrongful behaviour) compared with the more narrowly-drawn English torts. But in its judgement on March 16, 1990 in Keyer Robertson and Sport Newspapers Ltd., the Court of Appeal clearly ruled out the development of such a tort in English Law. Any remedy of this kind would now have to be provided by Statute.' The Committee then quoted from the judgement of Glide-well and Legatt L. JJ. in the said case where this point was raised.

After examining the five Bills introduced on this topic from time during the period 1961 to 1989, as also the draft Bill produced by Justice and the Natural Council for Civil Liberties and all other material and suggestions before them, the Committee concluded:

> '... an overwhelming case for introducing a statutory tort of infringement of privacy has not so far been made out and that the better solution lies with the measures set out elsewhere in this report. We, therefore, recommend that such a tort should not presently be introduced.'

The Committee made it clear that they were making their recommendation on the assumption that the improved scheme for self-regulation of the Press recommended by them in Chapter 15 of their report, will be made to work.

***New Press Complaints Commission :*** The Committee recommended: 'The Press should be given one final chance to prove that voluntary self-regulation can be made to work. However, we do not consider that the Press Council even if reformed as proposed in its internal review, should be kept as part of the system. We, therefore, recommend that the Press Council should be disbanded and replaced by a new body, specifically charged with adjudicating on complaints of Press malpractice. This body must be seen to be authoritative, independent and impartial. It must also have jurisdiction over the Press as a whole, must be adequately funded and must provide a means of seeking to prevent publication of intrusive material. We consider it particularly to emphasise the break from the past. The new body should, therefore, be called the Press Complaints Commission.' (Hereafter called PCC.)

It is further recommended by the Committee that the PCC should publish, monitor and implement a comprehensive code of practice for the guidance of both the Press and public. The PCC should operate a hot line for complaints on a 24-hour basis. The PCC adjudications should in certain cases, include a recommendation that an apology be given to the complainant. The precise form of the apology, including whether it should be given publicly or privately, could also be prescribed.

The PCC should have an independent Chairman and not more than 12 members, with smaller subcommittees adjudicating on complaints under delegated powers.

Appointments to the PCC should be made by an Appointment Commission with explicit freedom to appoint whoever it considers best qualified. The Appointments Commission itself should be independently appointed, possibly by the Lord Chancellor.

Complaints Committee should have delegated power to release adjudications subject to a right of appeal for either party to the full Press Complaints Commission before publication.

The PCC should not operate a waiver of legal rights. If the industry wishes to maintain a system of non-statutory self-regulation, it must demonstrate its commitment in particular by providing the necessary money for setting up and maintaining the PCC.

***Three New Criminal Offences Proposed :*** The Calcutt Committee has recommended that the following acts should be criminal offences in England and Wales:

(a) Entering private property without the consent of the law ful occupant, with intent to obtain personal information with a view to its publication;

(b) placing a surveillance device on private property without the consent of the lawful occupant, with intent to obtain personal information with a view to its publication; and

(c) taking a photograph or recording the voice of an individual who is on private property, without his consent, with a view to its publication and with intent that the individual shall be identifiable.

The Committee has further recommended that it should be a defence to any of these proposed offences that the act was done.

(i) for the purpose of preventing, detecting or exposing the commission of any crime, or other seriously antisocial conduct; or

(ii) for the protection of public health or safety, or

(iii) under any lawful authority.

The Committee further suggested that the individual having a sufficient interest should be able to apply for an injunction against the publication of any of these criminal offences or, if the material has already been published, for damages or an account of profits. It also recommended that further considerations should be given to the extent to which the law in Scotland needs to be extended to cover the proposed offences and civil remedy and how this might best be done.

The other important recommendations made by the Committee, are as follows:

***Legal Restrictions on Press Reporting***

(a) The statutory prohibition on identifying rape victims in England and Wales should be extended to cover the victims of the sexual assaults (such as procurement of intercourse with a woman by threats, or by false pretences or by administering drugs, intercourse with girls under 16 or with mental defects, incest, buggery, indecent assault on female or male etc.).

(b) In any criminal proceedings in England and Wales, the court should have the power to make an order prohibiting the publication of the name and address of any person against whom the offence is alleged- to have been committed, or of any other matters likely to lead to his or her identification. This should only be exercised if the court believes that it is necessary to protect the mental or physical health, personal security of the home of the victim.

(c) After consulting the Press and the broadcasting authorities, Press Complaints Commission should is sueearly guidance on jigsaw identification.

***Right of Reply***

(d) A statutory right of reply should not be introduced.

***Tort of Infringemen t of Privacy***

(e) A tort of infringement of privacy should not be introduced.

***Statutory Complaints Procedure***

(f) If the Press fails to demonstrate that non-statutory self-regulation can be made to work effectively, a statutory system for handling complaints should be introduced.

(g) If maverick publications persistently decline to respect the authority of the Press Complaints Commission, the Commission should be placed on a statutory footing. It should be given sufficient statutory powers to enable it to require any newspaper, periodical or magazine to respond to its enquiries about complaints and to publish its adjudications as directed. It should be able to recommend the payment of compensation.

(h) The Government should set the budget for any statutory Press Complaints Commission and provide the money which it should then reclaim from the industry. The industry should set up a funding body which would apportion the cost between and collect the money from, various industrial bodies or individual publications.

*Press Complaints Tribunal*

(i) Should the Press fail to set up and support the Press Complaints Commission or should it at any time become clear that the reformed non-statutory mechanism is failing to perform adequately, this should be replaced by a statutory tribunal with statutory powers and implementing a statutory code of practice.

(j) There should be two separate triggers for the replacement of the Press Complaints Commission by a Press Complaints Tribunal.

(k) A Press Complaints Tribunal should perform two distinct functions. First, it should attempt conciliation and investigate complaints. Second, where necessary, it should resolve disputes by ruling whether there had been a breach of the code of practice. This should be reflected in its structure and procedures.

(1) The Press Complaints Tribunal should be able to award compensation. Unless the complainant can show financial loss, the amount of compensation should be limited by statute. This limit should be periodically reviewed.

(m) In privacy cases, the Press Complaints Tribunal should be able to restrain publication of material in breach of the code of practice by means of injunctions. No injunction should be granted if the publisher could show that he had a good arguable defence.

(n) The Tribunal Chairman should be a judge or senior lawyer appointed by the Lord Chancellor. He should sit with two accessors drawn from a panel appointed by the Home Secretary.

The Calcutt Committee has also proposed a code of Practice for the Press. Since infringement of privacy cannot be considered in isolation from other norms of ethics.

**Analysis**

Some aspects of the Calcutt report have been the subject of worldwide criticism. The chief target of criticism is that part of its recommendations as a result of which the new body i.e., The Press Complaints Commission which has replaced the erstwhile British Press Council has not been entrusted with the responsibility to preserve the freedom of the Press. This recommendation rests on the specious argument that defending the freedom of the Press and adjudicating on complaints are distinct functions which sit uneasily together, there being an inherent conflict between the two.

Mr. Blom Cooper, Chairman of the erstwhile Press Council, maintained that the twin functions are not merely compatible but also interlocked. He submitted that in this respect the report of the Calcutt Committee was fundamentally flawed. In support of the view that these twin functions were inextricably linked with each other, Mr. Blom Cooper referred to a passage in a speech delivered by Lord Devlin, the first independent Chairman of the British Press Council, that to censure effectively misconduct by the Press, it is essential that the Council seeks to preserve the established freedom of British Press and work as to maintain its character in accordance with the highest professional standards.

At the international Conference held in Stockholm on 11-15 June, 1991 on the occasion of the 75th anniversary of their Press Council, delegates from several countries assailed this recommendation of the Calcutt Report and consequent debarment of the new Press Complaints Commission from entertaining complaints of infringement of Press freedom. Eminent among those critics included, Mr. Olle Stenholm, former Chairman of the Swedish Newspaper Publishers Association, Mr. Kenneth Morgan, Director of the British Press Complaints Commission and Professor David Flint, Chairman of the Press Council of Australia.

All of them were firmly of the view that preserving Press freedom and maintaining Press standards, were inseparable as two sides of the same coin. Professor David Flint described the British experiment in setting up the Press Complaints Commission as an ill advised attempt to divorce Press freedom from Press responsibility.

Since Mr. Kenneth Morgan was the best informed person about these developments in UK it will be worthwhile to refer to some of the points made by him in his speech.

In his opinion, the main contributory cause of the death of the British Press Council, was 'that characteristically English disease, obsession with privacy and obsession with privacy in two paradoxical senses'.

Explaining the background of this development, Mr. Morgan said '...the British have no law at all protecting personal privacy. In, say the last twenty years, there has been recurrent concern among politicians, but among others too, about whether she would have such laws, particularly to curb intrusion into people's privacy by the Press, or rather part of the Press, bent on gratifying other peoples' curiosity. The developing chorus of criticism at newspapers during that time has not been directed at all newspapers though its effect may be felt by all of them....

'It is a paradox that while condemning newspapers' focus on private lives, the public rushes out in millions to buy these very newspapers. The argument of proprietors and editors—and it has some force—has been that the sales figures demonstrate that they have been giving readers what they want, whatever politicians, pundits and moralists may say they ought to have. Wearing its

Press freedom hat, the Press Council shared the Publishers' antagonism towards new legislation which would be likely to inhibit proper investigation and inquiry by the Press as well as curbing the improper intrusion into private lives at which it is aimed.

Mr. Morgan further reported: 'The Council's view like that of many similar bodies elsewhere, was that while new restrictive laws were undesirable, individuals had a moral right to privacy about their private lives and affairs which editors ought to recognise. The right extended not only to wholly private citizens but also to the people in public life unless what they were doing in private bore directly on their ability or fitness for their public role.

Mr. Morgan lamented that while the Calcutt Committee's report adopted many of the Press Council's own proposals, it suggested the Council's abolition and replacement by the Press Complaints Commission having no role as the Press Council had in defending the freedom of Press. The lopsided suggestion by the Calcutt Committee in Mr. Morgan's view 'was the most significant central flaw in a report which contained many valuable suggestions'.

Mr. Morgan criticised the Calcutt proposal to create the new criminal offences of which in practice only journalists could be guilty.

He further disclosed that the new body, PCC has a code of practice to enforce but not one of its own making. The code, 16 points running from accuracy through privacy and harassment to protection of confidential sources was devised for the newspaper and magazine industry by a Committee of editors led by Miss Patricia Champan, editor of *News of the World*. Commenting on this code, Mr. Morgan said: 'It cannot be denied that a code of this type presents problems. It is to be applied in the spirit not merely in the letter but it is taken to be comprehensive and it thus restricts criticism of conduct which was not thought of by the authors of the code. We cannot all hope to be as farsighted as the Almighty at Sinai when trying to envisage possible human fraility and sin or editorial responsibility. The code will require extension or its restriction of what complaints may be made will have to be relaxed as the years go by.'

Incidentally, these comments are in line with the view consistently taken by successive Press Councils of India, that it is neither necessary nor feasible to formulate a rigid exhaustive code of conduct for journalists. In Press Council of India's view, any attempt at framing a code of this kind would result in a mere enunciation of a few basic principles only in general terms which would be of little help in applying them to individual cases: Because of their elusive, variable nature, these moral principles cannot be reduced into rigid formulas. Ethics being dynamic principles, abhor Procrustean approach.

Questioned as to whether the new Press Complaints Commission on probation was working more effectively than the erstwhile Press Council in ensuring high professional standards of newspapers on self-explanatory basis, Mr. Morgan felt that it would be difficult to devise a more severe test of the new system in Britain than that this commission faced in its first month. He illustrated this point by referring to the complaint of Ms Clare Short, MP, before the PCC, alleging infringement of her right of privacy by the *News of the World.* The complaint 'combined a minefield of issues which are, some of them both in public interest, of interest to the public and crucial to the operation of a system of self-regulation of the Press running alongside the law'. Facets of that single case included:

*Question of Privacy :* The question arose whether the private life of a politician, and a leading woman politician at that, was a legitimate subject for newspaper inquiry and report?

The suggestion in the newspaper report was that nearly twenty years ago she had a relationship with a man with a serious criminal record who was eventually shot dead in the street in what may have been a gangland killing. Did the newspaper, as she asked, 'to crawl over' her private life of long ago, invade the privacy of her former husband, a former psychiatric patient, and intrude on the privacy of her present husband, himself a former Member of Parliament and a seriously sick man? Was what emerged an information which ought to be disclosed in the public interest or no more than information which might interest the public?

***Question of Pornography :*** Should newspapers publish pornographic or near nude pinup pictures? Was this newspaper pursuing Ms Short as part of a vendetta because she had led a campaign to ban by law the publication of page-3 type pictures, an art form made famous by its sister newspaper?

***Problem of Possibly Conflicting Jurisdictions***

*Parliamentary Privilege;* Part of Ms Short's complaint was the way the newspaper reported a speech she made about it and newspaper ethics in Parliament. Part of its case was that she misused her privilege in Parliament to attack the paper and its reporter. She complained of a breach of Parliamentary privilege.

***Police and the Police Complaints Authority :*** Was the *News of the World's* source for some of its material about Ms Short's private life, information from disaffected members of the West Midlands Police Serious Crime Squad whose record she had attacked in the House of Commons? She complained about this to the Chief Constable and the Police Complaints Authority.

***Civil Law :*** Could the new Press Complaints Commission be expected to deal with her complaint against the paper when her lawyers were already in correspondence with the paper and a legal action looked imminent? The old Press Council had asked complainants to waive their legal rights. The new Commission was not going to do that. Then the overall question that arose was: Could the self-regulating Commission hope to deal fairly and squarely with all these issues on a complaint that the *News of the World* broke the industry's own code on privacy and accuracy? The editor of the Paper, Miss Chapman, was a member of the Commission and Chairman of the Committee which framed the code.

The Commission dealt with these issues, upheld the complaint and the *News of the World* published it's condemnation fairly and in full, taking up a whole page.

'The new Commission has no more sanctions, no more penalties at its command than the old Council. Its greatest strength has in two factors—commitment and fear. Commitment by newspaper and magazine owners and editors to support it and make it work and fear of the threat by government and opposition of what will befall the Press if the test of the last chance is failed.'

# 6

# Applied Ethics

## Select Cases

***Boy Bank Robber Story*:** A small boy toting what appeared to be a pistol robbed a New York City Bank of $118 one wintry afternoon. When a nine-year-old boy surrendered to the FBI in the case two days later, and his lawyer called a news conference, reporters for newspapers and television staged a publicity carnival. The ethics of both lawyers and journalists were widely questioned, particularly after each blamed the other for creating a circus like atmosphere about a child's misfortune.

A teller at the branch of the New York Bank for Savings at Avenue of the Americas near 47th Street was stunned on the morning of February 25,198 1, when be saw a small boy pointing what seemed to be a pistol at him. After the teller gave the child $118, the robber ran from the bank and vanished. Two days later, someone tipped off a New York Post reporter that a suspect was about to surrender to the FBI, requested that other reporters be informed and directed the press to a lawyer, Must A. Sachs.

***Reporters Move in*:** The boy, identified as Robert M., was 4 feet 5 inch, weighed 90 pounds and was dressed in blue jeans, a tan shirt and a tie. When he appeared at FBI headquarters, he had $20 on him and Sachs, his lawyer, said the rest had been spent on hamburgers, French fries, a movie and a $29.95 wrist watch that plays a tune. Dan Collins, a UPI reporter, set the scene.

"Have you ever seen 30 reporters and photographers bent over to the waist trying to interview a 4 foot 5-inch boy and waiting for one word to drop?"

Collins remarked, "U.P.I. was there because A.P. was there, and added that he had felt "caught in a competitive situation." 'Mat was to be the general excuse among reporters for the way they handled the story—competition.

E.R. Ship, a court reporter for the New York Times, said she believed that "most of the reporters here were offended" by what she termed " a Must Sachs production." Nevertheless, she concerned that she had been told by her editors "to get as much as we could," and she did her job.

*First Spiurge :* Television was in on the story, of course, and went with it, Pictures and all. The New York Times ran the story on the first page, second section, with a picture. Under normal conditions, the metropolitan editor, Peter Millions, said, the Times would not have used the picture but, since it already had been on TV and everybody else had it, he thought omitting it would be pointless.

He New York Daily News and the New York Post both used the boy's picture on Page I and gave generous coverage, to the story inside. The News had the name and address of the boy but didn't use them; however, so many details were used, including the name of the business of the boy's grandmother, that anybody who knew the boy could have identified him without the picture.

There was some soul-searching. Stephen. J. Cohen, news director of WCBS-TV, argued that he would not normally have displayed pictures of a juvenile suspect but added, "Once it was on the front pages of the newspapers it was difficult for us to take the high road."

***Justice for a Nine- Year-Old :*** Hearings in juvenile cases in New York City are nearly always private, but Robert M. was spared nothing, At his lawyer's request, Judge Edith L. Miller of Family Court held an open hearing a few days later and an even larger corps of reporters and photographers attended. Courtroom sketch artists also were at work during the boy's arraignment.

The lawyer entered a "not guilty" plea for the defendant and contended that he had only been "playing" in the bank. The lawyer blamed unspecified TV programs for the boy's actions. A trial date was set and the child was released in the custody of his fairly. Eventually, when the uproar about the case died down some months later, a Family Court judge ordered Robert M. to attend school regularly, undergo therapy and "commit no action which would be a crime if he were an adult." Pending regular reports on his progress "for a year or two," the court then suspended judgment. However, before long Robert M. was hauled into court again on another charge and this time there was no publicity circus.

***Moral Problem :*** Jonathan Friendly, who reports on the news media for the New York Times, commented on the ethical issue as follows in one of his stories about the first arrest:

> .... Reporters covering the story and editors who have displayed the stories and pictures of "Robert" in their newspapers and on the most watched television news programs agree the story is a fine one. And if the coverage has overstepped an ethical fine that no one draws in quite the same way, they say, that is the fault of the boy's lawyers and the reality of news competition.
>
> In principle, the press has largely agreed with juvenile-justice authorities who say that children are too immature to judge the consequences of their own acts and should not be subjected to public scrutiny that could permanently mar their future.
>
> However, there are no legal bars to identifying such children, either as suspects or if they are convicted

> and the press reserves to itself the right to make a case by case judgement about whether to disclose a name or print a picture. There seems to be no disagreement on the news worthiness of the robbery itself...

***Limits of Press Morality :*** Since there is noisy to stop the news media from thrusting a child into the midst of a publicity hippodrome in the largest city in the land, it may well be asked whether there is a line, generally accepted by professional journalists, beyond which no reporter, correspondent, editor, news director or photograph should go.

***What is Permissible? :*** That question raises a number of others of a rather crucial nature. For example.

* What is there to stop a reporter from betraying a source he has promised to protect?
* Or violating a confidence on the theory that the story is too good to pass up?
* Or making up stories and manufacturing phony personalities on the theory that nobody will ever know the difference?
* Or inventing a quote on the theory that a speaker should have said it even if he didn't?
* Or invading private homes and offices and grabbing papers and pictures that might have a bearing on an investigation?
* Or having a love affair with a news source on a story in which both reporter and the source are involved?
* Or trading information between sources, such as obtaining a list of defence witnesses in confidence and then trading them to the prosecution in return for an exclusive story?
* Or assuming false identities in cases where such actions
* amount to nothing other than crass deception for no purpose based on public policy?
* Or accepting gifts and other largesse from news sources, advertisers or both?

In 56 years as a practitioner and teacher in the news profession and business, I have known of journalists who did such things-and some of them got away with it. Fortunately, they were few in number and not typical. But the very fact that evil practices are possible in journalism underlines the weakness of accepting mere news-worthiness as a standard of judgement for morality, in whole or in part.

In reality, news worthiness is the very worst standard for deciding whether an act is ethical or not. The questions about what is permissible all dealt with situations that were, at the time, a part of major news developments. In each case, the reportorial acts were committed on the theory that "getting the story" is the only rule that matters.

However, the time for that kind of irresponsible journalism has long since passed. Even if some ill-advised reporter were to steal pictures or lie or cheat to get a big story, the consequences of such actions once they were revealed-would lead to ultimate disgrace for the person and the news organization involved. Both the courts and the public are holding the news media to much stricter standards of conduct today.

What Price First Amendment? There is nothing to stop journalists from doing anything that could be an affront to common decency, short of violating the law. The First Amendment makes it impossible for Congress or any other legislative or regulatory body in the land to pass a law licensing journalists, binding them to an acceptable code of conduct and devising suitable punishments-such as loss of a license-for infractions large or small.

Unlike physicians, lawyers or even plumbers, journalist cannot be regulated by any outside body, and the codes of conduct that profession societies adopt cannot be enforced. If journalists cannot act responsibly themselves, or if their news organizations cannot force them 16 do so under pain of dismissal, nobody else can do anything about it, unless they commit a crime or become involved in a civil court action in connection with their work.

It follows that self-control, responsibility and a decent sense of restraint ought to be stressed as important elements in the practice of journalism and, quite generally, they are. Most journalists of character and experience do profess to practice a certain amount of responsibility in dealing with the news. Here is one such instance.

***"I Don't Ambush People" :*** William Owner, a 23-year-old reporter for the Gainlessness (Florida) Sun, was just one yea out of journalism school at the University of Florida when the city editor asked him to take a telephone call.

At first it seemed like much ado about very little. An irate father complained that his little girl had been hit on her nose with a stick by another little girl while an older boy held the hands of the victim. The reporter sympathized but wondered aloud what the paper could do about it. The father announced that although the assailant was only six years old, he was having her arrested and brought to trial.

Bill Owney began taking notes furiously. Then he told the city editor he wanted to go out on the story and soon was on his way. He talked with the father who had telephoned in the complaint and learned that the lawyer for the six-year-old defendant withstanding a jury trial which, under Florida law, would've to be held in an adult court.

***Different Approach Owner was Appalled :*** He did something that is very different from the go-go-go image the public has of a reporter hellbent on getting the story no matter who was hurt. The reporter said to the father "Look, going public with a story like this will put you and your wife and your little girl in the centre of a lot of public attention. It may be very unpleasant. Do you really want to do it.".

The father insisted

Owney then went to see the family of the six-year-old defendant. To let him tell his own story of what happened:

> They were throwing great quotes around about not being afraid to put their little girl before: jury but I just bad to stop them. I asked them, too, if they knew the consequences for the children in the case and for

> themselves. I don't ambush people. I want them to know what they're getting themselves. I don't ambush people. I want them to know what they're getting themselves into. But the defendant's parents, like the father of the other little girl, wanted to go through with it, no matter what happened.

***Settlement* :** On March 25, 1982, the Gainesville Sun carried Bill Owned's piece on under the headline "1st Grade Girl To Go On Trial." It became a nationwide sensation for a few days until the local prosecutor, with good sense, insisted on an out-of-court settlement and refused to let a little girl face the jury. Instead, the case was put back in the Juvenile Court where it should have been settled in the first place. And eventually, the injured girl's parents received half the cost of their medical expenses, or $20, from the parents of the little girl who had wielded the stick.

It suited Bill Owney and it pleased his paper. Had he succeeded in convincing both sets of parents not to got to court, he would have had no story. And that, he said, would have been all right, too.

***What the Polls Show* :** The attitudes of journalist towards the news, and the manner in which they deal with it, inevitable have an effect on the public's assessment of the news media. In the 1980s, a Gallup Poll of 760 persons showed that journalists maintain a respectable credibility rating among professionals, with the clergy standing first among the respondents with 71 percent, followed by physicians, 58 percent, police, 52 percent; journalists, 38 percent; businesslike, 31 percent; members of Congress, I percent, and advertising executives, 12 percent.

***Credibility of the News Media* :** However, in the same Gallup Poll, 61 percent of respondents said they believed "very little or only some" of the news, 33 percent agreed that most news reports are varied and only 5 percent believed everything they read or heard in the news media.

Another Gallup Poll, taken a few months earlier, showed that of 1,524 respondents 37 percent believed that the current curbs on the press in the United States are not strict enough, 32 percent believed the restriction were "about right" and oniy 17 percent said they were too strict, the rest having no option. The restrictions included fibel laws, findings of contempt of court and regulations having to do with police news and court coverage.

On accuracy in the news media, the same number of repentant were polled and 34 percent concluded that facts were inaccurately reported, 47 percent believed facts were accurately presented and 19 percent gave no answer.

It may be seen, therefore, that there is a dichotomy in the public attitude toward the news media as a whole and a sharp split between belief and non-belief, credibility and lack of credibility. The First Amendment protection of the press, moreover, does depend on public support and, if that support should vanish, the press will be in deep trouble.

***Public and the First Amendment :*** It is not at all reassuring, in conscience, that the Gallup Poll of 1,524 respondents showed that only 24 percent were able to name correctly what the First Amendment is or what it deals with, among the college educated, only 42 percent were able to do so.

The ethics of journalists and thermopile position, therefore, are not mere theoretical matters. They are very important in helping to form public judgements of the profession and maintaining public confidence in the news media themselves. If either should ever disappear, then the First Amendment will go down with it.

***"Jimmy's World" and the Journalists' World :*** On September 28, 1980, the Washington Post published a story under the by-line of Janet Coke with this headline:

Jimmy's World:

8-Year-Old Heroin Addict Lives For A Fix

This is how the story began:

> Jimmy is 8 years old and a third-generation heroin addict, a precocious little boy with sandy hair, velvety brown eyes and needle marks freckling the baby-smooth skin of his thin brown arms.

He nestles in a large, beige reclining chair in the living room of his comfortably furnished home in southeast Washington. There is an almost cherubic expression on his small, round face as he talks about life-clothes, money, the Baltimore Orioles and hero. He has been an addict since the age of 5.

His hands are clasped behind his head, fancy running shoes adorn his feet and a striped Izod T-shirt hangs over his thin frame. "Bad, ain't it," he boasts to a reporter visiting recently. "I go time size of these."

Jimmy's world is a world of hard drugs, fast money and the good life he believes both can bring. Every day, junkies casually buy heroin from Ron, his mother's live-in lover, in the dinning room of Jimmy's home. They "cook" it in the kitchen and "fire up" in the bedrooms. And every day, Ron or somebody else fires up Jimmy, plunging a needle into his bony arm sending the fourth grade into a hypnotic nod...

The story continued in this manner for more than two columns. It was accompanied by a blood carding pen and link sketch of a tiny black boy wincing in pain as a big hand grasps one thin arm and another hand plunges a hypodermic needle into a vein.

***What Price Pulitzer Prize ? :*** The story won a Pulitzer Prize, but the celebration was short-lived at the Washington Post. Due to discrepancies in her published biography, Janet Cooke underwent night-long questioning by her editors and finally confessed that there was no Jimmy and that the story had been invented.

"Jimmy's World" shook up the world of the journalist as no other story has since the New York Sun's "moon hoax" in the early 19th century. It raised serious questions about journalistic ethics and journalistic morality that no one has answered to the satisfaction of the profession. It also demonstrated to what lengths young people can be driven by striving for a major journalism award.

***Washington Post's Reaction :*** The reaction of the Washington Post was to publish an 18,000 word analysis of what happened and why it happened by William Green, the paper's ombudsman, who since has returned to his academic post Green began his account.

"Jimmy" never existed, but his story convulsed the city and humiliated the Washington Post-proud house of Watergate investigation.

The story was a lie and, after all its celebrated achievements, the Post owes its readers an accounting of its spectacular failure.

How did it all happen? Why?

This account was prepared from 47 interviews, primarily with members of the Post's staff. It was written by the Post's ombudsman, who is the fifth person to occupy the position of reader representative since it was created by the newspaper in 1970.

This is essentially a story of the failure of a system that, in another industry, might be called "quality control." On newspapers, it is called editing.

The fabrication of Janet Cooke's story eluded all of the Post's filters that are set up to challenge every detail in every news story the paper Publishes. From the time she applied for a job, questions were not asked. Editors abandoned their professional skepticism.

This narrative reconstruction suggests that "Jimmy" moved through the cycle of news reporting and editing like an alien creature, unimpeded by ordinary security devices. This account has available the marvelous tool called hindsight.

It is also the story of a young and talented reporter, flaming with ambition, who showed irresistible promise of achievement. The Post accelerated her success, and may thereby have hastened her failure... For Cooke, it was a personal tragedy. For the Post, it was inexcusable...

*How the Story Got By :* It is worth summarizing, from the Green account, how the Cooke story got by and actual won a prize, with the deflation of all concerned when it blew up. These are the signposts along the way:

* Nobody at the Post asked Janet Cooke to identify "Jimmy" and his family for the confidential information of the editors and nobody even asked Jimmy's" address while she was on assignment.

* Nobody questioned the story when it was written or suggested the boy should be given help. Bob Woodward of Water gate fame, the top editor for metropolitan affairs, called it a "great piece." Ben Bradlee, the executive editor, said it was a "helluva job."

* Cooke was told, before the story ran, that it would be controversial, that she might be called before a judge to give her source and identify the boy and that she could back out and kill the story. She agreed it should be run.

* After the story was published, the mayor and police chief of Washington, D.C., launched a mammoth investigation to locate "Jimmy." They didn't find him and denied his existence.

* The Post sent a staff member, Courtland Milloy, with Janet Cooke to the neighbourhood where "Jimmy" supposedly lived and they drove around for seven hours without result. Milloy came back, openly skeptical. But the post's publisher, Don Graham, wrote Janet Cooke a note of congratulations.

* Others at the Post began voicing doubts, among them her immediate editor, Milton Coleman. But the Post decided to submit the story for the Pulitzer Prize.

* In the Pulitzer proceedings, the story didn't win the jury verdict in the news reporting category in which it was entered. By when the Pulitzer Prize Board met, the board itself shifted the story from the news category to the feature category and then voted it the feature writing prize. One or two board members, reportedly, voiced doubts about the story, but the majority did not.

* When the prizes were announced, the AP correspondent in Toledo, Michael Holmes, was notified by the Toledo Blade that the APIA biographical information on Cooke

> did not check with the blade's. The AP had simply picked up the Washington Post biography, forwarded with her entry, and made public at Columbia University by the Pulitzer Board. Cooke bad prepared it. It showed she had, indeed, graduated from the university but had no master's degree. When Holmes reported that to his New York office, the AP checked Cooke's claim to a degree from Vassor and study at the Sorbonne in Paris. Result: She had no degree from Vassar. As for her claim to have studied at the Sorbonne, she couldn't even speak decent French.

The Post finally decided to question Cooke. First she admitted she had made apart of her background. Then, after an all-night session, she signed this statement.

"Jimmy's World" was in essence a fabrication. I never encountered or interviewed an 8-year-old heroin addict. The Sept. 28, 1980 article in the Washington Post was a serious misrepresentation which I deeply regret. I apologize to my newspaper, my profession, the Pulitzer Board and all seekers of the truth. Today, in facing up to the truth, I have submitted my resignation to Janet Cooke.

Rocking the Journalists' World many a newspaper throughout the land and all TV news programs featured the Cooke story when it broke with the Post's announcement the "Jimmy's World" was fake. For more than a year, every meeting for journalists argued over the case, philosophized over it and deplored it. More candid critics of the press had some sarcastic observations about journalistic ethics.

As a result of the Cooke hoax, today's journalist taken as a whole have the deepest concern about their own reputations and their own integrity. It is perhaps the paramount reason for the most general criticism of the profession, its defensiveness and its resentment of outside inquiries into journalistic conduct and journalistic morals. There is no doubt that such criticism persists. A recent Washington Post poll concluded that the public is "sharply critical" of the national press, mainly because of just such considerations.

Ethics, in short, is not just a sometime thing. There may be no enforceable yourself professional conduct for journalists, but every ethical violation that comes to public attention receives a stiff share of public, censure. If enough of that piles up, Congress one day will take action and it will not be pleasant.

***Aftermath of "Jimmy's World" :*** It would be heartening to point out that the overkill coverkill coverage of the nine year old bank robber in New York and the expose of the mythical eight-year-old heroin addict in Washington had immediately beneficial results, but it wouldn't be true.

Only a few weeks after the disclosure that "Jimmy" didn't exist, the New York Daily News sadly announced the forced resignation of one of its columnists after a British newspaper accused him of faking a story about a shutout between British troops and a youth gang in Belfast.

Within a month, under pressure of a large libel suit, the Toronto Sun announced one of its reporters had been fired and another was forced to resign after they admitted having no documentation for charges that a high government official had made stock profits by using inside government information

***New York Time's Hoax :*** On February 22, 1982, the New York Times admitted in story that a 24-year-old American free-lance writer had confessed that he had made up an article published in the paper's Sunday magazine about a trip he took to live with the Khmer Rouge guerrillas incompliant. Moreover, the writer confessed that he had concocted the article without ever leaving Spain, where he was living at the time. In an editorial headed "A Lie in the Times," Executive Editor A.M. Rosenthal said, "We do not feel that the fact that the writer was a liar and hoaxer removes our reproducibility. It is our job to uncover any falsehood or errors ... I regret this whole sad episode and the lapse in our procedures that made it possible."

It may be true, as many in journalism contend, that these were isolated incidents. But when the whole tab was added up, it amounted to a substantial amount of doubt that too many sharp practices still exist in Journalism and something had better be done about it beyond passing resolutions of regret.

These are some of the results:

* Editors are more vigilant now about unsourced stories and are quicker to demand proof from reporters, including names, date and places where interviews took Place, plus better documentation of charges.
* More newspapers are checking statements made in their newspapers. John R. Harrison, president of the New York Times Group, a chain of small newspapers, says each member newspaper checks the quotes in at least two stories every week and publishes the results on office bulletin boards. It may arouse a certain amount of resentment among reporters whose accuracy is questioned, but Harrison believes the check is necessary. It is no more than leading magazines have been doing for a long time.
* More efforts are being made to develop a set of ethical standards in the profession that will be broadly acceptable, beyond those published by the American Society of Newspaper Editors and other organizations. But many editors still believe codes are useless.
* The existing embossment on about a score of American newspapers are receiving more attention from editors, but there is little indication that such a post ever will be universal adopted or even that it will increase in popularity.
* The National News Council, as an independent and privately funded body looking into the conduct of the news media, has received more attention bug its support in the profession remains spotty.
* The Pulitzer Prize Board decided to abandon its practice of awarding a dozen newspaper prizes and seven non-newspaper prizes in a one-day meeting, to avoid the appearance of undue haste. Instead, the 15-member board voted to hold two-day sessions to go over the jury reports in all categories. In addition, the board agreed to consult the respective juries before moving an exhibit from one

category to another if a prize was likely to result from the exchange. It was also the sense of the board that there would be greater consultation with the juries on other matters, in particular on reversing jury verdicts.

* The National News Council got into the Pulitzer act by criticizing an award to Teresa Carpenter, a free-lance writer for the Village Voice, a New York weekly, who was given the prize the Washington Post returned. However, the Pulitzer Board let the Carpenter award stand, holding, that the council's criticism applied to an article about a murder that Had not been the principal award-winning work.

Despite these attempts to make sure that nothing like the cooke case ever happened again, there was a distinct air of unease during the 1980s among American journalists in general and among students and other newcomers to the profession. As one student put it in an ethics class at the University of Florida, "How do we know how much faking is actually going on and how can it be stopped?" It was a disturbing question and there were no easy answers.

One this was certain, Editors aren't likely for some time to accept any story on faith, and they are even less likely to yield their authority over the run of the news to an impetuous and demanding reporter.

## Analysis

J. Montgomery Curtis, the former director of the American Press Institute, believes that ethical considerations in journalism have greatly expanded in recent years. This is his overview of the current position:

*Invasions of Privacy :* Is it ethical for news reporters to invade private homes, the private grounds, and indeed the private presences of innocent people caught in highly emotional situations? I think not. We continue to alienate a considerable part of the public by picturing innocent people in prose and photographs at moments when they should be allowed to grieve in private.

***TV Icusions into Privacy :*** If anything, television is much worse than the print press in invad privacy. But what the TV people do with their microphones and cameras inevitably curbs off on the print press.

***Objectionable Advertising :*** Is it ethical to print advertising for pornographic, X-rated movies? For nude theaters? For massage parlors that are used for prostitution? I don't believe it is. I think the press has a responsibility to refuse such advertising.

## Senseless Reporting

Occasionally, young reporters with little sense and editors with even less sense print articles that depict certain unethical, immoral and certainly illegal practices in a highly favourable light. Two example. Not long ago, a famous Sunday newspaper magazine came out with a cover showing two attractive youngsters, a boy and a girl, sniffing cocaine through straws, The article inside the magazine quoted several people by position, not by name. [A Congressman banker, a manufacture, an educator], to the general effect that cocaine had benefited them through daily usage. To me, such an article is totally unethical. The same paper a few years ago used an article about Miami Beach call girl who was supposed to have made between $ 35,000 and $ 40,000 a year. It was not the type of thing to recommend to the impressionable young girls who might be reading the paper. This also tanks as totally unethical, in my view.

***No Gifts, No Freebes :*** Curtis has always advocated a strict policy for newspapers against the acceptance of gifts and other freebies by staff members. He recalls bow Biol. Terry, while managing the New York Giants years ago, informed the New York baseball writers who were travelling with the team that they had no right to criticize the players because the Giants paid travel expenses for nearly all of them. The exceptions were the New York Vines and the. New York Daily News Curtis went on.

When I started work on the Buffalo Evening News. I was surprised that the paper accepted no free tickets for movies, the theaters, sporting events or anything else. We paid our own way.

The one newspaper that accepted no freebies of any kind, ours, is still in business today and quite healthy. Two rivals merged and two others went out of business.

The truth is that if a newspaper engages in unethical practices, the word soon gets around. People quickly know whether editors and reporters on the take or not. This includes such things as excessive Christmas gifts from news sources, free meals for restaurant reporters, free trips to distant tourist centres and hotels and so on. And when word gets around people lose respect for the paper.

***Obligations of Journalists :*** There is general agreement within the profession on the basic obligations of journalists. Briefly stated, they are as follows:

* To cover the news fairly, thoroughly and accurately
* To present the news truthfully
* To explain what the news means
* To protect sources wherever necessary
* To respect confidences if they are freely offered and willingly accepted
* To act at all times in the public interest and to be influenced by no other consideration
* To respect the law and the rights of privacy of people in the news and to deal with them with forthrightness and honesty
* To acknowledge error when it occurs and to make suitable corrections as quickly as possible.

Like all procedures, these can be abused or neglected by complacent reporters or sources given to perverting the truth or entirely withholding it. This does not make the measures any less necessary. Beginning reporters soon learn that they are judged by their colleagues, their editors and their sources on how well they observe these ground rules, how effectively they use them and how faithfully they observe them. There is, in journalism as in life itself something more important than getting the big story and zinging the opposition. That is the preservation of a decent respect for the good of the profession in general and for one's own self in particular.

It is so easy to state these high moral principles but sometimes, when reporters are on the job, it is difficult to decide where the line should be drawn between what is permissible in news gathering and what is entirely unethical. And there aren't any philosophical calipers to measure the difference.

***When Reporters are in Danger :*** A reporter for a major metropolitan newspaper, assigned to investigate the Mafia, once asked his editors with a trace of sarcasm: Do you nearly expect me to identify myself as a reporter for this newspaper whenever I go and explain what I am doing and what I am doing it?"

The editors, who had been properly concerned about widespread reports in the city of the infiltration of the Mafia into legitimate business, also wanted to safeguard the integrity of the newspaper and didn't like the idea of having the reporter masquerade as a hoodlum. What finally happened was that the reporter went on the assignment with permission simply not to identify himself unless he blundered into a confrontation and was asked who he was, what he was doing and why he was doing it.

That was one Mafia investigation that didn't get very far. There aren't many Sunday School characters in the underworld, and reporters, like informers, can run into rough treatment.

Several reporters for the Detroit Free Press had an even more difficult and dangerous probe. While why were investigating Michigan's mental hygiene system they came across information suggestion that a number of mental patients-including four killers-were at large and their was no indication that police were searching for them.

This was a ticklish matter. Was it really the business of reporters to do police work? And yet if they didn't find the apparently missing persons, how could they prove the truth of their story?

After a lot of soul-searching, a top-level editorial decision was reached to try to locate 10 of the patients involved. The reporters, of necessity, has to adopt various guises to get information. But they determined in advance not to use quotes obtained from innocent persons while posing as someone other than a reporter. And they worried over possible invasion of privacy in the cases of social workers they inter viewed and the ethics of obtaining confidential records in such circumstances.

In the end, all worked out well, Seven of the 10 persons on the Free Press list were locate by the reporters, including the four killers. The deficiencies of the state's mental hygiene system were exposed. And widespread reforms were instituted.

***When is Deceit Justified :*** Free Press has exposed abortion clinics, a surgery mill, discrimination against blacks by real estate agents and quack medicines by permitting reporters to assume disguises. While Neil Shine was the paper's managing editor, he defended the practice saying.

Our responsibilities to get information and if we can do it legally, we'll do it. I wouldn't let a reporter say he's a policeman. That's illegal. But I don't draw many lines. When our young medical writer heard about a guy selling phony arthritis medicine, she didn't go up to him and say, "Hi, I'm the medical writer from the Detroit Free Press. Are you a charlatan."?

The reporter pretended to have arthritis, bought $200 worth of medicine from the quack, then exposed him.

But Gary C. Schuster, Washington bureau chief for the Detroit News, got into trouble when he posed as a Michigan congressman so he could expose tax security the signing of the Israeli-Egyptian peace treaty on the White House Lawn. After he wrote his story next day under the flaring News headline, "Greasing a Moment in History," the Standing Committee of Correspondents in Congress rebuked him.

The Wall Street Journal isn't exactly a gung-ho paper bent on sensation, but it did publish a story about company—union conflicts by Beth Nissen, a young reporter, after she had worked for three weeks on the assembly line at the Texas Instruments plant in Austin. Laurence O'Donnell, Managing editor of the

Journal at the time, explained, "Three was no other way of getting the story and the information was worth getting."

This, too, was the justification for two other investigations by major papers, the Los Angles Time and the Chicago Sun-Times. The Los Angeles paper ran a piece about psychiatric care at Metropolitan State Hospital, based on the two weeks a woman reporter worked there posing as a graduate student in psychology. The Chicago Sun Times expose was the celebrated Mirage Bar operation, which was run by reporters and served to disclose Wide scale bribery among Chicago official dom.

"We couldn't have gotten the information any other way, "said James Hoge, then the editor-in-chief. He conceded such campaigns should be conducted "with extreme caution and selectivity and only when certain standards are applied."

The New York Times is one of the relatively few major newspapers that refuse to let their reporters adopt disguises. Instead of being praised, a Times reporter was censured for putting on mechanics' overalls to try to interviews the wife of a Russian defector while she was begin detained in an aeroplane.

Reporters should not masquerade" said the executive editor, A.M. Rosenth. And yet when the Times believed it to be in the public interest, it printed top secret government papers that had been stolen and delivered to a Times reporter.

What is ethical for some, quite clearly, depends on how big the story is, now strongly the editors feel about it, how effective the reporters are and the urgency of the public issue that is involved. The problem of whether reporters should disguise themselves seldom arises on a small city daily or weekly because somebody in town would almost certainly recognize the reporter and ask, "Hey, Joc, what are you doing working in a garage? I thought you wuz a reporter."

To quote an old time editor, Casey Jones.

"Newspapermen sitting around talking about ethics are like women discussing their virginity. If you've got it. And if you've lost it, that's your fault and you ain't Genoa get it back."

***Phonies, Freebees and Payoffs :*** There are three areas, however, in which an ethical line can be clearly drawn between what is right and what is wrong. These are, not necessarily in the order of importance, the phony story and the phony quote or "composite person", the acceptance of free tickets, free trips, free vacations and free clothes, and an agreement, sometimes unspoken, that if a certain story is done in a certain way the reporter will never have cause to regret it.

***Whatever It's Called, It's Still Phony :*** There have been reporters who made up quotes and even faked whole interviews and didn't seem to think anything was wrong about it one woman, a reporter at a famous court trial, was sent to interview the defendant when the lights went out in the cell block where he had been held overnight. She returned with a complete interview in about 15 minutes, fast work in any league. The editor meanwhile had learned from a wire service that the defendant had slept through the entire ruckus.

"How come you got an interview when the AP says the guy slept through it all?" the editor asked.

The reporter shrugged. "Mat's what he would have said if he'd been awake."

Sometimes this same rationale is clothed in high-sounding phrases and noble rhetoric. For example, Ray Mongo, a figure in the antiwar movement of the 1960s, argues that facts are less important than truth and illustrates his point with an article in a Boston publication, Avatar, called "Report from Vietnam, by Alexander Soienson." This purports to be an eyewitness account of torture in a Vietnamese village during the Vietnam War. However Mango says the report is fiction and Sereneness doesn't exist, but he contends:

> ... Because it has happened in man's history, and because we know we are responsible for its happening, and because the story is unvarnished and plain and human, we know is it true, truer than any facts you pick up from the New Republic.

Based on that premise, the argument could also be made that Janet Cooke's story about "Jimmy's World" was the truth because somewhere, somehow, children are introduced to illicit drugs; any she wasn't able to find such a child, Jimmy or anybody else. At me point, during her interrogation at the Washington Post, she called "Jimmy" a 'composite."

These "composite" figures, a favourite device sometimes when writers can't find quite the type of person they want to illustrate a particular story, can cause more trouble than they are worth. Gail Sheehy's "Redpants," a prostitute about whom she wrote in New York magazine, was a "composite," only her editor eliminated that fundamental point from her article. Thus "Redpants" was made to appear to be a real person when, actually, she didn't exist.

The main point cannot be mistaken. Either an interview is rel and honest and true or it is not, Either people in the news are real or they are to. You can't make things up to prove a point unless you are writing something clearly labeled fiction.

*Role of Freebees :* Automobile, film and flour companies and travel organizations have sponsored media events for many years to attract large numbers of journalists. Countries like South Africa have offered editors and reporters expenses paid trips, hoping for favourable notice in their publications. Assorted companies with something to sell offer everything from cocktail parties to moonlight cruises, to cause the assembled journalists to think well of them.

In New York City, it would be possible for a reporter to live entirely on such largesse if his news organization would let him do it. But most responsible news organizations these days try to keep freebees for their staffs to a minimum, and some bar them entirely. The basic premise is that you don't get something for nothing in the news business or anywhere else. The acceptance of a favour implies that something of value will be given in return. And in the current state of journalism in the United States, that is more than most detectors can tolerate.

Some reporters argue that it's necessary for them to have a drink with a news Source once in a while, or to go to dinner with an influential person. That may well be true. But the cocktail-and-dinner circuit can be overworked and usually is, which is why it isn't very popular in the higher reaches of journalism. The more effluent papers have a policy of buying everything from theatre tickets for their critics to trips for their travel writers; the smaller and less affluent ones have a choice of appearing to be bought or keeping their reporters at home.

For the beginning reporter or the reporter who is new to a news organization, the only recourse is to ask what the policy on freebees is and then take care to observe it. This is one of the touchiest subjects in journalism, and for good reason. No news organization can afford to have staff members living high at someone else's expense. The rule is to avoid even the appearance of impropriety.

***Relations with News Sources :*** Experienced reporters know that they must keep a decent distance between themselves and even the best of their news sources. If it becomes known that a certain reporter is too chummy with influential Republicans, for example, opposing Democrats quite rightly may have grounds for suspicion. If a business reporter is seen too often with a powerful company president or board chairman, and then writes favourably about the firm's newly issued stock, others in the business community are bound to draw unfavourable inferences. If a film reviewer pays more than occasional visits to the home of a film star and enthusiastically plugs the star's pictures, that also becomes the subject of comment gossip.

Some years ago, a first-rate woman reporter for a good newspaper in a large Eastern city was assigned to the local political beat and became friendly with influential political leader. She accepted lunch and dinner dates with him. Travel with him on assignment sometimes and even accepted a fur coat from him, Eventually, they had an affair that ended when the reporter left the paper and accepted a post with another paper in another city. She appeared to be doing well in her news job until the influential politician who had been her lover was indicted on fraud charges and the prosecution was determined to call her as a witness in the case. Her former paper, alerted that the story was about to break in the opposition paper in town, ran the whole story in depth, with the result that the woman lost her job of the out-of town paper.

Feminists argued that a male reporter or would never have been punished in similar situation had he become involved with a female news source. But it was pretty difficult to establish a case of discrimination it this instance.

***Standards are Strict*** **:** After the arrest of Kathy Boudin, caught while fleeing from the scene of a botched Brinks armored car robbery in which two policemen and a guard were killed, it was teamed that she had been living in a New York City apartment under the name of Lynn Adams with a reporter for the Staford (Connecticut) Advocate as her roommate. Boudin, a fugitive from justice for more than 10 years, told hey roommate that she was working as a waitress to support her year-old son.

The reporter in turn informed her employers at the Advocate, a Times Mirror group newspaper, that she had not known of Lynn Adams's real identity, but she also was too distraught, she said, to write anything, abut her rest while roommate After a month-long investigation by the Advocate, which found nothing to corroborate or refute the reporter's story, she was discharged.

Kenneth H. Brief, executive editor of Connecticut Newspapers, controlling the Advocate, contended that there is "an inherent clash between an individual's constitutional rights and a reporter's responsibilities." He went on:

> By the nature of the job, a reporter is a reporter all the time ... If a reporter has a relationship with somebody who has done something unethical or illegal, what is the reporter's responsibility? The more the issue is addressed, the healthier it will be for the profession.

He contended the information the paper had published about the reporter and Boudin had not been "totally accurate" but did not specify what fault, if any, had been committed by the reporter. It was a harsh judgement, but not many editors said they would have acted differently under the circumstances.

***Is Sports Reporting, a Special Case?*** **:** Younger sports writers who are fortunate enough to be assigned to travel with professional team have been known to contend that they must have a closer relationships sports figures than city side reporters and their sources. This, sports reporters argue, is vitally necessary because they so often must develop feature pieces for newspapers and magazines after television has covered a game in its entirety.

Most editors are willing to grant that there is something to the argument, but not many sympathize with it. Professional athletes, by reason of the earning power, have become very large figures in the news and it is unlikely that any of them will single out particular reporters and bestow all their favours on them. Sports, like all other kinds of coverage, calls for something more than a few quick quotes, a smile and a pat on the back for a young reporter. And reporters cannot feel very comfortable if they have close ties to a few favoured athletes on one team. The field is far too large for that kind of intimacy.

This is, fundamentally, the disadvantage of having the professional clubs pay for the salaries and upkeep of the TV sports broadcasters who cover the team's home games. No matter how broadcast journalists may protested they are still independent figures and can call em as they see 'em, not many fans are likely to believe them. Too many cameras have been shunted away from too many embarrassing situations on the field, where that kind of reporting relationship exists, for broadcasters to establish a forthright claim of journalistic independence-

***When to Omit News Detail :*** A country editor in Tennessee likes to tell the story of a woman, apparently some six or seven months pregnant, who came into his office one day and asked him not to publish news of her marriage, which had taken place the day before. It didn't take long for the editor to make up his mind. He agreed not to publish the news of the marriage. In a small town, where people, would know the story anyway, he reasoned that it would serve no good purpose to publicize the marriage and thereby add to the womanly pain and embarrassment.

***Withholding Names in the News :*** Most news organizations don't use the names of rape victims or the addresses of people who have received threats or are otherwise endangered.

Now and then, a case develops that tests editors' judgement sin a different way. One was the plight of a retarded teenager whose parents wanted to sterilize her because she could not understand the consequences of sexual relations and, the parents said, she could not have cared for a child if she had one.

The news broke when the parents asked for a private hearing and a New Jersey court granted their request. Because the judge's decision was made in open court, UPI carried the names of the parents and their retarded daughter. H.L. Stevenson, the editor-in-chief, pointed out that, even if the name had been withheld, there would have been requests from other clients to disclose it. UPI's senior news editors, in fact, were about evenly split on whether to use the name or withhold it.

## Code of Conduct

American journalists have always been wary of codes of conduct. While they may generally agree with the principles of such codes, they have invariable raised the possibility that government in some fashion will try to enforce them. That, of course, would lead directly to the licensing of journalists and the end of the free press.

Thus, in the following code that bears on the standards of journalists, it should be borne in mind, its enforcement is possible.

*ANSE Statement :* The following Statement of Principles was adopted in 1975 by the American Society of Newspaper Editors to replace its 52-year old Code of Ethics or Canons of Journalism.

# 7

# Social Morality

Ever since partition, India has been rocked by communal, caste, linguistic or regional violence. Of this, communal riots have assumed dangerous proportions from the beginning of the eighties. For example, the rise of Bhindranwale, the tragedy of Operation Blue Star, the genocidal riots of 1984, the Hashimpur-Malliana massacres of Muslims by PAC in U.P. and the Ram-janmabhoomi-Babri Masjid issue have sharpened the communal divide.

In the nineties, we were witnessing an emotional upsurge in the country which is added to the communal tension.

### Caste and Communal Factors

The Press has not covered these events dispassionately and objectively. During the anti-Mandal agitation, news and articles were planted in the newspapers against the Mandal report. The coverage of anti-Mandal stir by the video magazine 'Newstrack' was totally partisan. Not a word was said on the cause and what one came across was an intense hatred for Prime Minister V.P. Singh.

On the Mandir-Masjid issue, the Hindi Press played a damaging role by inciting passions against the government and the minority community.

On January 22,1991, the Press Council of India censured four Hindi dailies: *Aaj, Danik Jagran, Swatantra Chetna* and *Swatantra Bharat* for their gross irresponsibility and impropriety violating journalistic ethics in covering the events relating to the Mandir-Masjid issue on and around October 30,1990.

Simultaneously, the Council expressed serious concern over the authorities taking recourse to punitive and preventive action in excess of the demands of the situation. It deplored the U.P. government in invoking provisions of non-existent Press (Objectionable Matters) Act, 1951 and *misapplying* provisions of the Press and Registration of Books Act, 1867, in suppressing freedom of the Press.

In order to assess the Press coverage of Mandir-Masjid issue, the Council Committee set up a Committee on November 8, 1990. The Committee consisted of Mr. N.R. Chandran (Convenor), Dr. N.K. Trikka, Mr. K. Vikram Rao, Mr. P. Raman, Mr. Satish Khurana and late Mr. Raghubir Sahay.

The Committee came to the conclusion that the aforesaid papers were guilty in promoting mass hysteria on the basis of rumours and speculation, through exaggeration and distortion.

They were guilty in a few instances of doctoring pictures, such as drawing prison bars on the photograph of an arrested mahant, fabricating casualty figures, adding 1 before 15 to make 115 deaths. Some of the examples are:

*Aaj* (Ranchi). October 26,1990: *Ayodhya mein Ram Mandir toda gaya* (Ram Mandir demolished in Ayodhya).

*Aaj* (Kanpur) in its issue dated November 3,1990 carried the headline: *Nihatthe Ram bhakton ko gher ker ghanton firing*— 200 *maray Kartik Kay snan par khoon se nahaye Ayodhya Jallianwala Bagh kaand bouna pada.*

(Hours of firing on the unarmed worshippers of Ram after rounding them up—200 die, Ayodhya bathed in blood on Kartik-day bath, Jallianwala Bagh episode becomes petty against this.)

*Aaj* (Bareilly), November 4, 1990: *Ram bhakton ne DIG ko peeta, Magistraton ki bagavat, DM Chutti le bhage.*

(Ram Bhakts beat up the DIG, revolt of magistrates, D.M. goes on leave.)

*Aaj* (Agra) published an evening bulletin with headline, *Ayodhya Mein Firing, Sainkadon hatahat, Sarkar dwara khandan, mritak sankheya panch batayee.*

(Firing in Ayodhya, hundreds injured, denial by government, gives out figure of dead as five.)

*Aaj* (Varanasi). The Varanasi edition of the paper of October 22, 1990, carried an item stating that the President of India was unhappy and astonished at the statements of Chief Minister Mulayam Singh and that Mulayam Singh will not be given assistance of the army to strike terror in the state.

*Aaj* (Lucknow). The Lucknow edition of November 22, 1990 carried a headline: *Sou se adhik lashein Saryu mein fainkee gayein.* (More than hundred bodies thrown into river Saryu.)

The same edition announced that armed kar sewaks will now be pressed into the movement. A special report carrying a list of missing persons, released by the VHP was published with the headlines: *Yadi balidaan nahin huye, to kahan gaye ye 307 kar sewaks* in its issue of November 1, 1990. (If there were no sacrifices then where did these 307 kar sewaks go.)

The same newspapers carried widely divergent versions from different publication centres and even different editions of the same paper ran widely varying accounts of the same event. An example of this is the November 2, 1990, issue of *Aaj* giving different figures of casualties from different centres of publication as below:

| | |
|---|---|
| Varanasi | 100 dead |
| Ranchi | 400-500 dead and injured |
| Agra | 100 killed |
| Kanpur | 200 killed |
| Bareilly | 500 killed |

*Dainik Jagran* (Lucknow): *Har gaon ko Ayodhya maan kar sangharsh karein.* (Consider every village as Ayodhya and fight out.)

In its special bulletin in the afternoon of November 2,1991, it carried a news saying: 'One hundred kar sewaks had died on the spot in indiscriminate police firing on Ram Bhakts.' The figure was reduced to 32 in the regular morning edition of November 3.

On November 18, it carried an item set in double column with the heading: *Shri Ram Kranti Brigade agale maah tak Mulayam ke haath pair kaat degi.* (Shri Ram Kranti brigade will cut off the hands and feet of Mulayam by the next month.)

The item was based on the anonymous letter which also said that a thousand police and army personnel who are Ram Bhakts were leaving their jobs and would support the brigade's activities.

In the issue of November 15, 1991, the paper wrote in a 4 column report that Chief Minister Mulayam Singh was very angry that not enough bullets were fired on unarmed Ram Bhakt *kar sewaks* at Ayodhya.

A sub-heading said that the police was not in favour of firing at the unarmed kar sewaks. Next day, i.e. November 16, the paper carried another item which said that Chief Minister Mulayam Singh had repeatedly tried to pressurize the Chief of Army's Central Command, Lt. Gen. Billimoria, to order his troops to fire at the unarmed kar sewaks from all sides in Ayodhya on October 30. After visiting the areas by helicopter, Lt. Gen. Billimoria refused to obey the orders of the Chief Minister. The Chief Minister then contacted the Central Government and requested it to get orders for Lt. Gen. Billimoria from the Army Headquarters.

In a report of communal dash, the paper's Agra edition openly identified persons of the two communities involved. A Faizabad Bureau report published across eight columns was slugged *'Har gaon ko Ayodhya moan kar sangharsh karein'*. (Consider every village Ayodhya and fight out) and was headlined: *Ram Mandir ke liye dus lakh ka ladakoo dusta baneinge* (Ten lakh strong militant force shall be built up for the Ram Temple). This was based on a statement but no attribution was made to any source in the heading, nor did it carry any quotation mark.

*Swatantra Bharat* (Lucknow) reported the incident of November 2, 1990, with these headlines: *Nihatthe kar sewakon ko bhoon dala: 100 tak ke marne ke aashanka: 25 lashein baramad: Hazaaron ghayal.* (Unarmed kar sewaks massacred: up to one hundred killed, 25 bodies found, thousands wounded.)

In the body of the story, the 'paper wrote that anywhere between 50 and 100 people are feared to have been killed. It also gave other figures from different sources: State's Home Secretary—14, news agencies—15, BBC correspondent who had returned from the spot—between 30 and 50.

Though the paper was fair in giving figures from several sources including the official, it gravely erred in putting the figure of 100 in bold headlines.

In order to avoid sensationalism, particularly when the atmosphere is emotionally surcharged, it is always advisable to say 'at least 50 killed' instead of saying 'up to 100 killed'.

*Swatantra Bharat* (Varanasi) November 4, 1990: *Ayodhya mein...kar sevakon par firing*—115 *mare, darjanon ghayal* (Firing on kar sevaks in Ayodhya—115 dead, dozens injured).

The paper had originally given a figure of 15 dead on November 2 in a special bulletin that afternoon, but at the last moment: '1' was inserted by hand to make it '115'. The item remained credited to the news agency 'Univarta' even after this change. This is unethical, in addition to being totally irresponsible.

This paper also carried an item under the heading: *'Gorakh Nath Mandir ke gate per kabza, Saadhuon mein dahashat, mandir ke pramukh dwaar par virodhi jhande pheraye gaye'* (Gate of Gorakhnath Temple seized, tenor among sadhus, opponents' flags unfurled at the main gate).

The news was contradicted by the temple spokesman. It may be noted that this shrine is headed by Mahant Avaidya Nath, M.P., who is the Chairman of the Ram Janmabhoomi Mukti Yagna Samiti. Therefore, such a news had a very serious implication from the communal and political point of view. It should not have been published without confirmation at least from the Temple authorities.

***Role of Authorities :*** The Press Council not only examined the role of the Press during the October-November 1990 happenings in Ayodhya, it also examined the complaints of the Press against the authorities.

The complaints can be broadly classified into two groups: One, Government trying to deny opportunities for covering events; its officers not being available for not being sufficiently communicative; press /curfew passes being denied to newspersons, Press photographers and newspaper hawkers passes not being honoured by the police; and deliberate disinformation being spread by the authorities.

Two, pre censorship sought to be imposed; newspapers prevented from being published; printed copies seized or not allowed to be transported/distributed; and journalists, managers and hawkers beaten up, arrested and maltreated.

In regard to the first part, several correspondents, editors and a Press photographer repeatedly alleged that access to news sources had been blocked by the state authorities and it was not their intention to allow unhindered reporting.

On the most crucial dates of October 30 and November 2, newspersons were prevented from reaching spots of action. Whatever was published regarding the incidents of these days was the result of their enterprise which they undertook at great personal risk after defying the police.

Similarly, they were not allowed to personally verify the information about the removal of canopy at the *shillanyas* site and tampering with it in other ways. In the circumstances, they had to rely on secondary source.

They said that despite a newspaper advertisement published by the state government inviting requests for special passes to cover Ayodhya, even the accredited Press photographers were first refused passes and asked to contact the Home Department. The Press Photographer's Association passed a resolution condemning the attitude of the state government in this regard and threatened to boycott official functions. It was after a memorandum was submitted to the Chief Minister and an altercation took place between him and same photographers and other Press persons that passes were issued to the photographers on October 25, on the condition that the photographs would be taken only between 8 a.m. and 5 p.m. in Ayodhya and flashlights would not be used.

But despite having these passes they were not allowed to photograph the shilanyas site nor were they permitted to use their cameras themselves in the shrine.

On October 30, a number of camera persons were attacked by the police; their cameras were snatched and damaged. A woman photographer of the PTI was saved by others. They were prevented from taking photographs on October 31 also.

Journalists were also not allowed to visit Shilanyas site after the rumour about its having been tampered with spread. Obstacles were placed all along the rout to the site. After passing many such obstructions, news persons could go only up to the Bada Sthan. Their passage was totally blocked beyond that point.

Press persons going from Lucknow, including those from Delhi were made to wait for five hours at the Barabanki-Faizabad border before being allowed to proceed further towards Ayodhya. Some were sent back. They could return only after contacting higher authorities.

All Press passes were suddenly cancelled at Ayodhya/ Faizabad at about 7 p.m. on October 29. New passes were issued only after 1 a.m. on October 30. Some journalists got the passes later in the morning of October 30.

Those who made these complaints included correspondents/ photographers of *The Hindu, The Statesman, The National Herald, The Dainik Jagran, The Swatantra Bharat, The Nav Bharat Times and The Maya.*

The fact that the journalists/photographers were not allowed to visit the Shilanyas site after the rumour of its being tampered with spread and was published by a newspaper was corroborated even by those newspapers who otherwise did not make any complaint against the authorities.

The District Magistrate of Faizabad said that he was not responsible for this as he was away in Tanda, a town in the district. On that day about the cancellation of the passes in the evening of October 29, a local editor said that the new passes would be issued by 10 p.m. but the D.M. confirmed that they would issue passes only after 1 a.m. and most of the distribution was completed by 3 a.m. on October 30. All those who held the earlier passes were given new ones.

It is strange that the authorities did not think of issuing passes with the holder's photograph affixed on them to guard against their misuse. The new passes were issued to everyone who had held the earlier pass and the system of holder's photograph was not introduced even in the case of new passes. The cancellation of the old and the issuing of the new passes made no real sense except causing inconvenience to the Press persons and preventing them from covering the situation during the critical hours between 3 p.m. and 1.30 a.m.

This lends credence to the charge that the crude method was devised to deny the Press an opportunity to cover the situation on an important night before the crucial day of the proposed *kar sewa.*

Asked about arrangements by the government, the UP Government Chief Secretary, the Home Secretary, the Information Secretary and the Special Secretary (Home), all told the Council that they and the Commissioner and District Magistrate of Faizabad were available to answer any queries that Press persons wanted to make and that the Home Secretary was regularly holding Press briefings in the evenings at Lucknow.

Similarly, Commissioner, Faizabad, had been addressing the Press at Faizabad. A Deputy Director Information was also posted at Faizabad to help the Press. Director of Information and Public Relations was also present there on important occasions.

But all these officers conceded that apart from this no special arrangements were made. No Press Camp was set up in Faizabad/ Ayodhya to give authoritative information to the Press. No high-level spokesman of government was posted there to give immediately the information to the Press, answer their queries and confirm or deny reports about any incident that might occur.

The result of this became clear on October 30 when rumours were field that day in the absence of any official briefing at Ayodhya or otherwise any official information being given about the fate of the shrine when the kar sewaks stormed it. The only infirmation the official media, particularly the AIR, gave was that the people attempting to cross the Saryu Bridge were pushed back after a police lathi-charge in which some persons were injured.

The special afternoon bulletins went into print with the agency copy which reported that the kar sewa had begun after a large number of kar sewaks pushed their way into the main Temple-Mosque-structure and caused damage to it. Some papers even said that parts of the mosque had been broken and saffron flags unfurled on the top of all its three domes.

No officer made himself available to the Press at Ayodhya at the time of these happenings to say what exactly the position was.

The availability of such an officer was necessary because Press persons/Press photographers were not allowed to go towards the disputed site. Only a couple of journalists could reach there by sheer impact of the surging crowd which was heading towards it.

They conveyed to other journalists what they had seen. Afternoon editions carried their own accounts, some of which gave the impression that a determined attempt was made to demolish the mosque and that even some security personnel had colluded.

Instead of taking the Press into confidence, the authorities, both state and the district, first kept quiet and then adopted totally negative attitude. They did not allow Press persons to see for themselves the extent of damage.

The Commissioner of Faizabad, Mr. Madhukar Gupta, cancelled his Press Conference scheduled for 4 p.m. while agencies were reporting in their evening leads that hundreds of kar sewaks had succeeded in entering the Ram janmabhoomi-Babri Masjid premises and had tried to damage it. The Home Secretary, Mr. A.K. Rastogi, chose only to say, late in the evening, that 'some people had attempted to enter the premises but they were arrested'.

Chief Minister Mulayam Singh also maintained this stand till the next day. The Central Government spokesman in New Delhi, however, conceded a little later that about 700 people had entered the sanctum sanctorum and some climbed on to the top of the structure but the security forces had removed all of them.

But the next day, some newspapers published photographs showing at least 17 people on the domes and a photo showed a flag hoisted on them. In his Press Conference that evening, the Chief Minister conceded that people did enter the shrine and caused some damage which would be got repaired. This disingenuous and tactless approach of the government gave a body-blow to its credibility with the Press.

The Press Council Committee itself saw the extensive damage caused to the outer wall and the chipping of the plaster at one or two places of the main structure and the slight damage caused to the top of the domes during the attempt to hoist the flag. No lesson seems to have been drawn from the failure of October 30 in spite of the Press reports of the possibility of further attempts at kar sewa resulting in greater trouble. Special arrangements were still not made to inform the Press on time to catch immediate editions.

According to the State Home Secretary's statement in Lucknow in the evening of November 2, 12,000 kar sewaks had tried to move towards the Ram janmabhoomi-Babri Masjid site at 9.30 in the morning. At Ayodhya, the Commissioner of Faizabad told the Committee that police action which included lathi-charge, bursting of tear gas shells and firing of bullets began at 10.27 a.m. Deaths had occurred within the next one hour.

This was the most important time for reporting major events in the afternoon editions, special or regular. Speculation of heavy casualties had widely set in, which was certainly known to the authorities in Ayodhya. But no formal attempt was made either in Ayodhya or at Lucknow to establish communication with Press persons. State Information Secretary, Mr. Nripen Mishra, told the Press Council's Committee that he had personally rung up between 1 and 2 p.m. the editors of papers in Lucknow, Kanpur, Agra, etc. But the fact is that all these efforts had become in-fructuous because the *Dainik Jagran* with a figure 100 dead, was already on the streets of Lucknow. In fact, these officers got into action after they got the copies of the special bulletin of the *Dainik Jagran*.

It is clear that lack of proper arrangements and planning on the part of the administration in respect of giving information to the Press has cost the people and the government dearly. What the Home Secretary said in reply to a question about the arrangement made in this regard, speaks for itself. He said: It was not a very satisfactory arrangement but at least a framework was there. He added: 'Nobody came to us for confirmation of the information.' But some correspondents told the committee that their attempts to get information from officers either evoked no or very inadequate response.

No briefing was done at Faizabad / Ayodhya on November 2. In Lucknow, the government gave in the evening a figure of nine dead, whereas a news agency continued to maintain in every new lead that the figure was fifteen dead according to non-government sources. More than one editor said that a news agency had reported that about 100 persons were feared to have been killed according to unofficial sources (Perhaps it was withdrawn later).

***Press Suppression :*** The special bulletins of Lucknow papers were quickly seized by the authorities and the Home Department asked the district magistrates all over the state to see that such news did not reach the people in their areas. No clear guidelines and no specific instructions were given to them as to the manner in which this was to be ensured.

Some of the methods resorted to by several district administrations were not adopted even during the Emergency when fundamental rights had been suspended and censorship clamped by a specific notification. A common pattern emerges in respect of one method which was employed not only in several publication centres in UP, but also at Ranchi in Bihar. Under this, police officers went to newspaper offices in the evening of November 2, and the night of November 2-3, 1990, and asked journalists on duty to show them the negatives and the plates of the matter being prepared for publication in the next edition.

A magistrate led the police at some places whereas only an inspector or a sub-inspector of police did this elsewhere. At some places where editors or journalists in-charge of the shift refused to show the material, the material was seized or destroyed. Bundles of moffusil additions which were already printed were either not allowed to leave or were seized inside or outside newspapers offices by force. Where the vans and taxis carrying newspapers had already left for various cities and towns, they were intercepted on the way and either forced to return or seized. Drivers of the vans were taken into custody along with bundles of newspapers at some places. Papers were not allowed to be distributed on the morning of November 3 at various places where they had reached somehow. Hawkers who tried to distribute copies were beaten up, driven away and the copies were seized/destroyed at several places.

These complaints were made to the committee by journalist of Muzaffarnagar, Agra, Lucknow, Kanpur, Bareilly, Gorakhpur, Varanasi, Allahabad and Ranchi. At Allahabad, the police forcibly stopped the printing press of a paper in the midst of printing. A similar complaint was made at Varanasi. No search/seizure warrants were shown anywhere. Nowhere Press persons were told under what legal powers these steps were being taken. No distinction between one paper and another was made at some places and blanket action was taken against almost all of them, as at Varanasi.

Another method adopted was not to issue or to delay the issuance of curfew passes to the hawkers. At one publication centre, the authorities admitted that no hawker had a curfew pass from the evening of October 30 to the evening of October 31. They pleaded practical administrative difficulties for this, but the fact remains that hawkers could not legally operate on the streets on these important dates when people were keen to know as to what had happened at Ayodhya and elsewhere in the State. While at some places, the district authorities orally asked the newspapers not to publish special evening bulletins on November 2, the deputy commissioner of Ranchi issued a formal letter 'requesting' them not to publish such bulletins. No paper, however, published any special bulletin there, but the *Ranchi Express*, carried the Deputy Commissioners letter along with its comments calling it an attempt to dictate to the Press.

The district administration at Gorakhpur in U.P. also 'requested' through a formal letter on November 2, the local editors of the *Aaj*, the *Dainik Jagran* and the *Swatantra Chetna* to cooperate with the administration by not publishing special evening bulletin that day. The *Swatantra Chetna* ignored the letter and did bring out an evening edition after which its Chief Editor, Mr. R.C. Gupta was arrested.

In the course of the enquiry some district officers said that the magistrates and the police officials had visited the newspaper offices not to browbeat them but as a friendly act and in order to know what was going to be published so that the administration could prepare itself to deal with its possible fallout. When asked whether it would not have been better to achieve this claimed objective by sending the officers of the Information Department rather than of the magistracy and police as their presence in the newspaper premises is looked upon with suspicion, apprehension and, sometimes, with anger, the officers of the Home Department of Bihar agreed.

Various district officers told the committee that they had taken action of seizure, etc. under Section 153 A, 124 A and 505 IPC but they admitted that no warrants were issued/shown before the-aforesaid steps were taken. The district authorities of Allahabad said that they had simply issued orders under Section 144 Cr.P.C. The District Magistrate of Gorakhpur cancelled the declaration of the *Swatantra Chetna* invoking subsection 2(d) of Section 5 of the Press and Registration of Books Act, 1867, and under substation 2 of section 14 of the Press (Objections Matters) Act, 1951, stopped its publication. The district administrations contention was that the publications of special evening bulletin constituted a change in the periodicity of the publication, thereby violating Section 5(2) (d) of the Act. Its declaration was, therefore, liable to be cancelled. In the district administration's view, publication of an evening bulletin of a newspapers required filing and authentication of a separate declaration.

It is important to note that section 153 A and 124 A IPC do not authorise the administration or the police to enter newspaper premises or search and seize newspapers. All copies of the publications in which matter considered actionable under the above sections is carried, can no doubt be confiscated, but only after following the procedure laid down under Section 95 Cr.P.C. This procedure requires issuance of a notification by state government clearly declaring its intentions to do so and by stating what it considered objectionable in the published material. Without such notification, no seizure can be made and no warrant for seizure can be issued. No such thing was done in the above cases. Therefore, their legality was not beyond doubt apart from their being arbitrary.

The facile device of invoking Section 144 Cr. P.C. to impose the worst type of pre-censorship like stopping of printing of newspapers is all the more appalling. Under no circumstances should the police feel encouraged to take such steps against the Press by invoking section 144 Cr. P.C.

What the district administration of Gorakhpur did is indeed shocking, in that, it invoked in the *Swatantra Chetna* case the provisions of an Act which was buried long time ago and no longer remains on the statute book. This is the ignominious Press (Objectionable Matters) Act. 1951, which was revised during the Emergency but was again repealed in 1977. The Press and Registration of Books Act also seems to have been wrongly applied in this case.

If the district administration's contention that publication of a special evening bulletin changes a daily's periodicity and it is, therefore, illegal, then no daily newspaper can legally publish its various editions, like the dak editions, the city and late city editions, etc. without filing separate declarations for each one of them. It appears that the district administration was groping for some law under which it could stop the publication of this paper and just caught hold of these two Acts without giving serious thought to their applicability in this case. Some editors and journalists were also arrested in the two states. Some were beaten and some others were unnecessarily harassed.

One editor in UP was handcuffed after arrest and another in Bihar was lodged in the condemned prisoners' cell in the jail. About two hundred newspersons courted arrest at Varanasi and a number of journalists took out a march at Agra protesting against alleged excesses by the authorities.

Police entered a newspaper office and beat up Press persons for which the district authorities later expressed regret. The editors of the *Aaj,* the *Dainik Jagran* the *Swatantra Bharat,* the *Pioneer* and the *Swatantra Chetna* complained that their advertisements had been stopped by the authorities.

Mr. Shekhar Agrawal, Special Secretary (Home), U.P. justified the arrest of the editor, Mr. R.C. Gupta, for publication of exaggerated figures of casualties at Ayodhya on November 2, but he admitted that handcuffing of the editor was wrong and apologised for that. He also admitted that it was improper to stop the distribution of newspapers and said those who did that exceeded their brief.

The Committee felt sad and anguished that an influential section of the Press, particularly in UP, has conducted itself in a manner, which has seriously offended against ethics of journalism. It needs no emphasis to state that news can be a highly inflammable commodity that may set the society afire if not handled with the greatest sense of responsibility.

Similarly, intemperate and incisive comment on communal and social issues may lead to serious strife engulfing the nation. The Committee, therefore, called for strict adherence to the Council's guidelines of 1969 on communal and social writings.

Corrections should be promptly published with due prominence and regrets expressed in serious cases, and it will help a great deal if an in-service training is given to journalists for inculcation of all these principles.

It also needs to be stressed that a judgement can be no better that the information it is based upon. Therefore, it is the bounded duty of the state not only never to try to choke the channels of information but to make positive and conscious efforts to help the Press and the media to get the necessary information on all questions of public importance. Such an effort was found grievously lacking on the part of the authorities in the context of the extremely sensitive issue of Ram janmabhoomi-Babri Masjid.

The state administration in UP failed to anticipate the situation and to evolve ways to see that a true picture of things and happenings gets reflected in the Press. It did not act imaginatively when the situation appeared to take a serious turn. It left it to the district administration to tackle without suggesting any guidelines and parameters within which they should have acted, resulting in certain acts which tantamount to curbing the freedom of the Press.

The Committee suggests that the Council may express displeasure and caution the authorities over these trends while reprimanding the defaulting section of the Press. Also, (a) authorities should beware not to act against the Press outside the powers given by law; (b) they should make adequate arrangements to inform the Press in time to catch editions and to give it all legitimate facilities for coverage whenever major events of news value are likely to take place; (c) editors /correspondents should be immediately taken into confidence, without being partial or discriminatory, and their help sought in an amicable manner whenever tension may appear to build up or incidents affecting communal peace and harmony may take place.

## Suggestions

At the meeting held in November 1968, the Press Council considered complaints by governments, particularly by the Government of Mysore, regarding the objectionable nature of as many as 18 articles and news items which appeared in certain dailies and weeklies published in their respective states. In view of this, the Council considered it proper to frame certain guidelines with reference to which it would judge communal writings coming up before it. Besides affording guidance to the Press, the guidelines, it was felt, would also tend to impart objectivity to their own decisions.

In framing the guidelines and in determining what shall be considered as 'objectionable communal writing', as contrasted with writings which were calculated to unify the diverse elements in the nation's political life, three documents were given special consideration. These were Appendices II and III to the decisions of the National Integration Council of 1962 and 'the Code of Ethics for the Press in respect of reporting and to commenting of communal incidents' formulated by the All India Newspapers Editors Conference (AINEC) at its meeting in Srinagar in 1968.

The re-constituted National Integration Council which met at Srinagar in 1968 had appointed a sub-committee as regards matters relating to mass media but no conclusions were drawn by it. With the assistance afforded by the formulations in these documents, the Council reviewed the problems and the following represents the basis on which the Council proceeded:

> The function of the Press may be considered from two aspects. The first is what might be called the positive role. It is this that is emphasised in most of the declarations contained in the three documents referred to above. They refer to the principles which should guide the Press to achieve national unity, which would be to emphasise those aspects of cur national life which tend towards unifying the communities, not unifying in the senses of abolishing distinctions, or identities or making them indistinguishable from one another, but emphasising the common features of the diverse faiths and religions and the subordination of sectional interests to the interests of national unity and integrity. This one might say is the positive aspect of the role of the Press.

This, however, is not the aspect with which the Council is most immediately concerned in framing these guidelines. In doing so, what it is concerned with is not so much as to what the Press should do, as to what the Press should not do. When adjudicating upon matters under Section 13 of the Act, the Council is concerned principally with transgressions from proper standards of journalistic propriety, in other words with what the Press should avoid. In this context, reference has first to be made to two paragraphs in Appendix in to the National Integration Council resolutions of 1962. These are paragraphs 4 and 5. They run:

(4) Journalists shall observe restraint in reports likely to lead to violence;

(5) Journalists shall endeavour to ensure that information disseminated is factually accurate. No fact shall be distorted and no essential fact shall be suppressed. No information known to be false or not believed to be true shall be published.

Reference may next be made to the relevant portion of the code as laid down by the AINEC of 1968 which are clauses (a), (c) and (d) of paragraph 3 of (iv) and (v) and these run:

3.(a) All editorial comments and other expressions of opinion, whether through articles, letters to the editor, or any other form, should be restrained and free from scurrilous attacks against leaders or communities, and there should be no inducement to violence.

(c) Likewise, generalised charges and allegations against any community or unfair discrimination amounting to inciting communal hatred and distrust, must also be eschewed.

(d) Whereas the truth should not be suppressed, a deliberate slanting of news of communal incidents should be avoided.

3.(iv) Condemn unreservedly incitement to violence or advocacy of violence as a means of settling differences.

(v) Refrain from giving tendentious treatment to news of disturbances involving caste, community, class, religion, region or language groupings.

Having considered these principles, the Council felt that they required some modifications and some additions before they could satisfactorily be applied to the actual problems which crop up before the Council. One has to remember that the Press does not act in a vacuum but voices the feelings and sentiments of the groups. Of course, when these feelings and sentiments are prejudicial to the public weal, they have to be suppressed. But one should be quite sure that they are against the common good before thinking of banning them. If the circumstances that India is composed of diverse groups and faiths is a fact of life on the basis of which alone everyone has to act, then there should be liberty to voice the feelings, sentiments and aspirations of groups and communities constituting the body politic. In this context it has to be mentioned that communities could and do have legitimate grievances which they must bring to the notice of the general public as well as of the authorities in order to have them redressed. That would be a democratic right which in view of the freedoms guaranteed by our Constitution could not be denied.

The Press should have a useful role in ventilating these grievances. Only the language employed should be sober, the sentiments expressed should not lead to acerbities (acrimony) between communities and the means of redressal of grievances suggested should not include resort to violence, riots or disorder. It need not of course be stated that grievances should not be invented nor exaggerated. The Council should, therefore, be on its guard not to characterise as communal writings or writings contrary to journalistic ethics what merely sets forth or explains the grievances of a community—be it in any field: social, political of economic— which is voiced by a newspaper and means suggested for its redressal by peaceful, legitimate and legal means.

Digressing a little, the same would also apply to writings which are meant to ventilate grievances of particular regions or particular linguistic groups; all these would be governed by the same principles. The Council considered that if these were adhered to, a sense of nationhood, unity and integrity, which is the ultimate guarantee for all sections of communalities would be furthered.

Based on the above principles and criteria, the Council drew up the following:

Recognising that the Press which enjoys the utmost freedom of expression has a great and vital role to play in educating and moulding public opinion on correct lines in regard to the need for friendly and harmonious relations between the various communities and religious groups forming the fabric of Indian political life and in mirroring the conscience of the best minds of the country to achieve national solidarity, the Press Council of India considers that this object would be defeated, communal peace and harmony disturbed and national unity disrupted if the Press does not strictly adhere to proper norms and standards in reporting on or commenting on matters which bear on communal relations. Without attempting to be exhaustive, the Council considers the following as offending against journalistic proprieties and ethics:

1. Distortion or exaggeration of facts or incidents in relation to communal matters or giving currency to unverified rumours, suspicions or inferences as if they were facts and base their comments on them.
2. Employment of intemperate or unrestrained language in the presentation of news or views even as a piece of literary flourish or for the purpose of rhetoric or emphasis.
3. Encouraging or condoning violence even in the face of provocation as a means of obtaining redress of grievances whether the same be genuine or not.
4. While it is the legitimate function of the Press to draw attention to the genuine and legitimate grievances of any community to have the same redressed by all peaceful, legal and legitimate means, it is improper and a breach of journalistic ethics to invent grievances, or to exaggerate real grievances, as these tend to promote communal ill-feeling and accentuate discord.

5. Scurrilous and untrue attacks on communities or individuals, particularly when this is accompanied by charges attributing misconduct to them as due to their being members of a particular community or caste.
6. Falsely giving a communal colour to incidents which might occur in which members of different communities happen to be involved.
7. Emphasising matters that are apt to produce communal hatred or ill will, or fostering feelings of distrust between communities.
8. Publishing alarming news which are in substance untrue or make provocative comments on such news or even otherwise calculated to embitter relations between different communities or regional or linguistic groups.
9. Exaggerating actual happenings to achieve sensationalism and publication of news which adversely effect communal harmony with banner headlines or in distinctive types.
10. Making disrespectful, derogatory or insulting remarks on or reference to the different religion or faiths or their founders.

In addition, the Committee made the following suggestions in the light of the findings of this inquiry and expect newspapers to act upon them:

(a) Provocative and sensational headlines should be avoided;

(b) Headings must reflect and justify the matter printed under them;

(c) Figures of casualties given in headlines should preferably be on the lower side in case of doubt about their exactness and where the numbers reported by various resources differ widely;

(d) Headings containing allegations made in statements should either identify the person/body making the allegation or, at least, should carry question marks;

(e) Comments and value judgements in presentation of news should be avoided;

(f) Presentation of news should not be motivated or guided by partisan feelings or should it appear to be so;

(g) Language employed in writing the news should be temperate and such as may foster feelings of amity among communities and groups.

***Anti-Reservation Stir :*** The Editor's Guild received sometime in March-April 1987 reports alleging bias and distortion in local coverage of the anti-reservation agitation in Gujarat. The Guild sent a fact-finding team to Gujarat.

The team included Mr. M.V. Desai, Mr. Inder Malhotra (former Resident Editor, *The Times of India,* Delhi), Mr. K. Narendra (Editor, *Daily Pratap,* Delhi) and Mr. B.G. Verghese (former Editor of *The Hindustan Times* and *The Indian Express).* They were supposed to find the truth so that professional norms may be upheld.

The agitation in Gujarat was sparked off by resentment on the part of caste Hindus in the matter of reserving appointments to posts and seats in medical colleges to members of the scheduled castes and tribes. Trouble started on December 25, 1981, when the Harijan youth was allegedly severely beaten in Jetalpur Village, some 25 km from Ahmedabad. Disturbances followed and as frequently happens in such situations, snowballed to unprecedented proportions. The question was whether the events were reported accurately and fairly.

The fact-finding team considered it important to find out exactly where, how, why or to what extent there was bias and distortion, so that such lapses could be avoided in future. Unless this was done by some self-regulatory mechanism of the Press itself, such as through its professional associations, one of the two things would happen: either the government would seek justification in such dereliction to impose censorship as in Assam, or an angry public would take the issue to the streets by attacking newspaper officials and manhandling newsmen and photographers as had sometimes happened.

The team looked into six major dailies published in Gujarat: *Gujarat Mitra* in Surat, *Loksatta* in Baroda, *Phulchhab* in Rajkot and in Ahmedabad, *Jansatta* (part of the *Express* Group).

The findings of the team are not flattering to the Gujarat Press. Among other things, the team observed:

(1) Backgrounding of the issue of reservation generally and of the post-graduate medical students' demands in particular, was weak with the result that emotion triumphed over fact-perspective was lost.

(2) Government's concessions did not receive the notice and elaboration. They merited...agitation grew on folk lore.

(3) Coverage of day-to-day incidents left much to be desired.

(4) Government contradictions were carried in an abbreviated form in the inside pages.

(5) An unsubstantial report of a Harijan attack on the Guru Nanak Bhavan in the University Campus was published while nothing appeared on the burning down of the Christian-Harijan houses in Uttarasanda village in Kheda district.

(6) Quite a large number of reports of alleged Harijan violence against denominational institutions proved baseless.

(7) Newspapers (many cases cited) failed to make their own independent checks and published whatever was told to them by anybody.

(8) While hard news was always carried, credence was given to rumours and casual pronouncements by all and sundry. Notices of bandhs in different parts of the city (Ahmedabad) were printed without any effort to assess the authority or worth.

(9) Government efforts to reveal the truth were frustrated, forcing it, to buy advertisements space to tell its side of the story.

(10) The leading citizens including the venerable Gandhian Ravi Shankar Maharaj (Father Wallace and another) were misquoted as supporting the anti-reservationists' cause. Their clarificatory statements were not published.

(11) Some of the newspapers, through their leading personalities, changed their role from witnesses to actors having got embroiled in interparty and intraparty rivalries.

(12) The absence of a strong professional leadership was manifest in failures to assess news, mistaking rumours for news, playing up trivial items, not following up stories, failing to publish corrections and allowing prejudice to get the better of sober news judgements.

The fact-finding team's report added: 'It is with deep regret that we have to conclude that a section of the Ahmedabad Press did not rise to the occasion when the state was undergoing an agonising trial. Many of the failures of omission and commission may have been the result of subconsious factors, rather than deliberate prejudice. Even so, the results were no less tendentious and injurious to public good. This said, experience shows once again the need to set and observe higher professional standards.

A touchy Gujarat Press reacted somewhere strongly on the team's presence and probing. Critical reports of the Gujarat Press by other journalists like Arun Sandhu of *Statesman*, M.J. Akbar of *Sunday*, Janardan Thakur in *Janmabhoomi Pravasi* and an IFWJ team denounced in clarity.

The Gujarat Press, it was held, had been maligned by the English Press and by visiting newsmen who had no knowledge of die Gujarati language or any background to the issues at stake. Chimanbhai S. Patel, Editor of *Sandesh*, in a letter to K. Narendra of Editors Guild made the point that the fact finding team's observations were based on cursory check-up of facts and onesided representations or limited cooperation of the section of the Press. Will the leading lights of Indian journalism sign its own death-warrant through the public follow-up of this report? 'Let not this report be remembered at least for this', Mr. Patel concluded by way of warning.

Another case was that of the Editor of *Deccan Herald* who also showed his indiscretion in allowing a short story to be published some time in July 1985, which bore a striking resemblance to Mohammad with a derogatory reference. This sparked off communal riots in Bangalore in which about 20 people were killed and newsprint worth rupees one crore belonging to the *Deccan Herald* was burnt.

8

# Moral Code for Media

The official media in this country is devoid of credibility. Former Prime Minister, Indira Gandhi, was extremely authoritarian and did not allow any measure of autonomy to the media. The only time this media breathed fresh air was when V.N. Gadgil was removed as Minister for Information & Broadcasting in 1986 and Bhaskar Ghosh was brought in as Director-General, Doordarshan and Gopi Krishna Arora as Secretary in the Ministry of Information & Broadcasting.

But as Opposition pressure grew on former Prime Minister Rajiv Gandhi in 1987, both Doordarshan and AIR were criticised for pandering to the opposition and not playing up the official line.

The official media touched its nadir with the appointment of K.K. Teary as Minister for Information and Broadcasting in 1989. Fairness and objectivity, if there was any, was thrown to the winds and this media degenerated into a Congress propaganda machine.

During the Blue Star Operation in Amritear in 1984, most of the people were listening to B.B.C for news as the Doordarshan and AIR were concentrating only on the government propaganda. Even Rajiv Gandhi made an admission of this fact. In early 1986, the Central Government hiked the prices of essential commodities on the budget-eve. This was considered as an undemocratic act and there was widespread resentment against it as people thought that any increase in taxes should first be debated in Parliament. The opposition parties organised a bandh in Delhi as a protest against price hike. The bandh was total and was truly reflected in all the newspapers. But for AIR the bandh was a partial success, for TV it was a complete failure, although it showed pictures of half-a-dozen DTC buses stoned and battered and Delhi's main markets presenting a deserted look. The picture scene betrayed the news.

In March 1986, fifteen Hindus were shot dead by extremists in a deluxe bus near Muktsar in Punjab. The TV bulletin, while giving brief details of the incident, harped on the fact that people of both the communities have been killed by the terrorists, whereas the fact was that only Hindus were the sole victims of the carnage.

In the same year, Charles Sobhraj, a notorious smuggler, made good his escape from the Tihar Jail—a high security prison—after drugging the jail officials. The TV bulletin chose not to mention the escape at all, although it was the major news of the day. On persistent enquiries from the Information & Broadcasting Minister as to how the TV missed the news, the government merely gave an assurance that a probe was being made and such lapses would not be repeated. Incidentally, when Charles Sobhraj was held in Goa, a month later, the TV gave it as the lead news with photographs and all to give an impression to the viewers that the government was very effective and the law and order was completely under control.

The following *Times of India* editorial published on February 2, 1986, vividly sums up the distorted coverage of Delhi Bandh by Doordarshan:

***'White Lies and Worse' :*** The protest launched by the opposition parties against Doordarshan's distorted coverage of

Monday's Delhi bandh is wholly justified. Its strength is evident from the arrest on Wednesday of 59 leaders of the Bharatiya Janata Party in Delhi, including 29 members of the Metropolitan Council, the Municipal Corporation and the Delhi Cantonment Board, as well as the public sympathy it has generated. The events preceding the arrest are themselves noteworthy as an index of the deplorable methods adopted by Doordarshan's bureaucrats in dealing with the protestors' delegation. The delegation had apparently sought an appointment with the Doordarshan Director-General, Mr. Harish Khanna, and was given one for 12.30 p.m. When it reached the compound of the office, however, it was told that Mr. Khanna was not present and hence its members would not be allowed to enter the building. Expectedly infuriated, the delegation squatted in the compound in protest. Its members were manhandled and arrested so that they could be evicted from the premises.

This manner of dealing with protest deserves to be condemned strongly. But its repugnance fades into insignificance when compared with the way in which the national television network depicted the Delhi bandh on Monday evening.

## Doordarshan Lying

There cannot be the slightest doubt that Doordarshan was lying when it claimed in its news bulletins that 'the Delhi bandh called by the opposition parties to protest against the recent price hike in certain essential commodities failed to evoke any response'. In reality, as the entire Press reported, the bandh was a considerable success: most shops, factories, office and business establishments, as well as schools were closed. A high proportion of the buses that plied (or were made to run—92 per cent of the Delhi Transport Corporation fleet or over 100 vehicles more than on a normal days) ran empty: DTC's earnings slumped by over 50 per cent despite the increase in fares. But Doordarshan's bureaucrats could speak a white lie and managed to do so with a straight face only because they had resorted to the crassest form of manipulation of the camera and of its coverage. This trick, a form of deception to which TV as a medium is particularly amenable, was played with full premeditation by placing the camera in strategic—false or unrepresentative position. This kind of deception represents utter disgrace. Not only has it exposed Doordarshan's abjectly servile relationship with the government, it has also revealed on the part of Doordarshan and the I&B Ministry nothing short of contempt for the people. That contempt is the stuff of which the world's Goebbelesses are made.'

Again, Jack Anderson, an American film producer, was given all facilities by the Government of India to make a film entitled 'Rajiv's India'—a film showing India on the threshold of major changes. The film was supposed to greatly educate the Indian public. At a preview, the film was seen by K.C. Pant, then Minister for Steel and Mines, Chairman of the Policy Planning Committee in the Ministry of External Affairs, G. Parthasarathy, Minister of State for External Affairs, K.R. Narayanan, Minister of State for Welfare, Rajendra Kumar Bajpayee, and Mohammed Yunus of the Trade Fair Authority of India. The picture was applauded for its educative value. It was decided to screen the film on TV. It was sponsored by *Press Trust of India* (PTI) whose Chairman, Ram Nath Goenka (Proprietor, Indian Express Group), had hosted a preview party. But the screening was cancelled at the last moment.

But the man, Yashpal Kapoor—former confidante of Mrs. Gandhi—took the credit for stopping the telecast. Kapoor, who attended the preview, disclosed that he had protested to Goenka and Gadgil (the then Minister for Information and Broadcasting) that the film denigrated Indira Gandhi and gave free publicity to Goenka's *Indian Express* chain of Newspapers. 'Is this Rajiv's India or Goenka's Indian Express?', asked Kapoor. It was stated that other characters in the film also made outrageous statements. Khushwant Singh remarked that Rajiv was just a 'namsy pamsy Avro pilot who would make an ass of himself and take the country to ruin'. He said Rajiv was better than his mother and grandfather. Nusli Wadia (Bombay Industrialist) was introduced as the grandson of Jinnah (Founder of Pakistan) and the other big shareholder of Bombay Dyeing, Madhavrao Scindia was introduced reading a 'ten-minute lecture' about the Gwalior royal family's service to the people. *Sunday Mail* wrote that after the preview 'Tytler was heard loudly exclaiming: this is India through the eyes of a Press tycoon, industrialist and Maharaja'.

The incident illustrates the complete dependence of Doordarshan on government. *The Times of India* editorial dated February 11,1986 said:

***Rajiv's India'*** **:** In cancelling the screening of Mr. Jack Anderson's film 'Rajiv's India' at the last minute after the film had been publicised as a great media event, Doordarshan has once again demonstrated that it is not its own master. Only a couple of days before the scheduled screening, Mr. V.N. Gadgil, Minister for Information and Broadcasting, had described the film as one which would not only 'entertain the audience but also educate them'. Clearly, it had his approval. But we shall let that pass since no one suffers from any misconception about the independence of either Doordarshan or the Information and Broadcasting Ministry. We are interested in the wider issues this episode has raised. Regardless of whether the film is laudatory or critical of the present government, and regardless of whether it is censorious of or objective about Mrs. Indira Gandhi, surely we do not need foreign producers to tell us what we should think about either the present Prime Minister or his predecessor. Such films, it should be obvious, are made for foreign audiences. They are not meant for the Indian audience and they cannot be edited to suit our needs. They can serve only one purpose. Which is that they can tell us what some particular foreign producer and his team think of us. If that was the purpose for which the film was to be screened on Doordarshan, then there could be no case for removing certain allegedly offensive portions. There is enough talent in the country which can not only help project and sustain the Prime Minister's and his government's image but also focus attention on serious social problems such as bride-burning or harassment of Harijans.

Earlier foreigners in search of 'mysterious India' used to look for snakecharmers, yogis and maharajas. Currently they look for different kind of celebrities who perhaps tell them that they want to hear about this country. That is their business. But they inflict such views on fellow Indians with the endorsement by foreigners. Reports have it that the film was cancelled following protest to the Prime Minister by some-Congress leaders who had been invited to its screening by the chairman of the PTI Board of Directors. If this is in fact the case it reflects very poorly on how decisions are taken. Mr. Rajiv Gandhi has in this case exposed his information and broadcasting minister and others who cleared the film to unnecessary humiliation. Surely heavens would not have fallen if certain remarks critical of Mrs. Indira Gandhi had been allowed to be put on the screen.

*The Statesman* offered the following comment on the bandh and the cancellation of film on February 16,1986, in its editorial entitled 'Distortions on the box':

> It was possible to sympathise with those BJP workers who protested in front of the Delhi Doordarshan Kendra against the distorted reporting of the bandh in the capital on February 16. Despite the regrettable violence that marked the day of protest, there was virtual unanimity, at least in the Press, that the bandh was by Delhi standards, almost total. Yet Doordarshan chose in its news bulletins to claim that the bandh had no effect on the city, coming close on the heels of the sudden decision not to telecast Jack Anderson's 'Rajiv's India' because of 'unforeseen' but still officially unexplained circumstances. Doordarshan was once again drawn into the firing line. Perhaps it is naive to expect accurate and objective news coverage of national politics from the state controlled media which have in the not-too-distant past distinguished themselves in their role as the mouthpiece of the ruling party at the Centre. Doctored information, sometimes plain falsehoods, disseminated by radio and television over the years are still too fresh in public memory to expect any sudden and drastic change.

***The Indian Express on March 5,1986 wrote :*** The withholding of the film 'New Delhi Times' from the telecast over Doordarshan last Sunday is the second time in barely three weeks when a programme announced with much pride and fanfare, even as late on the evening before, was suddenly and mysteriously cancelled. As in the case of the American-made documentary 'Rajiv's India' earlier, the film had been seen and approved by the authorities concerned. In fact, the former I&B Secretary, Mr. S.S. Gill, during whose tenure the film—which shows the nexus between politicians and the underworld—had been bought by Doordarshan had reportedly described it as a fine political film and hoped that it would be telecast. Sadly it was not. As on the earlier occasion, nobody apparently even knows why the film was withheld. The current I&B Secretary pleaded ignorance and properly directed the questioner to Doordarshan. But neither the DG of Doordarshan nor two of his senior colleagues were aware of the cancellation and one of them thought there must be technical problem.

The following was The Times of India comment on March 4,1986 on the cancellation of the screening of 'New Delhi Times' on TV:

> Doordarshan has done it again. In a blatant display of censorship, it cancelled the film 'New Delhi Times' a day before it was to go on air. The film, which was scheduled to be shown last Sunday, deals with the nexus between politicians and criminals. Whatever be their preconceptions about such a nexus, TV viewers have been denied access to even its fictionalisation. With 'Rajiv's India' being cancelled earlier and now 'New Delhi Times' meeting the same fate, there can be little doubt about the nexus between Doordarshan and those in power. The people were beginning to believe that Doordarshan was being given a relatively greater degree of freedom in selecting and scheduling its programmes. Except the Prime Minister and a few of his cohorts, no one, it seemed for a while, was holy. Thus, even a Chief Minister was attacked

> in a sponsored programme on TV and he then had to rush to clarify his government's position. Some Doordarshan's own programmes exposed ministers and government departments to critical, and at times embarrassing scrutiny. The emphasis, it seemed, was on exposing everything—warts and all. The hope inspired by these programmes about the government media has, however, turned to be short-lived. The first signs of this came with the abrupt cancellation of 'Rajiv's India'. It showed that the government's sensitivity to criticism had been extended to include any criticism, justified or unjustified, of Mrs. Indira Gandhi too. While Mr. Rajiv Gandhi could attempt to bury his predecessors with impunity at the Congress Centenary celebrations, clearly the government media was not to be allowed to do so, particularly, at the time when the euphoria about the new leadership had started subsiding. But even by the old/new standards cancellation of a feature film is a different matter. It would seem that even common politicians are now to be counted amongst the holy cows of Doordarshan and that 'power brokers' can be so described only by Mr. Rajiv Gandhi. For the rest, they must remain above all criticism—even in fiction.

What to talk of avoiding adequate TV coverage to opposition leaders and Chief Ministers of non-Congress (I) governments, the TV officials even started either ignoring or scantly covering functions presided over by President Zail Singh in 1985-86 when the relations between the President and the Prime Minister were at the lowest ebb.

Invited by President Zail Singh to witness Republic Day celebrations in Delhi in 1987, Mrs. Anita Pfaff, daughter of Subhas Chandra Bose, felt bitter about her experience with the official media which totally ignored her. She doubted whether Doordarshan would ever telecast the interview she gave to them in Calcutta.

Two encounters with TV had left her cold on January 26, 1987, when she accompanied the wife of President Zail Singh, in the same car to the VIP enclosure at Raj Path, TV commentaries did not identify her. She was shown on the TV but not named. 'That was the compromise—to show me in the crowd, but not to say what I was', she said.

Doordarshan refused to send a team on January 31,1987 to Rashtrapati Bhawan, where a reception was held in her honour. The function was kept out of Doordarshan's English news bulletin. Perhaps, the presence of Mr. Prakash Mehrotra, Mr. Inder Gujral, Mr. Bhanu Prakash Singh, Mr. Vijay Kumar Malhotra, Mrs. Pramila Dandavate and the grand daughter of Mahatma Gandhi (leaders either in disfavour or belonging to opposition) kept Doordarshan away.

Mrs. Anita Pfaff observed: 'I do not think Mr. Rajiv Gandhi could have issued instructions for this blackout. But those more loyal than the King who want to please the Prime Minister, are behind this pettiness.' She added: 'As far as I know the Minister for Information and Broadcasting is a Bengali (Panja) and I would like to know his reactions to all this.'

She also noticed the niggardly manner in which TV covered the Netaji award presentation in Calcutta, posthumously awarded to Maj. General Mohammad Zaman Kazani, a Commander of the Netaji's Indian National Army on the Imphal border during the freedom struggle. It was the widow of the former IN A officer who had come all the way from Pakistan to receive the award.

All India Radio on May 19, 1987 (Tuesday) wittingly or unwittingly kicked off the Haryana election campaign for the ruling party in the state. In a gross violation of its own code, AIR went on the air with a Haryana newsletter programme eulogising the state Government's performance.

The Hindi programme 'Rajyon se Chitthi' (letters from the states) was put out at 9.10 a.m. as part of its daily news broadcast from different states. The lead carried the declaration of elections (Haryana) and in the next story the AIR reporter went on to inform listeners that Haryana was the first state to implement the Fourth Pay Commission recommendations. The newsletter programme is broadcast every morning immediately after the news in Hindi.

The code of conduct clearly states that as soon as the elections are announced by the Chief Election Commissioner, no political party taking part in the election is allowed access to AIR facilities except for specific time allowed by the Election Commissioner. Secondly, and more important, the code does not permit AIR to broadcast a news or a feature programme which is either laudatory or critical of any political party.

If a political party needs to go on the air, then it is treated as an election broadcast and the listeners are informed about it.

The programme which was aired for the full duration of five minutes, had its quota of praise for development work done by the state government. Measures for industrial development taken by the government were described in sharp detail.

## Lacking Professionalism

Even N.L. Chawla, former Director-General, Doordarshan, admits that TV totally lacks professionalism and more than that often succumbs to bureaucratic and political pressures. In an article in *The Times* dated November 19,1986, he observes:

> The newly appointed Minister of State for Information and Broadcasting, Ajit Panja's concern for improvement of Doordarshan news programmes should be welcomed as also his observations that 'radio and TV should not sermonise or be propaganda machines only'. This raises the hope that Mr. Panja is seriously concerned with the wider issue of professionalism and credibility of the government controlled media which has suffered an erosion in recent years.

Since news and current affairs programmes are at the interface between broadcasting and politics, they are invariably at the centre of controversy. The combination of picture and sound makes TV news particularly vulnerable to a temptation for self-publicity and to political pressure. There is no dearth of instances of Doordarshan having surrendered professional ethics and discarded guidelines in favour of commands from bureaucrats and politicians. The professionals in the media, who have often complained against interference, have also been guilty of playing safe. How else can one explain the omission of some newsworthy events or coverage of seminars and conferences focusing on ministers or of formal calls on the President, the Prime Minister and other ministers. The criticism that Doordarshan has indulged in an overkill in projecting the Prime Minister has never been satisfactorily answered.

The Media Advisory Committee prepared in 1982 a policy document as a guideline for AIR and Doordarshan. It was formulated to guide the professionals in the live newsrooms and to enable them to resist pressures. The document was also presented to Parliament.

Apart from providing guidelines on specific situations like strikes and bandhs, riots and disturbances, national calamities, sex and crime, the document set out a basic approach to the broadcast programmes of news and current affairs which will do any media under government control proud.

Since this policy paper has not had much of exposure a few relevant paras from the document are being quoted:

'There has to be a clear understanding of the difference between news and views. The reporting of news has to be factual, accurate and objective and only such views as make news should find a place in news broadcasts. There can be no editorialising in broadcast news: each news story should be judged strictly on the basis of its news value.

'In the selection of news received from wideranging sources and in news editing, AIR and Doordarshan should be guided by the highest possible professional standards. While newsworthiness will determine the selection of news, its treatment and presentation should be directly related to the special characteristics and potential of each medium as well as the target audiences.'

There are two other points in the document which are important in the present context on the responsibility of news media to reinforce the fundamental principles on which national policies are based. It says 'the fundamental principles' include territorial integrity, national integration, secularism, maintenance of public order and upholding the dignity and prestige of Parliament, state legislatures and the judiciary.'

On the reporting of pronouncements by the Prime Minister and other ministers, the document says: 'Ministerial statements on policy matters, particularly those of the Prime Minister, are important in as much as they enable the people to understand national policies. Similarly, implementation of government programmes should be given proper place in the news. The focus should be on information rather than on individual. It is also necessary that views of official policies and the manner of their implementation should find adequate time.'

The question is that ever since the guidelines were formulated, AIR and Doordarshan professionals have had the freedom to apply them. No, this should be clear to those news managers of the government who wish to establish the credibility of the government media.

In fact, the government news managers do not want the Doordarshan and AIR staff to have a professional approach towards this media as they apprehend that this might lead to exposures and embarrassment to the government.

In March 1986, H.Y. Sharda Prasad, Prime Minister's Infirmation Adviser, addressed a marathon close-door meeting of Doordarshan news staff. At the meeting which lasted for about three hours and was held in the room of the Chief News Editor of Doordarshan, Sharda Prasad stressed the need for introducing professionalism in news coverage by the television network. A number of producers from Doordarshan's news staff and the Director General, Harish Khanna were also present.

According to some Doordarshan staff members who attended the meeting, the Prime Minister's top media aide pointed out instances when the network coverage had looked lopsided. However, he parried a question on what the 'government thought was "professional journalism".'

Despite the falling standards in the credibility of journalists, newspapers continue to be reliable and dominant source for news and current affairs among households with TV sets, while TV is fast emerging as a major source of news, radio evidently has lost its ground.

These are some of the major findings of a survey conducted by Operations Research Group in 1986 among TV households in the metropolitan cities. Fifty-nine per cent of adults in TV households of the four Metros—Bombay, Calcutta, Delhi and Madras affirmed their reliance on newspapers as a major source for news and current affairs and this is more apparent in Calcutta and Bombay, where over 65 per cent of adults pointed out papers as their source.

Also papers continued to be relied upon more by the more educated in the TV households.

The following petition was admitted by the Supreme Court of India on April 29, 1987, challenging the Union Government's use of AIR and Doordarshan as a nonexclusive voice of the ruling party. It sums up the state of official media in India. The petition was filed by Romesh Thapar, former Editor of *Seminar*, and one of the doyens amongst the journalists in India.

A division bench, comprising the Chief Justice, Mr. R.S. Pathak and Mr. Justice Ranganath Mishra issued a notice to the Union Government returnable on July 21, 1987. This is the first time in the history of India that the Supreme Court has addressed itself to such issues.

The petition had argued that the manner of functioning of AIR and Doordarshan violates the fundamental rights of citizens enshrined in Articles 14, 19 and 21 of the Constitution which guarantee equality before the law, right to freedom of speech and protection of life and personal liberty. The petitioner had asked the Court to direct the government to refrain from violating his rights.

The petitioner argued that the 'fundamental right to freedom of speech and expression includes the right to receive information and the right to know without imposing any unreasonable impediment or restriction on the exercise of the said rights.' The monopoly given to AIR and Doordarshan, it said, is a national asset to be used exclusively for public purposes in accordance with the Constitution.

Thapar, who was represented by the well-known constitutional expert A.G. Noorani, cited several examples and argued that the two official media organs have been reduced to propaganda instrument for the ruling party, the Congress and Prime Minister Rajiv Gandhi. This, said the petition, violates every Indian citizen's fundamental right 'to insist that the significant differences of opinion on important questions of public policy be allowed fair and equal access' to the public media.

As a precedent, the petition quoted the judgement of the US Supreme Court in the case of Red Lion Broadcasting Company versus the Federal Communications Commission where the Court had ruled that though the government could be justified in restricting licences for broadcasting, 'it is the right of the broadcasters which is paramount.'

Arguing mat there had long been widespread 'dissatisfaction' over the working of AIR and Doordarshan, the petition gave the history of his dissatisfaction, starting with the establishment of the Chanda Committee and the government decision to turn down its recommendations granting full autonomy to AIR and Doordarshan.

Quoting a later Committee (1982) headed by Dr. P.C. Joshi, the petition argued that the two official media did not even have 'functional freedom' since they have to function under telephone calls regarding news coverage.

The petition pointed out that unlike all other democratic countries where the status, objects, functions and television are defined by law, there exists no such legislation in India. What is more the two media organs violate guidelines set by the Union Government itself.

In effect, said the petition, Doordarshan and AIR are run according to the wishes and to promote the interests of the political party in power at the Centre and its leader Rajiv Gandhi.

The petition cited several instances to support its contention of bias in the official media. Some among these are—Justice V.R. Krishna Iyer's letter to the then Union Information and Broadcasting Minister V.N. Gadgil, protesting against Doordarshan's censoring of his views on India's nuclear options; newspaper editorials criticising Doordarshan's coverage of the 1983 assembly election results in which the Congress had lost in Andhra Pradesh and Karnataka; its biased reporting when Dr. Farooq Abdullah, Jammu and Kashmir Chief Minister and N.T. Rama Rao, Andhra Pradesh Chief Minister were dismissed by Mrs. Indira Gandhi's government, its lapses as documented by former Director General Iqbal Malik, in the reporting on 'Operation Blue Star' (Military action in 1984 to flush out the Sikh extremists from the Golden Temple and other places in Punjab).

The two media organs, it argued, were so obsessed with the doings of the Prime Minister and other ministers that they had no inclination to record the struggle of the common man. The petition quoted Dr. Joshi's report lamenting 'that a television system which is not only publicly funded but was also directly run by the government, on the ground that this was necessary to make television serve the purpose of development in the direction of socialism, should show so little orientation towards the common people in its news and current affairs programmes.'

The petition quoted Rajiv Gandhi's frequent expression of dismay at Doordarshan's obsession with him but charges that the continuation of the malady is because of the 'lack of any institutional protection of independence or autonomy of the professional or provision for accountability'.

The petition wanted the court to declare the two medias functioning according to citizen's fundamental rights.

***Role of K. K. Teary :*** Soon after Rajiv Gandhi came to power in October 1985, he gave certain measure of freedom to the electronic media. He also gave a statement that he wanted the Press to be free. In pursuance of this goal, he sacked V.N. Gadgil in 1986 for allowing political use of Doordarshan. Rajiv issued instructions that TV be made a real mirror of the nation.

Bhaskar Ghosh and Gopi Arora revolutionised the news coverage of Doordarshan with balanced reporting. Fairfax, Bofors and other such controversial issues were discussed threadbare on TV and even the views of prominent critics of the government were telecast fearlessly.

But as the opposition pressure on him grew during the year 1987, both Doordarshan and AIR began to receive flak for pandering to the Opposition.

Consequently, Ghosh was sacked as Doordarshan Chief in October, 1988 and later Arora was shifted from Information and Broadcasting Ministry to the Finance Ministry.

The General Elections were to be held in 1989. In order to shape Doordarshan and AIR into an election winning weapon, Rajiv inducted K.K. Teary as an Information and Broadcasting Minister. The doughty Ramnath Goenka's *Indian Express* under the stewardship of the crusading Editor, Arun Shourie, through combination of harangues and exposes had been giving Rajiv and his government sleepless nights.

The Congress Party concluded that credibility was only an urban concern and there was no risk in issuing relentless propaganda to woo the rural electorate.

It is not as if electronic media had not been used for partisan purposes. But never had the misuse by the ruling party been so blatant, so systematic, so purposeful, so single minded and so ruthless.

A two-pronged strategy was drawn, to use the official media to the ruling party's advantage and deny to the Opposition an effective, even if limited, counter in print.

This line of reasoning was reflected in several government actions during this period. While Government extended liberal financial aid to the electronic media, the screws were relentlessly tightened on the print media. From the period 1984-89 the Government spent Rs 800 crores on the I&B Ministry's growth and expansion programmes.

Due to the fiscal concessions extended to the TV industry, the TV was made accessible to most people. Today TV covers 85% population with 25 million TV sets as against less than half the number five years ago. In 1989, Doordarshan covered 75% of the population as compared with just 18 per cent in 1986. On the other hand, the Government during the period 1984-89 pushed up the price of the newsprint by more than 200 per cent, stultifying the largely independent print media. The idea was to render the newspapers out of reach of the lower and middle class.

Once Teary took over the reigns of the Broadcasting Ministry, he went about his task in a most brazen fashion and surpassed the record of H.K.L. Bhagat and N.P.K. Salve in turning TV into the Congress Party's propaganda machine.

### The Distortion

Following his instructions, both AIR and Doordarshan made an ingenious use of an article written by veteran leader Madhu Limaye on the problems facing the Janata Dal to humiliate the Opposition.

In the piece published on May 28, 1989 in the *Sunday Mail*, Limaye had critically analysed the weaknesses of the Janata Dal and its leaders and had advised Chandra Shekhar and V.P. Singh to close ranks to defeat the Congress (I) in the forthcoming elections. Limaye concluded by saying that while the two Thakur leaders were busy fighting with each other like Prithviraj and Jaichand, Mohammad Ghori was waiting in the wings to finish them off.

Perhaps for the first time in their history, AIR and Doordarshan made a news item out of a newspaper article and that too, written by an Opposition leader and used it in all the news bulletins for two days. But while all the critical comments made by Limaye about V.P. Singh were given prominent coverage, whatever had been said against the Government was scrupulously edited. An impression was created to suggest that even a veteran Opposition leader like Madhu Limaye was disillusioned with the Janata Dal.

Limaye was piqued at this blatant distortion and on June 2, 1989, he shot off an angry letter to Rajiv Gandhi protesting against both AIR and Doordarshan. Wrote Limaye: 'Akashvani and Doordarshan have committed a sin against media morality and intellectual ethics. I feel that AIR and TV have taken final leave of fairness, objectivity and truth. It is a pity that your ministers and officials believe that these things can help the ruling party in the forthcoming elections to the Lok Sabha.'

The Prime Minister's Office (PMO) passed on the letter to K.K. Teary, who shot off a reply to Limaye on June 10, 1989. Teary praised Limaye for his 'significant, candid and nonpartisan' views. Little realising that the weekly newspaper that had published Limaye's article did not enjoy a wide circulation, he also added that the socialist leader's write-up had been read 'throughout the country with avid interest'. The Minister informed Limaye: 'Your incisive analysis and well-argued expose of the new outfit becomes interesting and noteworthy because nobody ever questions your bonafides on your ancient and age-old anti-Congressism.' But what about Limaye's views on the Rajiv Gandhi's government which the Doordarshan and AIR bulletins had conveniently ignored?

Teary dealt with this aspect too. He wrote to Limaye: 'In all humility, I may submit that your views on the Rajiv Gandhi Government are all too familiar to be really "news". Because of their reiteration *ad nauseum*, they have become almost tantological. I am sure by now you must also be feeling sick and tired of having to repeat the same views with such mechanical consistency.

Additionally, you may also not be oblivious of the boredom and fatigue caused to the discriminating public.

Stung by this ridicule, Limaye sent another letter to Rajiv Gandhi on June 14 in which he wrote: 'K.K. Teary's answer is as impudent in tone as it is irrelevant in content. The simple question that I raised was about fair reporting. Teary has nothing to say about it. He claims that my views on the Rajiv government are too familiar to be really news. He accuses me of repeating these views with mechanical consistency. He further informs me that the public is suffering from boredom and fatigue as a result of the reiteration of my views *ad nauseum.*'

Limaye went on to raise a few more questions. He asked Rajiv Gandhi: 'How many times have Doordarshan and AIR carried my views on the various issues that have arisen since you assumed power? How many news items were sourced to my articles on various issues and broadcast over the AIR and Doordarshan? it is sickening that your minister should indulge in misleading statements and false suggestions. What boredom and what *nauseam* is he talking about? May I say it is the blatant Congress propaganda that is causing nausea and boredom to the discriminating public'.

As a result of the Congress propaganda unleashed by Teary, V.P. Singh dubbed Doordarshan as 'Dushtdarshan' and Opposition parties belonging to the National Front along with two Communist parties staged a nation-wide protest on June 26, 1989 against the misuse of Government-controlled media. The Bharatiya Janata Party (BJP), too, observed June 25 as 'switch off Rajiv serial Day' and broke dummy television sets as a symbolic gesture.

Teary took the war into the *Express* camp. He harangued with greater acrimony, twisted news where the *Express* had merely slanted it and showed more disdain for the *Express* chain of newspapers than it had shown for the ruling party.

The prime target of attack of the Congress Party was Janata Dal leader V.P. Singh who was emerging as an alternate leader.

The policy of blacking him out on electronic media was replaced by bludgeoning him mercilessly. Till now V.P. Singh was anathema to Doordarshan. With the advent of K.K. Teary, track changed.

Now, every whisper of and opportunity to take a swipe at a Janata Dal leader was grabbed.

Some examples of V.P. bashing during prime time news during 1989:

*April 26,1989*

'He (Buta Singh) said that the party (Janata Dal) President Mr. V.P. Singh, got elected to Parliament from Allahabad with the support of the RSS and Haji Mastan (Bombay smuggler). He was indulging in double dealing with the supporters of Ram Janambhoomi-Babri Masjid to secure his win from Allahabad.'

*May 2,1989*

'In the Lok Sabha today a Congress (I) member, Mr. Harish Rawat, drew the attention of the House to the report along with a photograph published in *The Times of India* alleging that some opposition member of Parliament attended a tea party, hosted by an alleged heroin smuggler in Shahjahanpur in Uttar Pradesh last month. Mr. Rawat said: the Janata leader, Mr. V.P. Singh, was on the dias at the public meeting with the alleged smuggler.'

*May 4,1989*

Both Houses of Parliament today witnessed noisy scenes when ruling party members sought to raise the issue of alleged protection of smuggler by V.P. Singh when he was a central minister.

*May 5,1989*

The Congress (I) MPs pointed out that the heroin smuggler was admitted to the Congress Legislature Party by Mr. V.P. Singh when he was the Chief Minister in Uttar Pradesh. The Congress (I) threw him out of the party immediately on his arrest for heroin smuggling. But Mr. V.P. Singh and other Janata Dal leaders were contriving to hobnob with him.'

*May 6,1989*

A number of Janata Dal leaders have demanded the resignation of their Party President, Mr. V.P. Singh. In a statement issued in Delhi, they expressed their deep distress with the functioning of the party. They said the euphoria of Mr. V.P. Singh and the party Vice President, Mr. R.K. Hegde's so-called value-based politics is over. The signatories to the statement are Mr. Brij Mohan Toofan, Mr. Raj Kumar Jain, Mr. Ram Gopal Sisodia, Mr. Lalit Mohan Gautam, Mr. Suraj Bhan Gupta and Mr. Ravinder Manchanda.'

*May 10,1989*

When a correspondent drew his attention to Mr. V.P. Singh's charge that the issue of Panchayati Raj is a poll gimmick, the Prime Minister remarked: If your vision is up to your nose, what could I comment?'

*May 14,1989*

Eight Congress (I) MPs have in a statement said that the Prime Minister was anxious that power should go to the people in rural areas while Mr. V.P. Singh wanted it to remain with a small coterie.'

*June 2,1989*

'Four Janata Dal leaders have demanded the resignation of Party President, Mr. V.P. Singh, in a statement in New Delhi today. They accused Mr. Singh of an authoritarian attitude. The signatories are, Mr. Ram Gopal Sisodia, Mr. Ravinder Manchanda, Capt. Vikram Singh and Mr. Kulwant Gupta.'

*June 5,1989*

A group of Congress (I) MPs in a statement today have criticised Mr. Vishwanath Pratap Singh for describing the decision to send the Indian Peace Keeping Force (IPKF) to Sri Lanka as a mistake. They said Mr. V.P. Singh did not utter a word about the heroic deeds of the IPKF for the unity and integrity of Sri Lanka.

*June 10,1989*

'Replying to a question, Mr. Chandra Shekhar said he is not yet ready to accept Mr. V.P. Singh as a future Prime Minister of India. He said: He will decide about the candidature of Mr. V.P. Singh when the time comes.'

*June 18,1989*

'Mr. K.K. Teary has strongly criticised the Janata Dal leader, Mr. V.P. Singh, for making baselss charges against the Prime Minister. He said the Janata Dal President had run away when challenged to repeat his charge in Parliament to the acute embarrassment of his own partymen.

'Mr. Teary accused Mr. Singh of acting under the command of Hershman and other foreign agencies, using mother, God and the country as mere bargaining counters for that hallucinatory chair that will never be his.'

In an interview to *India Today* in its issue dated July 15, 1989, Mr. K.K. Teary defended his policy towards the electronic media. Prefacing the interview, *India Today* wrote:

Rhetoric in his rapier, and bombast his battering-ram, if there ever was an Indian politician whose major strength was his acerbic lung power, it has to be K.K. Teary, 47. And in the Ministry of Information and Broadcasting, the one-time professor of English literature from Bihar has found the perfect vehicle for his talents. He launched into a characteristic diatribe against the Opposition and the print media in the course of an interview with Senior Editor Prabhu Chawla at his luxurious house, once the official residence of former Prime Minister Lal Bahadur Shastri.

*Excerpts from the interview*

*Q.* Why have AIR and Doordarshan become blatantly biased instruments for promoting the ruling party's electoral interests?

*A.* This is a sweeping generalisation. In the last two years, there has been an attempt to violate all norms of national consensus. A section of the Press has been indulging in psychological warfare, no less lethal than nuclear warfare.

Q. Are you trying to pitch the official media against the print media?

*A.* There has been an attempt to undermine everything which this nation stands for. The Trojan horses of Indian media and their collaborators in politics have been misleading the nation. Their style has been to exaggerate their strength, and unleash confusion in the minds of their opponents. It has been a strategy aimed at undermining the nation's achievements and leadership.

*Q.* All this sounds like a cliche.

*A.* This is very unfortunate. No government anywhere has been able to achieve in such a short period what we have managed to in India. Yet the media only focuses on certain aberrations, projecting them as if they were the hallmarks of the Indian political system. It indulges in exaggerations, distortions and falsification. And is often sectarian and antichange.

*Q.* But the print media has no motives.

*A.* The aim is to grab political power. But its role is confined to providing material for keeping Parliament going in a particular direction. And those who are doing this are not professional media persons. They are economic offenders like Ramnath Goenka. I can accept the diseased and pathological prejudices of the M.V. Kamaths, Prem Bhatias and Kuldeep Nayars. They are not conscious subverters. But the Iranis and Shouries are, and they are leading the Opposition which follows them like obedient urchins. They're destroying the sanctity of the Press. Their role is anti-Press and anti-India.

*Q.* Doordarshan is no different. It is being used to hit out against opponents.

*A.* This is not true. It is the illegitimates of the system—the Arun Nehrus, Shouries, V.P. Singhs, Jethmalanis, Goenkas and Iranis—who have destroyed the system from within, who are subverting the Government, the Press and the Opposition. Doordarshan is, in fact, sustaining legitimacy. It has the mandate of the people.

*Q.* A mandate to destroy its credibility?

*A.* All criticism on Doordarshan should not be lumped with the fashionable credibility concept. Those who talk of our credibility never enjoyed any themselves. If we have lost credibility we will lose the elections too. We are accountable to Parliament, to the people, no one else.

*Q.* But why such excessive coverage of the Prime Minister?

*A.* Rajiv Gandhi is the Prime Minister of India. No one in India can claim equality with him.

Q. You seem to be depending on Doordarshan and AIR for election purposes.

*A.* The Congress is not an election-oriented party. We are a movement. I appeal to the Opposition not to suffer from any hallucinations. No amount of publicity can ensure victory unless backed with achievements.

Q. Then why blatantly slam opponents through the electronic media?

*A.* That is not correct. Has Doordarshan ever exposed Devi Lal's bandity? Has it ever recorded the plundering of Andhra Pradesh by N.T. Rama Rao? Did Doordarshan catch Hegde with his pants down tapping the phones of his opponents? Doordarshan will never get involved in political polemics.

*Q.* What about V.P. Singh bashing?

*A.* I have a valid explanation. If important leaders of the Janata Dal demand his resignation, it is news. How can anyone afford to ignore a well-known phoney like V.P. Singh?

Q. But do you find nothing positive to broadcast about the Opposition?

*A.* There is nothing positive about them. The Opposition is destroying itself?

Q. You want to project this?

*A.* No. I don't. They are already dead.

Q. Why do you oppose a guarantee ensuring fair use of official media?

*A.* The guarantee is Parliament. It can declare man a woman and woman a man. And Parliament is controlled by the people. If we misuse it we will be rejected by the people.

Q. This means you oppose granting autonomy to AIR and Doordarshan?

*A.* It is the people's media. What we require is autonomy for the print media which is owned by the Sethjis. How much do they share with their journalists? TV and AIR are government wings and cannot be autonomous. Is the print media accountable to anyone?

Q. Yes, to its readers.

*A.* But the same readers elect us as well. This vague accountability to readers is not enough. If there is any loss in circulation, you will make it up by putting in sleazy and sensational stories.

The following *Times of India* editorial published on June 6, 1989, sums up Teary's approach towards the electronic media. Teary never wanted electronic media to promote professionalism to encourage diversity of opinion. Since 1989 was the General Elections year, he wanted to project the ruling party in general and the Prime Minister Rajiv Gandhi in particular on the media.

***No-nonsense Teary :*** Whatever his other failings, Mr. K.K. Teary, the newly-appointed Minister of state in the Union Ministry of Information and Broadcasting, cannot be accused of lacking in candour. In the interviews he has given since assuming office he has studiously refrained from making platitudinous pronouncements about the government-controlled electronic media's commitment to promote professionalism or to encourage diversity of opinion on radio and television. Mr. Teary is clear about his goals and equally clear about how to go about attaining them. In an election year, his mandate is to ensure that the ruling party in general, and the Prime Minister in particular, are projected in the most flattering light. Given this single-mindedness of purpose, he has no use for the qualms of a professional's conscience. The word credibility has been banished from his lexicon. It is possible that Mr. Teary's language sometimes races far ahead of his ideas but even his most acerbic critics can scarcely make a case that they lack logic or internal consistency. The Minister's views are based on two clearly articulated hypothesis. The first relates to the fact that since the government has the sanction of the people and is, therefore, vested with legitimacy, it is only natural for the state-controlled media to propagate its achievements without let or hindrance. In other words, the government's record is fit only for what he calls 'creative projection', it cannot be subjected to critical scrutiny.

The second hypothesis is based on Mr. Teary's conviction that the opposition and some sections of the print media are nothing short of 'subversives' who, in cahoots with their collaborators abroad, are hell-bent on destabilising an elected government undermining in the process the unity and integrity of the country as a whole. To effectively counter the minister's arguments it is clearly not enough to denounce them as Goebbelsian rantings. The arguments would have lost much of their sting had the votaries of the 'free' Press candidly examined their own record during the past two years and more. It is not an unblemished one. But even such an examination, assuming it is undertaken, would not go far enough. Paradoxically enough, both Mr. Teary as well as those who have been at the receiving end of his barbs appear to share the belief that since information is power, journalism is no more than political warfare conducted by other means. In this respect a reminder that the post-Emergency Janata Government too backed out of its commitment to grant autonomy to AIR and Doordarshan may not be out of order. Under the circumstances, Mr. Homi D. Sethna's strong protest against Doordarshan's refusal to screen certain award winning, antiestablishment documentaries heard at the National Film awards ceremony in New Delhi on Wednesday, amounts to crying in the wilderness.

***Khula Manch Controversy :*** George Fernandes, Union Railway Minister in the Janata Government, appeared on TV in August 1990 on the second instalment of 'Khula Manch', a fortnightly interface between a single minister and the public with two presenters acting as moderators. He answered questions not just on railways but on the Pepsi deal, Kashmir, caste-based reservations and other topical issues. But all portions of the programme not relating to the railways were excised before telecast.

Union Minister for Information and Broadcasting, P. Upendra cited three reasons for hacking the programme: Fernandes had no authority to speak about portfolios that were not his, that if every minister started answering every question, there was no need to interview all of them, and that the other ministers had resented Fernandes talking about their areas.

The counter-arguments put forward by the others—that Fernandes had been talking about Pepsi and multi nationals for a long time, that he had, been a minister for Kashmir affairs, and that if the programme was censored it would create a furore—failed to persuade Upendra.

A communication gap between Doordarshan and the Information & Broadcasting Minister seems to have resulted in this fiasco. According to Karan Thapar, one of the presenters of the programme, Doordarshan had agreed to the idea of asking Fernandes questions about other subjects besides the railways.

On August 11,1990, non-railway questions were worked out at a meeting that HTV (Hindustan Times Television) and DD had with three journalists invited to the programme—Kewal Verma, Srinivas Raghavan and Binu John. It appears that Doordarshan failed to tell Upendra about this.

I have fought against censorship all my life and there is no question of my compromising on issues that I have fought for, Mr. George Fernandes told *Express News Service* during a 45-minute-long interview. 'The editing of the programme was not necessary', said the outspoken Railway Minister, adding that he had tried but failed to convince the Information and Broadcasting Minister, P. Upendra, on this point. But he also criticised Doordarshan for not laying down clearly the parameters of the programme and lambasted its co-host, Mr. Karan Thapar of HTV for his handling of the show, going so far as to describe Mr. Thapar as a 'kind of juvenile delinquent'.

These sanctions were cut on the orders of Mr. Upendra, who later told Parliament that this was not 'censorship' but 'editing' since the excised portions were outside the programme's ambit.

This was hotly contested by the Congress (I) which said that it was indeed censorship since Mr. Fernandes' candid replies to some questions and the TV audience's reaction to the Mandal Commission's recommendations had embarrassed the Government.

When asked if he accepted the distinctions sought to be made between censorship and editing in the present context, Mr. Fernandes said, 'No, I do not.' He also disclosed that he had told Mr. Upendra thrice after the recording of the programme that it should be shown in its original form.

### Censorship Flayed

Apart from the censorship question, the *Khula Manch* affair has also raised another controversy: Should ministers speak out publicly on issues concerning other ministries, especially when they have contrary views, as Mr. Fernandes does on some issues? This matter has been thrown into sharp focus by Mr. Upendra's reported comment, while making a case for the cuts, that other ministers had resented Mr. Fernandes' remarks.

Mr. Fernandes' answer to this is two-fold. He has firstly contended that he did 'not say anything on *Khula Manch* that was contrary to government policy' and secondly, that 'ministers are asked questions every day on all matters relating to government, so the question of encroaching on any minister's territory does not arise.' He said he was not aware of any resentment on the part of his cabinet colleagues and did not see why there should be any.

Defending his performance on *Khula Manch,* Mr. Fernandes said, 'I only aired my views in response to questions and that too, in a guarded way. I have a view and can express myself. Any minister worth his salt would have done the same.'

The Railway Minister said that the Government had not laid down any parameters that ministers should not answer questions on matters outside their ministries. Rather if they were part of government then they should, he argued, since ministers were constantly asked all sorts of questions at Press Conferences, while touring the country and at other forums.

He cited the example of his coming visit to Kerala. 'I will definitely be asked about Kuwait. Should I then say that these questions can only be answered by Mr. I.K. Gujral?' he asked.

Mr. Fernandes also cited the fact that the Prime Minister had asked ministers to tour sensitive states. 'There is only half a kilometre of railways in Arunachal Pradesh. Can I only talk about the railways?' he said. On *Khula Manch*, specifically, Mr. Fernandes confirmed that he had reiterated his well-known views against 'multinationals of the Coke and Pepsi kind' and had said in response to a question on whether Pepsi would be sold on railway platforms, 'Not if I have my way'. But on the larger policy issues of government such as Kashmir and the industrial policy, he denied that he had taken a divergent view, even though he had been confronted by a battery of questions on the differences between my view and the government's. 'I may have a different point of view within the government but out-side, I have to protect the Government,' he said.

He had initially declined to answer questions on Kashmir, and had yielded only when pressed on the issue, he said. He had also told a questioner that he would not discuss cabinet matters on TV, but he did answer a question on a statement made by him just after the elections that 50 per cent of the Kashmir problem had been solved with Rajiv Gandhi's defeat. 'I said I was not aware of the gravity of the situation then, as I am now. But I also pointed out that this was because I was not in the Government and did not have access to information that I do now', he said.

On the industrial policy, Mr. Fernandes said he had only pointed out that just as bills were subject to modifications, so too, was the policy, which was being debated both in Parliament at a national level. The Industry Minister, Mr. Ajit Singh, had said as much, argued Mr. Fernandes.

On the third issue raised by him during this interview—the manner in which *Khula Manch* was conducted—Mr. Fernandes made it clear that he personally did not object, in principle, to questions not relating to the railways. His point was that the ground rules were not defined. He 'did not have a clue' that such questions were going to be asked, while some journalists on the programme clearly did.

Mr. Fernandes said that the I&B Minister had told him some time ago that the programme related to specific ministries and that though Doordarshan personnel had a meeting with him a few days before the programme they did not tell him that it would be otherwise. 'They seemed more concerned with what I should be wearing', said Mr. Fernandes.

He also charged that many of the participants had also been kept in the dark on this point, and in fact, there was a big commotion on this issue after the recording was completed. Some participants, who had come with specific grievances on the railways, were furious at not being given a chance to speak despite sitting through a three-hour rehearsal, said Mr. Fernandes. The general complaint was that the programme had been hijacked by those wanting to ask political questions, mainly the journalists.

Mr. Fernandes' second point on the handling of the show was that it 'was orchestrated in a particular direction' with the co-host Mr. Thapar, acting as a 'choir leader'. He noted that some people, particularly a journalist, Mr. Kewal Verma, who asked 'nasty' questions, were given more opportunities to speak than others. On Mr. Thapar's role, Mr. Fernandes said, 'He was hostile that I got the impression that he was trying his hardest to run down the Government. Every gesture, every word, every question seemed designed to this end. It crossed my mind that the man was some kind of a juvenile delinquent-somebody who was used to street fighting but had got into the wrong place.'

The Railway Minister recalled that Mr. Thapar had first asked him why had he not resigned on the Pepsi issue and then accused him of practising 'opportunistic politics' when he said he could not resign on every issue. He had also demanded an apology from the Minister on a complaint relating to women's compartments in trains, after he had given assurance that the matter would be looked into. But what had really upset him, Mr. Fernandes said, was that the presenter had sought a vote on the Mandal Commission's recommendations from 'a captive audience in which almost everyone was upper caste'.

Mr. Fernandes' contention was: 'No sensible person would have asked this hand-picked group to vote on the issue in a national programme, when 52% of the people in this country belong to the backward classes.' He said he had pointed out after all members of the audience had unanimously voted against the recommendations that 'those who had vested interests in the matter were bound to approve them.'

On the whole, Mr. Fernandes felt that the programme was superficial, and had not grilled him enough on important and well-documented issues such as corruption in the railways. But he did not feel that *Khula Manch* should be discontinued. 'It must go on, but not in this way,' he said. 'It should lay down norms, and have a genuinely representative audience, and not be taken over by a few journalists with axes to grind.'

***HTV-doordarshan Deal :*** Doordarshan had entered into a deal with HTV to present six *Khula Manch* shows, but following this controversy, the Doordarshan, on September 8,1990, cancelled the other shows; Additional Director-General, Doordarshan, Shashi Kapoor wrote a brief letter to the HTV which said: 'In order to bring variety, it has been decided to have new presenters and consultants for the next few programmes.'

The HTV gave its side of the story as follows:

> 'The termination letter delivered to HTV came as a storm after the proverbial lull. For nearly four days before that, repeated efforts to contact the Doordarshan team were of no avail. The consultancy meetings which should normally have followed the third show (featuring I.K. Gujral) in preparation of the next programme were postponed (not cancelled) on one pretext or the other.

The Doordarshan officials remained inaccessible even after HTV received the termination order. Mr. Upendra in the meanwhile, had left on a tour of Andhra Pradesh and Mr. Suresh Mathur, Secretary, I&B did not care to respond to HTV's frantic efforts to contact him on phone. The Government lifted the cordon only on September 10—with Mr. Balagopal, the minister's Private Secretary informing that Mr. Upendra 'did not think it appropriate to meet' Mrs. Shobhana Bhartiya, Director of HTV and Mr. Karan Thapar. HTV was referred back to the Additional Director General of Doordarshan

***Double Dealing :*** Unfortunately, this incident is only the latest in a long saga of double dealing by Doordarshan and the ministry. When, after the first show, questions were raised in Parliament about the credibility of the audience, the minister blamed HTV; although he knew and Doordarshan confirmed, that the HTV's role was that of a consultant, and that Doordarshan chose the audience. The objective, clearly, was to score political points at HTV's cost.

After the second show featuring George Fernandes, which was cut despite HTV's strong protests, the company was accused of trying to run down the government. Such propaganda was encouraged despite the fact that the decision to question Mr. Fernandes on subjects other than the railways was taken jointly by Doordarshan and HTV a full week before the recording. Moreover, the people who asked the questions, including Mr. Kewal Verma, were selected by Doordarshan, whose officials vetted the questions. It was Doordarshan's responsibility to brief Mr. Fernandes. Having failed to do so, it sought to unfairly put the blame on the HTV whose presenters were publicly and unjustifiably attacked.

To add insult to injury, the Government made no efforts to set the record straight. The minister acknowledged that the 'censoring' of the programme had rendered the show lopsided, making the presenters seem needlessly aggressive, but refrained from coming to the defence of HTV. Doordarshan and the I&B Ministry officials simply watched the fun from the ring-side as Mr. Fernandes called the presenters names in interviews to newspapers.

When it came to the third show, Mr. Upendra personally telephoned Mrs. Bhartiya to invite her for breakfast. He wanted her assurance that nothing would go wrong. The minister appeared quite nervous. Mrs. Bhartiya told him that the previous problems were of Doordarshan's making and not HTV's. None-the less, she assured him that HTV would, in view of the present sensitive nature of India's foreign relations, exercise great caution. As is obvious in the final product, the company kept its word. Even Mr. Gujral would personally confirm this because the Joint Secretary (External Publicity) had asked for and was given a briefing by HTV. The Joint Secretary later expressed happiness that nothing had gone wrong. It is a sad commentary on the functioning of the Government that after all this HTV has been rewarded with the cancellation of the contract and that too in a shabby and deceitful manner.

From the very outset, the Government adopted double standards in dealing with HTV. After the first show, when there was controversy about the audience selected by Doordarshan, the Minister asked HTV to assume full responsibility for the selection of the audience. He asked HTV to add and delete names as it thought fit. The minister's views were expressed at a meeting attended by two other ministers, Mr. Satpal Malik and Mr. Jagdeep Dhankad, Mr. Suresh Mathur and Mr. Shashi Kapoor, besides several other senior Doordarshan and I&B officials. Later, the minister himself briefed the Press and informed Mr. Sunil Sethi, whose column is regularly published by *The Times of India*, while his Secretary, Mr. Balagopal, told Ms Seema Paul of *The Telegraph* of this decision. But when within days and before the minister's decision could be implemented, Mr. Upendra changed his mind and HTV was left to handle the Press and cover up for his indecisiveness.

### The Controversy

In fact, the confusion created by the minister's rapid change of mood led to a strange controversy over the audience of the third show. Exercising its newly given (but short-lived) power to choose the audience, HTV sought to invite both Mr. A.P. Venkateshwaran and Mr. S.K. Singh, former Foreign Secretaries. Mr. Singh declined the offer but Mr. Venkateshwaran agreed to appear in the programme. However, when Mr. Suresh Mathur learnt about Mr. Venkateshwaran being an invitee, he telephoned HTV in rage. He refused to speak to Mr. Thapar, demanding instead to speak to Mrs. Bhartiya. He told Mrs. Bhartiya that HTV has no right to unilaterally invite people to participate in the show and that HTV was unnecessarily inviting awkward people. When Mrs. Bhartiya pointed out that HTV had only acted in accordance with Mr. Upendra's earlier instructions, Mr. Mathur told he that Doordarshan would thereafter assume full responsibility and power to choose the audience and vet their questions.

Mrs. Bhartiya asked Mr. Mathur to send the new instructions to her in writing as they represented a change from the minister's position. Mr. Mathur promised to do so. But his letter is still to reach HTV.

As is evident from this episode, Doordarshan and the ministry have utilised every opportunity to ride roughshod over HTV. When questioned by journalists, the minister blatantly said that there was no commitment to give HTV six shows. When he found that criticism was being voiced about 'censoring' of the Fernandes show, he told that presenters could and would be changed from time to time, although no such proposal was in the knowledge of HTV. And long, long before the arrangement with HTV was terminated, Doordarshan officials were spreading the word that they were on the lookout for the new presenters.

Mr. Upendra and Mr. Mathur have even gone so far as to attempt to pressurise Mrs. Bhartiya into changing the presenters. Above all, they wanted Mr. Karan Thapar removed because they considered him 'unreliable'. The aim was to strike a crude bargain: HTV can keep its association with the *Khula Manch* series provided the presenters (or at least Mr. Karan Thapar) were dropped.

The Government's intention was to eat the cake and have it too. It wanted to continue with an independent and credible company like HTV as it would have corroborated its claim to have implemented real autonomy. At the same time, by having Mrs. Mrinal Pande and Mr. Karan Thapar dropped, the Government would have removed two irritants who, despite their perhaps aggressive style, had persisted in asking awkward questions. The objective was the appearance of autonomy as a cover for the reality of a doctored and controlled programme.

Hidden as they aren't any longer, such intentions raise serious doubts about the hopes and expectations that the Prasar Bharati Bill has raised. Two principal issues stand out.

Is Indian television on the threshold of a new dawn of open and objective broadcasting? And is the era of murky backroom interference and 'censorship' by double-dealing politicians and bureaucrats about to end? The story of *Khula Manch* would suggest that while there may be some doubts about the first, the answer to the second question must, for the time being, be a resounding 'No'.

The *Khula Manch* episode made a mockery of the National Front Government's rhetoric that they would grant autonomy to the electronic media.

***Chanda Committee Report :*** In order to evaluate the work being done by the various media units of the Ministry of Information and Broadcasting in the light of the high professional standards required of them, the government appointed a Committee in 1966 with Ashoka Chanda as Chairman and M/s Nath Pai, M.S. Gurupudaswamy, Dr. L.M. Singhvi, Kamla Chaudhri, Vidya Charan Shukla, Hasan Zaheer, Ashok Mitra, Chalapathi Rau and Dr. Hazari Prasad Dwivedi, as members.

The following were the observations of the Chanda Committee on the existing set-up of the All India Radio and their major recommendations for re-organisation:

# 9

# Ethics in Force

In the recent years, the partisan attitude of the journalists has eroded the credibility of the press. The journalists editorialise news and allow comments to go as news items on front pages forgetting that news is sacred and comment is free.

Stories are politically motivated. The language and the headlines are biased and say more than the story. This amounts to contamination of news. It is an extremely dangerous phenomenon and is devoid of ethics.

A journalist is a custodian of public interest; he bears the onerous responsibility to ensure that he does not contaminate the news at source by adopting biased and prejudiced view.

The Press is politicised. The journalists have been openly taking sides and planting stories and articles. During the Mandal Commission agitation, pro-Mandal stories were not published. During President Zail Singh's tenure, on Rajiv Gandhi versus V.P. Singh controversies, the national Press took a partisan attitude. The result was a series of articles or news items appearing during April-May 1987 which were either against or in favour of the contending parties. The division was more sharp during the Bofors gun payoff scandal and the St. Kitts issue.

Editors withhold stories and wait for the Parliament session to hog limelight. Often, the interest of the government is identified with the interest of the nation. Professional journalists have become a dying breed and are being replaced by managing editors. Journalists are accepting non-editorial jobs such as printers and publishers. They have become activists and have started participating in the decision-making process. The job of a Journalist is not of a mediator but of a communicator.

The journalists like politicians and bureaucrats have become a privileged class. They knuckle down under obligations. Businessmen openly talk of how journalists can be bought. Certain Pressmen are known to be lobbyists for industrial houses. Some are even rumoured to be on their payrolls.

**Select Cases**

*Bofors Issue and Ethics :* Bofors issue coverage by an important section of the Press blatantly showed how it was sharply divided and how it planted or rejected stories as suited it. We will briefly recall the important events connected with the Bofors history.

*April 17, 1987:* News agencies reported that the Swedish radio has charged Bofors with paying senior Indian politicians and key defence figures through secret bank accounts to get the deal.

*June* 4, 1987: The Swedish Embassy presented a copy of the Swedish National Audit Bureau Report confirming kickbacks.

*April 22, 1988: The Hindu* published its first set of papers on the Bofors documents, attempting to establish a connection between payments of Bofors to Moresco Pitco on the one hand and a relationship between Pitco and the Hinduja Company Sangam on the other.

*April 26,1988:* Joint Parliamentary Committee submits report absolving the government of wrong doing.

*June 22,1988: The Hindu* published another set of documents that firmly linked commission payments by Bofors to three front companies. Also established link between Win Chadha and Svenska.

*June 22, 1988:* The Indian Government asked the CBI to investigate the material published.

*July 29, 1988:* Motion moved in the Indian Parliament for setting up Joint Parliamentary Committee on Bofors.

*April 26, 1989:* Comptroller and Auditor General T.N. Chaturvedi signs report indicting the government for the manner in which the Howitzer deal was struck.

*July 24,1989:* Seventy-three M.Ps. including Arun Nehru and V.P. Singh resigned from the Lok Sabha on Bofors issue.

*October 31,1989:* Story from Chitra Subramaniam *(Indian Express* Correspondent in Geneva) and N. Ram (Associate Editor, *Hindu*) appeared in several newspapers, giving numerous details of the cover up from Martin Ardbo's diary.

*January 22, 1990:* With the National Front Government in power, an FIR was filed by the CBI on Bofors case.

*January 24, 1900:* Letter Rogatory presented to the Swiss authorities.

*January 24,1990:* Letter Rogatory referred back to the Indian authorities for defects of form.

*July 18, 1990:* Dagens Nyheter (a Swedish newspaper) apologizes to the Bachchans for attributing the sixth account to them.

*August 29, 1990: The Independent* (a *Times* group newspaper from Bombay) carried translation of diplomatic despatches showing Arun Nehru's role in the deal.

It is this last incident to which we would like to draw particular attention. *The Independent* broke the story that *The Indian Express* correspondent in Geneva Chitra Subramaniam had sent a story to its Editor, Arun Shourie, in which she gave details about Arun Nehru's conversation with Swedish official over the Bofors deal in June 1985 (nine months before the contract was signed), underlining that Arun Nehru might have played a crucial role in the negotiations.

The relevant points raised by the story were as follows:

1. At a stage when the defence experts in-charge of the technical negotiations were opting for the French Sofma gun, why was Arun Nehru taking it upon himself to assure Martin Ardo that Bofors could improve upon its position and have a realistic chance to win the competition ?
2. What did Arun Nehru mean when he said that 'the political aspect' is crucial in this context on Rolf Gauffir specifically asking him what it meant, Nehru's answer was ambiguous. He said he meant 'Political understanding' in the widest sense of the word. But obviously this aspect was so important that Nehru clearly stressed the fact 'if you reach an agreement on the political level, I am sure, you will be able to agree on the test....
3. Who authorised Arun Nehru, the minister of power in Rajiv Gandhi's Cabinet, to lay down a time schedule for the negotiations with the Swedish Government on a defence deal ?
4. Why was Arun Nehru so obsessed about keeping Rajiv Gandhi and his own name out of the whole business so much so that he virtually threatened the Sweden that the deal would be called off if there was any indiscretion on their side ?
5. What was so secret about the talks that Nehru had to stipulate that the Indian representative of Bofors should not be informed of the developments under any circumstances ?
6. Why were technical experts not involved in the talks ?
7. Why was only Arun Nehru authorised to inform the Swedish Government about whom the Bofors negotiator should meet when he came to India ? Why was the whole tenor of the discussions and, indeed, the negotiations so hush-hush ?

8. Nehru was clearly aware of who the Indian middlemen were but he did not speak up when the Bofors matter exploded in Parliament in April 1987.

Chitra Subramaniam's story along with other documents were made available to *The Statesman* also. Both papers did not carry the story. *Indian Express* Editor Arun Shourie, found the story damaging in view of the paper's new-found closeness to Nehru. It may be recalled that the *Express* and Nehru were partners in the campaign to get rid of Devi Lal from the Cabinet and also shared a common hostility to the then Prime Minister, V.P. Singh, over his decision to implement the recommendations of the Mandal Commission report.

Nehru's most powerful advocate is someone called S. Vinayak who writes for the newspapers from Delhi. Nehru's votaries described the documents variously as a 'red herring' part of an attempt to destabilise the V.P. Singh government.

The charge of self-censorship in the Press assumes an even wider dimension since Chitra claims that Ram had been shown in October 1989 a set of nine documents, including the two on Arun Nehru, which were placed before the Swedish Parliamentary Constitutional Committee, but were not carried by *The Hindu*.

The newspapers toeing the pro-Congress line demanded a probe in this matter.

The Legal Adviser to *Indian Express,* Ram Jethmalani, suddenly came out with a signed front-page statement in *The Independent* saying that V.P. Singh must sack Arun Nehru. The journalists questioned Jethmalani on the possibility of *The Independent* articles having been written at the behest of the Hindujas with whom its former Editor is reported to be close.

Calcutta's *The Telegraph* quoted sources close to Nehru as confirming the genuineness of the documents, but not implicating him in the kickbacks. The attempt on the part of the Congress party to embarrass V.P. Singh and leave alone Arun Nehru was also reflected in the coverage of this episode in the Press.

Chitra Subramaniam quit the *Indian Express* on the ground that her stories on Bofors were suppressed by Shourie when he found that Arun Nehru's name came into the picture. She says: 'The whole thing stinks. These documents are as authentic as any I have got on the Bofors case. But for one ostensible reason or another the publication of the documents was held back by *The Indian Express* since early July 1990. I am beginning to think that a debate on ethics in this profession is much needed. My sources in Europe are beginning to raise valid questions about the ethics of Indian editors.'

Arun Shourie dismissed the charge with characteristic contempt, 'Absolute bunk'.

In her first interview on phone since resigning from *The Express*, Chitra tells Coomi Kapoor of *The Illustrated Weekly of India* why she decided to resign.

The following are the extracts from the interview:

Q. When did you send in your piece on the Arun Nehru documents?

*A.* I sent in the article and documents around early July. At first, Arun Shourie praised the story and even said it vindicated a piece he had written for *The Express* earlier. But then, for one reason or another, the publication of the documents was held up. First, it was because the Devi Lal controversy was at its height and *The Indian Express* felt it might deflect from the other issue. Then I started getting messages to check the translation of my documents as they believed that some critical references in my translations had got dropped in the documents faxed to them. I was repeatedly asked to authenticate the documents and my sources, whom I kept going back to, accused me of playing games. It became a question of my own image with my sources. It was even claimed that my sources had misled me.

Q. How come the documents you sent to India are in circulation?

*A.* I don't know. And I am furious. A Swedish journalist Henrik Westander who was in India two weeks earlier was actually presented xeroxes of my documents and he telephoned me asking me to give him other documents. The whole thing stinks. I am fed up and have written yesterday to *The Express* that the arrangement is not working satisfactorily.

Q. When did you actually obtain the documents referring to Nehru?

*A.* I got them in October last year and they have been waiting to be published ever since then.

Q. That implies that even before *The Indian Express* sat over the documents they were not used by *The Hindu*.

*A.* That is correct.

Q. Why were only these two documents not published by both the newspapers?

*A.* You can draw your own inference.

Q. Were the documents not published because of genuine doubts about their authenticity?

*A.* They are as authentic as any document I have got on the Bofors case. All the documents I have are up for scrutiny for any serious efforts by investigators. If you genuinely doubt the authenticity, why do you have to leak it around? The whole thing just stinks.

It is ironical that the last government tried to suppress information on Bofors and in this government now, much of the same thing is happening. In the end there seems to be no difference.

Q. What do you feel about the government investigations into Bofors?

*A.* I am not passing judgement on the investigation. Who am I to do so? I am nobody. But I feel personally that the investigations should not just concentrate on getting the names behind the Swiss Bank accounts in Geneva. That is just one aspect.

The Swedish Parliamentary Committee which looked into the arms deal in 1988 collected as many as 700 documents. A year back the Swedish government had promised a white paper on the findings of the constitutional committee. Why is the Indian Government not pressing the Swedish Government to live up to the promise made and release the white paper?

*Q.* What about the role of the CBI in the investigations?

*A.* The CBI is doing a good job, but look what they are up against. Look at the kind of signals and pressures being put even on an outsider like myself. I am sure all kinds of people are breathing down their necks. I think they are in an unenviable position.

Q. What do you feel about ethics in journalism?

*A.* I begin to think that a debate on ethics in this profession is much needed. I am so tired of moral arguments. Whose morality are they talking about? The real morality comes when principles are put to the test. It is easy to point a finger at others but there are three pointing back at you. It is not just editors and proprietors who are entitled to have a sense of ethics. My sources in Europe are beginning to raise valid questions about the ethics of Indian editors. You realise that in the end you are just an employee. Working journalists don't get access to putting across their point of view. I think there is a major crisis in the Press. I think there is need for a debate.

Q. What about attempts in the Indian media to damage your credibility by insinuations that you are a Bachchan mole or a V.P. Singh plant?

*A.* I set certain standards for myself and the rest is all nonsense. My credibility is what I think of myself and how honest I am to my principles and how faithful to my

> profession. The test of my credibility is that my sources still have faith in me. In fact, they are laughing and saying, 'It shows you are hurting in the right direction.' If anyone has doubts about my integrity let them look me in the eye and say so, not make wild insinuations behind my back.
>
> In the middle of September 15, 1990, Seema Mustafa, Special Correspondent of *India Today* magazine resigned in protest when she found her story on the Bofors documents and Nehru being drastically altered in the night, just before the edition closed, without any valid explanations, reportedly at the instance of senior editor Prabhu Chawla and Executive Editor Inderjeet Badhwar. To her shock she found the altered story still carrying her by-line. When Seema objected and resigned in protest, her name was taken off the story and a more balanced version finally inserted in the magazine.

However, a printout taken earlier of a message sent by Prabhu Chawla to the News Editor and Seema Mustafa tells its own story. The nine-point message sent on September 10,1990, makes it clear that Mustafa's story had, among other points, to highlight the following: That the documents do not break any new ground and there is a serious fallout; it was to charge Chitra with being in league with the Bachchans and give documents which show that Arun Singh was also a part of the deal.

The first media victim of the Bofors controversy was N. Ram himself. Ram, who was Associate Editor of *The Hindu,* went to the Press Council complaining against 'systematic violation of professional norms in the 112 year old newspaper.' The charge was levelled against his uncle, G. Kasturi, Editor, *The Hindu.*

Ram alleged that Kasturi had, time and again, insisted that he 'abandon the Bofors expose in the interest of the family.'

To fight this internal censorship, Ram and Chitra took stories to *The Indian Express* and published them there.

Ram told a crowded Press Conference at Taj Hotel, New Delhi, on October 12,1989, that Kasturi's decision to block publication of the Bofors series was arbitrary, capricious and derogatory to the traditions, norms and values of independent, ethical journalism. From a moral standpoint, Ram could not accept such opportunistic censorship.

The first report in the Bofors series appeared on October 9, 1989, with the promise 'to be continued'. In this report Ram and Chitra disclosed portions from the Swedish National Audit Bureau (NAB) report which had been held back from the Indian Government. The second report was to be published on October 11,1989 but did not appear.

In an unprecedented move, Ram announced his decision to carry forward his fight through the 'unconventional' step of offering the withheld reports to other 'influential newspapers in a broad, representative basis.'

He said censorship by *The Hindu* should not prevent readers from learning about the latest findings on the Bofors Pay-offs.

Though Ram could not reveal the exact nature of the pressure put on *The Hindu* by the government, he said that the 'coup'—that is, a change in his editor's attitude towards the investigative reports was worked behind his back. He felt that the pressures must have been brought on the paper in September 1989.

Ram was ruthless in his criticism of Kasturi in having yielded to pressure. 'Mr. Kasturi has been a severe obstacle in the path of conducting this important journalistic investigation and especially the business of publishing documents and articles in detail of Bofors', he said.

Asked whether he would quit *The Hindu* in the light of his glaring differences with the Editor, Ram said: 'No. It was his right to attend office and carry on with his writing. And he would exercise his rights.'

Ram dwelt at length on the larger issues involved in this case. "The larger issue here is whether the people have a right to know on a vital and a major national and ethical issue and whether journalism must essentially fix its professional norms and values around this right. I am taking essentially an ethical stand on the intellectual and professional issues at stake. Therefore, I must speak out.'

It is said that the second instalment of the withheld reports which was to appear in certain newspapers on October 11, 1989, dealt with the meeting, a team of Indian officials, including the then Defence Secretary, Mr. S.K. Bhatnagar, and Finance Secretary, Mr. G.K. Arora had with Bofors officials, Mr. Per Ove Morberg and Mr. Lars Gothlin.

Ram and Chitra had been able to obtain a copy of the minutes of the meeting and were able to establish Swedish officials' connivance with their Indian counterparts to cover up the investigations of the kickbacks that were being carried out by the Indian agencies.

On his part, Ram did not divulge anything about the nature of his forthcoming reports at the Press Conference. He, however, gave a detailed account of how various officials, ministers and influential NRI businessmen met him in the course of his investigations, and some tried to persuade him to allow his investigative ardour to cool.

Among the people who met him were Rajiv Gandhi, K.C. Pant, G.K. Arora, the PM's Press Secretary, G. Parthasarathy, the CBI Chief, Mohan Katre, matinee idol, Amitabh Bachchan and NRI businessman, Gopichand Hinduja.

In chronological order, the first meeting was with G.K. Arora. This was soon after the first round of investigative reports. During the AICC Session in Madras, Arora met him and discussed the Bofors issue. He also put a series of questions to Ram. To his surprise, Ram found the same questions being put to him when he granted an interview to the Calcutta-based, *The Telegraph* (this paper became a mouthpiece of the Congress Party under the editorship of M.J. Akbar). He conveyed it to the official that his journalism was not negotiable.

Soon thereafter, Defence Minister K.C. Pant met him at a Defence Ministry function in Madras. The minister told him that the reports appearing in *The Hindu* were not quite correct. During the conversation Ram discovered that the minister had not even read the reports. He, therefore, told Pant: 'Why do you accept the burden of defending the indefensible?'

In June 1988 came the next feeler from the government. G. Parthasarathy rang up Ram to ask him whether he would meet Katre. Apparently, Katre sought his cooperation in getting to the bottom of the kickbacks. When Ram met the CBI official, the latter said he had told the PM that *The Hindu* documents were authentic. Win Chadha was linked to Svenska, one of the payoff recipients, he told Ram.

Later that month, when Ram was in Delhi, there was another request for a meeting with Katre. At this meeting Ram got the impression that the official was seeking to cover up the Hinduja's link with illegal payments. During the same visit, G.K. Arora wanted to meet him.

When he met Arora, the latter discussed the situation in Sri Lanka with him but at the end of the meeting asked whether Ram would stay for the night in Delhi and meet the Prime Minister. Ram agreed.

The meeting with Rajiv Gandhi lasted an hour and 20 minutes. The first part was devoted to Sri Lanka. Rajiv requested Ram to carry a message to the then Sri Lanka President, Mr. J.R. Jayewardena. Ram accepted the assignment. Subsequent discussion centred around the Bofors gun deal.

Ram told the Prime Minister that any effort to cover up the pay-offs would be futile. He already had some evidence on the pay-offs made to A.E. Services. On his part, Rajiv sought his cooperation in the investigations.

At the 100 minute Press Conference, Ram claimed that Kasturi had earlier taken great interest in the layout of the documents and materials and had made his own professional contribution to the presentation and highlighting of the material concerned in the newspaper's detailed expose of June 1988. 'But essentially after this, everytime the question of publishing something major and original on the Bofors scandal arose', the Editor countered by saying: What is really new about it?' Ram said.

Asked about the kind of pressures being put on the newspaper, Ram said: 'These were not as severe as those against *The Indian Express* or *The Statesman* but came in the form of cancellation of schedule for advertisements from public sector undertakings, the Railways and increase in the facsimile rates.'

***Kasturi's Statement :*** The Editor of *The Hindu* denied that any pressure had been exerted on him by the Prime Minister or any minister or official to stop the publication of stories relating to the Bofors deal.

He was commenting on a statement made by Ram earlier that there had 'clearly' been pressure from the government.

Kasturi said that most of what Ram had stated did not call for comment. It reflected 'gross indiscipline, lack of decency and elementary manners on the part of the individual'.

He made it clear in a statement that no decision had been taken 'to discontinue the expose of the Bofors Scandal' in his paper. All that was decided was not to publish the 'second instalment' as he felt that there was nothing in it that was vitally indicative of who might have been recipients of the Bofors pay-offs and of something that can be a fraud on the people of this country, high or low. Nor did it take the issue forward in any meaningful way. He added: 'Almost all members of the family of which I happen to be a senior member, were of the view that the second instalment did not merit serious enough attention to warrant publication.'

The holding of the Press Conference by Ram led to his suspension and a sharp division among the board of directors of *The Hindu*. As a result, *The Hindu* edition dated October 20,1989, did not come out. This is the fourth time in its 111 years of history the *Hindu* suspended its publication.

The immediate provocation for *The Hindu* General Manager, N. Murali (elder brother of Ram), directing the Press not to print the edition was due to Kasturi's proposal at the meeting of the board of directors to issue show-cause notice to Ram seeking explanation why disciplinary action should not be taken against him for his release of Bofors documents to other newspapers and also for the charges he had levelled against Kasturi at the Press Conference in Delhi.

General Manager Murali and the newspaper's publisher S. Rangarajan opposed the move for a show-cause notice to Ram and declared the board meeting illegal.

Ram did not accept the show-cause notice and went abroad. He was suspended. N. Murali and S. Rangarajan (the pro-Ram directors) obtained an interim injunction in the Madras High Court against Ram's suspension.

Here we have quoted this case exclusively to show how an editor of a paper tried to stop another to perform his function. In this case Kasturi bowed to government pressure and stopped Ram from publishing documents which gave vital clues to the pay-offs in the Bofors scandal.

It is unethical on the part of an editor to hold back information which gives an insight into the functioning of the government. The people have a right to know what all goes behind the scene in the government and the editors have the responsibility to inform the public. The Editors are only answerable to the readers and none else. Failure to do this is the abdication of responsibility and the editor's credibility can be questioned.

***St. Kitts Issue :*** St. Kitts issue abundantly established how deep politicisation has gone into the Press. The Press was sharply divided on this issue and took sides.

An Istanbul tabloid, *Golge Adam,* published documents indicting V.P. Singh's son, Ajeya Singh, a middle level banker with Citi Bank, New York, of stashing away $ 21 million in the First Trust Corporation Limited, an offshore bank in the Carribean Island of St. Kitts. The secret account number was given as 29479.

The tabloid furnished greater details of the controversy which had also been reported by the Kuwait-based *Arab Times.*

*The Telegraph* headlined this disclosure on August 22, 1989, and also published an interview with George Maclean, the then Managing Director of the Bank, now residing in Canada. A statement of deposits and withdrawals was also published, signed by Maclean and another director, Alon Tonks (anti-V.P.).

In the meantime, *The Indian Express* got into the fray. It carried a report where Terence Byron, the solicitor of the company, denied that such an account existed (pro-V.P.).

The situation was further complicated when *The Indian Express* published a report by Lynn Hudson, a senior journalist with the *India Abroad News Service,* where Tonks, the second director stated that his signature on the statements of accounts was forged.

Then *The Hindustan Times,* a pro-Congress paper, spoke to Tonks over the phone and both *The Telegraph* and *The Hindustan Times* published excerpts from his recorded conversation.

Tonks denied all that he meant to have told Hudson. His signature was genuine, he affirmed. He would not talk about the account. Maclean would know about the account, he added.

As the speculation continued to build up, the subject of the controversy returned to India. Indignant about the things that were being written about him, Ajeya Singh, V.P. Singh's son, promptly sued *The Hindustan Times* and *The Telegraph* on September 20, 1989. The latter received a legal notice which demanded that the stories published be retracted and an apology printed. He also made a declaration of his assets abroad.

In the case of *The Hindu,* Editor Kasturi tried to silence Associate Editor N. Ram in the Bofors case. But in St. Kitts case, the Congress Party and the proprietors of *The Hindustan Times* propped up senior Editor Subhbrata Bhattacharya to take on his senior H.K. Dua, Editor of *The Hindustan Times.*

Bhattacharya, who married around the time the St. Kitts controversy broke, is believed to have told Dua that he was proceeding to Udaipur for a holiday but landed instead in New York. From there he flew to Caribbean Island of St. Kitts where Ajeya Singh is supposed to have stashed away millions of dollars.

The basic purpose of Bhattacharya's trip was to prove that the Indian visitors to St. Kitts can escape the immigration stamp on their passport upon arrival there, which would, on the face of it, seem to demolish Ajeya Singh's argument. Ajeya Singh had never visited the Island and cited the lack of the immigration stamp as proof of the same.

Dua, according to *Sunday Observer*, learnt about his own colleague's trip abroad through the columns of the Hyderabad based newspaper *News Times* which had alleged that Bhattacharya's expedition was paid by persons close to the government. In a note to the management, Dua is reported to have asked: 'Who assigns stories to the staff? The Editor or the Prime Minister.' Dua resisted the publication of Bhattacharya's stories, but ultimately gave in.

Arun Shourie's writings in *The Indian Express* were vehemently criticised by a section of the Press. *The Indian Post* (now extinct) correspondent, Dhiren Bhagat, had said that *The Indian Express* under the editorship of Shourie had ceased to be a newspaper, it reads like pamphlets and its editorials seeming as though they had been dictated by Ram Jethmalani.

In 1988, *The Telegraph* Editor, M.J. Akbar, in his by-line column criticised Shourie's journalism accusing him of substituting innuendo for fact and abuse for comment. All journalists, suggested Akbar, need to be fair to those they write about. Shourie, he argued, threw fairness to the winds and preferred hysterics of the 'lies, variety.'

Akbar was an excellent editor once and was appreciated for his objective writings, but ever since he has started toeing the Congress line, his own credibility has come under doubt. He is no longer a journalist, but a politician.

An attempt was made by Rajiv's government to introduce a column by Akbar in *The Hindustan Times,* but it is learnt that Dua foiled this move. But the Congress government succeeded in introducing Akbar's column in *The Navbharat Times,* a widely circulated Hindi daily of *The Times* group. Dua resisted Akbar's column on the ground that the latter was an editor of a rival paper and, therefore, could not be allowed to write for his newspaper. Dua was functioning within his rights.

However, it is only fair to say that Akbar was editor of *The Telegraph* he continued to publish Nikhil Chakravarty's column, highly critical of the establishment. He did not censor any critical comments against Rajiv Gandhi.

It is well to remind everyone of the comments of the Press Council clarifying the role of the editor vis-a-vis the management. The Council proposed that in all matters relating to the administration of the editorial department, it would be obligatory for the managing director to act on the recommendations of or in consultation with the editor/resident editor.

The Council had given its ruling on a complaint brought to it by P. Rajan, the then assistant editor of *Mathrubhoomi,* the Calicut-based Malayalam daily. According to the Council, the responsibility for maintaining discipline in the editorial department of all branches of *Mathrubhoomi* shall be delegated to the editor / resident editor.

**Battle On**

The latter part of 1986 witnessed a fierce battle fought by the two textile giants-Dhirubhai Ambani, Chairman, Reliance Industries Ltd., and Nusli Wadia of Bombay Dyeing through the medium of the proprietors of the Press. This kind of battle between the two corporate rivals is not the first in the history of the corporate sector in the country, but the weapons such as Press employed by them on a large scale and in an unethical manner are certainly without a parallel.

This shatters whatever illusion we have of objective journalism in a business controlled Press. This also gives a vivid picture of close nexus between the politicians and the captains of industry on the one hand and the industrialists and the Press persons on the other.

*The Indian Express* spearheaded the campaign against Reliance followed by *Blitz* and *Imprint* (Wadia held shares in *Imprint*). *The Times of India*, on the other hand, took up cudgels on behalf of Reliance while *Onlooker* magazine and *The Patriot* launched an offensive view against Wadia.

The root of the Ambani-Wadia conflict lies in the astonishing growth chart of Reliance which threatened to sound the deathknell of its older competitor in the textile field. In a matter of a decade, Reliance grew at a phenomenal pace.

What irked Wadia was not merely the fierce competition in which Ambani had left him behind, but the reported political patronage that the latter enjoyed from the Congress (I). Wadia is not lacking in the art of seeking political patronage.

During the brief Janata regime, through the good offices of the RSS leaders, Wadia managed to establish links with the top echelons of the then ruling party. Unfortunately for Wadia, the Janata rule did not last long.

With the return of Mrs. Gandhi to power in 1980, Reliance managed to get into the good books of the Prime Minister and Finance Minister Pranab Mukherjee and the official machinery turned in Ambani's favour. The latter was rumoured to have literally financed the Congress (I).

But thanks to Wadia's equation with Madhavrao Scindia, who has a large share in Bombay Dyeing and who was made the Minister of State for Railways in the Rajiv Gandhi Government, roles were reversed once again after the assassination of Mrs. Gandhi in 1984 and the fall from political grace of Pranab Mukherjee. It was Wadia's turn to rule the roost once again. But the fact remains that Reliance is way ahead of Bombay Dyeing in politicking.

The Reliance-Bombay Dyeing competition intensified particularly after the decision of both to set up plants to manufacture raw material for the making of polyester yarn and fibre during the Janata rule (1976-79). Wadia managed to procure a letter of intent for the manufacture of di-methyle terephthalate (DMT), one of the raw materials for making polyester yarn. But with Charan Singh replacing Morarji Desai as Prime Minister later during the Janata period, the influence of RSS waned, and Wadia could not succeed in getting the Letter of Intent converted into industrial licence. It was only in the subsequent rule of Mrs. Gandhi that Wadia could manage the licence through the good offices of Scindia.

Meanwhile, in 1982, Reliance got the licence for setting up of a plant for the manufacture of an alternate raw material, Purified Terephthalic Acid (PTA) for the making of polyester yarn. PTA is relatively more modern technology. Bombay Dyeing had immense teething problems with the commissioning of its second hand plant purchased from Harcofina, USA.

To add to Wadia's woes, Ambani, according to business circles, floated rumours that the raw material produced with outmoded technology by Bombay Dyeing was defective and could not be used to produce quality yarn.

In 1986, Reliance suffered severe jolts under Union Finance Minister V.P. Singh.

Sometimes in April 1990, *Illustrated Weekly* editor, Pritish Nandy interviewed Chandra Shekhar when V.P. Singh was the Prime Minister. The former made accusation against the latter in confidence that his telephone was being tapped and his house was bugged. It is good of Chandra Shekhar to have owned the statement and not to have borne any grudge against Nandy. Those belonging to the old school of journalism would certainly not approve of what Nandy did. Confidences must be kept. Anything said in confidence to the Press is never published and is regarded as violation of journalistic ethics.

On September 25,1991, the Press Council recorded its disapproval of a story, 'Open War, written by the former Editor of *The Indian Express*, Arun Shourie, in his paper in 1990.

The article was about an alleged conspiracy to topple the V.P. Singh government.

The Council, which investigated two separate complaints by Madhu Limaye and Har Kishen Singh Surjeet (CPM) felt that Shourie had committed two violations. He never tried to check with the people who were likely to be affected by the publication of the story. Also a statement that *The Indian Express* stood by its story was appended below the rejoinder published by the paper.

Shourie had alleged in his story that Madhu Limaye and Chandra Shekhar had hatched a conspiracy to topple the V.P. Singh government and replace it with a national government to be headed by Jyoti Basu and that Basu had shot down the proposal discussed at a Politburo meeting of the CPM.

Press Council Chairman Justice Sarkaria said efforts should be made to obtain the viewpoints of people whose esteem is likely to be affected before publishing a story. If there were doubts about some portion, that portion should be deleted. And if there were doubts affecting warp and woof of the story its publication should be withheld.

Mr. Justice Sarkaria observed that if an editor had evidence that a rejoinder was wrong, he could append his claim about his story to the rejoinder.

Mr. Sarkaria said that Shourie went on saying obdurately that he had relied on his sources. Shourie claimed that he felt no need for checking his story, as his experience shows that politicians always denied stories and nobody disclosed facts.

He (Shourie) wanted us to believe that he and his supporters had 'supernatural powers and omniscience of God', said Mr. Justice Sarkaria. He felt that the story could have been reported in a different tenor, mentioning perceptions about conspiracy. The

Council found that participation of Madhu Limaye and Harkishen Singh Surjeet, the complainants in such a conspiracy, was doubtful and improbable.

**Perks and Privileges**

There is a rampant corruption in the profession at all levels; the journalists vie with one another to carry favour with politicians and bureaucrats in order to avail the maximum facilities that the government could offer to them.

To mention a few, out of turn allotment of government accommodation, scooters, cars, telephones, free jaunts to foreign countries, and the honour to head the panels of discussion on current subjects on the AIR and Doordarshan.

In the states, the Chief Minister is the Sultan and is in a much better position to distribute largesse to the Pressmen. Press representatives in the states, besides enjoying medical, housing and travel facilities are also given free lunch when the state assembly is in session. There are numerous instances where a pleased Chief Minister has allotted land in posh areas at throwaway prices to journalists.

The Sunday Observer, dated July 7, 1985, a weekly periodical published from Bombay, carried a three-column article by a journalist on the controversy regarding the journalists' trip abroad which was financed by former Maharashtra Chief Minister Vasant Dada Patil from the Chief Minister's fund. The item focused attention on the journalists' proximity to the ministers in order to obtain unofficial favours. The journalists association is provided with the free use of government mini-buses, favours of gifts, presentations, free stay in government guest houses, etc.

The story revolves around a senior journalist of UNI and President of the Journalists Association of Bombay who took Rs 5000 from the Chief Minister's Relief Fund for a trip to the Soviet Union and Europe without informing any member of the executive committee. This Sparked off trouble in the association. While the President took the plea that he got the money in his individual capacity, the association contended that he had misused his office for such favours from the government. In support of their contention the association members pointed out that the president applied for the loan which was promptly sanctioned by May 11 whereas earlier in 1984, when another senior film journalist had requested the Chief Minister to help him to attend a conference abroad, the latter had declined.

In April, 1985, about five journalists in U.P. were paid Rs 75,000 from the Chief Minister's fund for a visit to Korea and Czechoslovakia which was described as a study tour. The UP government also issued licences to these journalists to purchase revolvers. Later on these journalists bought revolvers from Czechoslovakia for Rs 4000 to Rs 5000 each and sold it in India for double the amount.

It is interesting at this point to quote Khushwant Singh on the aforesaid trip in The Telegraph a newspaper published from Calcutta. He wrote:

"I do not understand the logic behind the tirade against our artists performing in South Africa. In what way do Lata Mangeshkar, Jalotas or Jagjit-Chitra's singing in Durban, Johannesburg or Cape Town before entirely Indian born audiences compromise our stand against apartheid? It is the same with journalists. They should be free to go wherever they wish, provided no restrictions are placed on their reporting as they please. Only two conditions must be fulfilled. They must be told beforehand what they are being invited for and if anything is expected from them in return for hospitality.

This brings me to the visit of Indian Pressmen to Pyongyang (North Korea). The invitation came from the Korean Journalists Association to K. Vikram Rao, President of the Indian Federation of Working Jounalists. I have seen the circulars Rao sent to the 26 journalists who responded. They mention attendance at the May Day rally in Moscow's Red Square, visits to the ILO headquarters in Geneva, UNESCO headquarters in Paris and offices of other organisations in London, the Netherlands,

West Germany and Belgium. They say little or nothing about the visit to North Korea.

I am pretty certain that apart from the leader, none of the other delegates were told that they would be in Pyongyang to participate in the birthday celebrations of Comrade Kim II Sung.

Businessmen these days openly talk of how journalists can be bought. Their PROs now are pretty women who scurry in the newspapers offices and at their houses with gifts. It is a regular feature that on festival days, such as Diwali and Christmas, packages of sweets, dry fruits and liquor are distributed to them. The industrialists even finance these journalists for pleasure trips abroad. It is indeed not surprising that a section of journalists lobby for industrial houses. Food and liquor at Press Conferences organised by companies is an accepted minimum hospitality. At these Press Conferences costly gifts are given to journalists the scent of which draws more than one journalist from a newspaper.

The gifts range from pants, shirt pieces, suit lengths, cassettes, mattresses, sarees and fountain pens to calculators (given by AT & T and DCM computers), suit lengths and sarees (only Reliance Ltd.), brief cases (United Group), bed sheets (Cosmo Ferrods) and even cheques for Rs 101 (Usha Rectifier Corporation).

A curious tale was also reported in *The Business Standard*, when a company manufacturing portable television sets, had displayed its wares at a Press Conference, an enterprising journalist on his way out simply picked one up and nobody had the temerity to question him. Besides shares and debentures, a company manufacturing say motor cycles, scooters and cars, is 'known to have given out-of-turn allotment and sale discounts to scribes. No wonder then that young entrants to the profession when asked why they have opted for journalism, almost inevitably reply: there is glamour in it. Even those who join prefer field jobs to desk ones for obvious reasons.

'No whisky Mr., a leading Bombay industrialist was asked by a group of senior journalists, after he had addressed a Press

Conference and invited the journalists to join him for lunch at the Taj. Lost for words the young industrialist asked the hotel to serve liquor regretting his decision not to have brought the scotch bottle along because there the company would only have to pay corkage instead of paying the hotel by the expensive peg.

The industrialist in question leads one of the most successful consumer product companies in Bombay. He advertises in almost all the major papers in a big way. He does not feel the need in any way to seek publicity by providing inducements to the Press simply because his product invites publicity on merits and the newspaper owners are in any case indebted to him for advertising campaigns. And yet, the gentlemen of the Press, out of sheer and incorrigible habit, 'demand' liquor which as a host he would not refuse.

'We have come to reconcile to such corruption to the extent, that consumable items like food or drinks are accepted as the done thing. So long as you do not give presents to carry home ... I now avoid Press Conferences and do not give presents', said the industrialist.

Top editors of newspapers and magazines lend approval to this practice by attending select cocktail Press Conferences. One such cocktail conference hosted by a leading industrial house to announce a product of vital social significance had senior editors and others in its glittering galaxy of Press VIPs.

Is it really shocking then that PR men should ring up editors and while requesting them to attend a briefing by some top boss or other, bluntly throw the bait, 'and it's with cocktail Sir, so you must come!' How many are the editors who like one of their younger colleagues have as bluntly told these PR men 'You have given me one reason why I should not attend. I go for Press Conferences, not cocktail conferences.

After seeing the Scotch and Cognac that flows freely in homes of journalists who can barely afford to buy half as many bottles of the Indian variety, one cannot blame Morarjibhai (former Indian Prime Minister 1976-78) for his sparing charge during an interview with the editor of a Bombay tabloid that journalists drink only because they get it free, otherwise they simply cannot afford to drink.

Most businessmen and PR men, however, cynically accept the fact that the Press only needs to be looked after to ensure quick and positive coverage. It is indeed sad that they should have to resort to this method even when their product itself deserves publicity on merits. Take the case of India's first electronic typewriter launched a couple of years ago by Network. It was an item that merited coverage at a Press Conference that had no cocktails thrown in. But the promoters decided to play safe and not to antagonise the Press. They had a cocktail followed by lunch and even presented a foreign ball-point pen with a timepiece inset in it, but packed in an Indian box. One journalist who was leaving after the Press Conference, was literally pulled back by other colleagues who whispered in his ear: 'Wait, till the end. They are giving a present'.

'We invite two people, but they come in dozens,' said a managing director of a leading advertising agency about Pressmen in Bombay. 'We cannot obviously ask them to go back, instead, we hold back the gifts.'

Very few of the journalists who attend these conferences have done their home work to care to ask questions. Stupid questions only attract ridicule from their colleagues between whom waiters keep running relay races with glasses of Scotch. At the release of Music India's *chal disco chal disco,* the media manager of the company had to coax Pressmen to ask questions to singer Sharon Prabhakar.

At a cocktail conference to launch Doburg's canned beer called Seagull at Hotel President, the attendance was 200. All leading newspapers and magazines were represented by more than one person. And one group of newspapers was represented by as many as eight even when the paper was itself on strike. Among the representatives of the group was one belonging to a trade magazine which had ceased publication.

The most agonising part of the cocktail was Pressmen scrambling for the complimentary beer cans at the end. The management was embarrassed beyond words since the stock was already exhausted. The rest were, however, assured crates of canned beer the next day. And at the end of it all, only two newspapers carried token coverage of a para each on the fifth and eighth pages, respectively.

Another Press Conference organised some time back by Shri Brij Mandal (a religious organisation), to mark the beginning of Krishna Leela celebrations had a very thin crowd. The invitations indicated: vegetarian lunch at the Bristol Grill restaurant. While 22 invitations were sent out, only four Pressmen turned up. The organisers were visibly upset. One of them tried to rationalise saying, 'youngsters do not take much interest in religious activities these days. They must be busy elsewhere.'

Was it the absence of liquor ?

'Perhaps', was the reply.

The four Pressmen who attended were each given a silver coin and the rest were taken back by the organisers.

Public relations officers of even government departments and public undertakings take recourse to the wining and dining technique, sometimes because their case is weak and at other times they genuinely believe that the Press will not give coverage unless it is plied with food and liquor, said a public relations officer of a State government 'unless you throw the lunch in the journalists do not consider it to be a formal invitation to a Press Conference'.

A more telling example of the weak case backed up by strong spirits (Black Dog Whiskey and food at the Claridges Hotel) was that of Hindustan Latex Chairman who called an informal Press Conference to promote the public sector undertakings new product, lubricated condoms. The Pressmen were all given a package which contained a teak wood box (which the journalists estimated to be worth Rs 80) containing a packet of newly lubricated condoms worth Rs 2.75. Along with the gift was given a booklet entitled 'National population Advisory council—First Meeting on July 7,1982, some reflections and suggestions on the national family welfare programme—Chairman, Hindustan Latex Ltd.' Inserted inside the booklet was an elaborate biodata of the chairman which among other things pointed out how he had not yet been rewarded for his services by the ruling party.

The Chairman was working at the Pradesh Committee level with the Congress (I) after joining the Party in November 1980, though he was yet to be assigned a formal party position. He has been accepted by the party leaders as a selfless and dynamic worker and leader.

Having known that they had been invited expressly for the purpose of promoting the Chairman's political image (there was no purpose for this cocktail conference) the journalists who partook of the hospitality and almost without any exception collected the present might like to search their consciences to find out whether they gave the Chairman his due. (A wag commented that the journalists without exception collected the condemns in order to prove they are active at least in one field.)

It is not unusual for commercial journalists to give undue publicity to companies, floating shares and debentures. The enterprising among the tribe often get the shares and the debentures allotted to them from the managing director's personal placement.

A senior economic journalist who had nearly twenty-five years of experience of working in the news agencies and newspapers could have made lakhs if he wanted to. He told us that a liaison officer of the company offered him 100 shares at Rs 10 when the ruling price of the share was somewhere around Rs 78. When this journalist refused to oblige, the contact man flourished a list of six economic journalists who had already accepted the offer.

*The Sunday Observer* dated August 17, 1986, carried a story about a top journalist taking a huge bank loan to buy Reliance debentures. The loan was taken at 17 per cent interest whereas the debentures would have yielded 15 per cent only. The guarantee for the loan is said to have been given by Reliance Chief Dhirubhai Ambani. Subsequently, the Government of India did not allow the non-convertible debentures to be converted into equity.

In 1981 a Press Conference was held by DCM for the issue of convertible debentures at the residence of the DCM chief. About 25 people were in attendance. The DCM chief explained the details of the debentures issue and questions followed. Soon after, the Press moved out to the drawing room where drinks were served. Pressmen stood in clusters and even as the first peg was drained out, one senior Pressman felt inspired to suggest to his colleagues that a request be made to the DCM chief for a 'Press quota' of debentures, considering that there was a premium on them.

There was an instant agreement and immediately two senior journalists promptly went to the chief and made the demand. The chief explained that it would be difficult for him to find out from debenture applications as to which of the applicants were journalists. He also expressed his reservations about such an arrangement. However, the journalists ultimately prevailed on him and told him that a list of journalists desirous of getting debentures would be presented to him so that he could allot debentures.

'Let us write the names now itself, suggested a senior in the profession. Another was ready with a pencil and pad. A majority of those present wanted to be on the list. Someone among the journalists wrote to the DCM chief saying that he should not allot any quota for Pressmen as it was neither desirable nor correct. The Press Association was also requested to look into the matter and requested him not to allow any such quota for Pressmen. Press Association President S.C. Anantaraman called a meeting of the Press Association Executive and fully endorsed the stand taken by the journalists. He also wrote to the DCM chief.

The main point is whether these junkets can in any way colour the judgement of the scribe who is covering a public issue, merger, or the latest advances made by a particular company. Can a length of suiting get a bigger, bolder write-up with a bigger heading? Explains Prem Shankar Jha, former Editor, *Hindustan Times*, and a reputed financial writer, "There is a very firm dividing line between a general gift given to 300 writers as a part of the image-building exercise and specific individual gifts. I think a journalist knows instinctively when a gift is being given to extract a favour and when that is being done he has to deal with his own conscience'.

Reacting to gifts, a spokesman from BHEL said, 'In fact, we find that it is those journalists who refuse gifts that give the company a more detailed write-up. So there is no question of quid pro quo between a gift and a favourable copy. 'So are gifts redundant?' Considers the spokesman sheepishly. 'It is better to give something and have it refused than to upset journalists who expect some sort of souvenir. In any case these momentos are very cheap, almost all are under Rs 60.'

However, there are companies which take Press relations even a step further by making presentations to the spouses of scribes as well.

One often comes across stories datelined somewhere on the Western or Eastern front which eulogise the fighting spirit, and the armed might of our defence services. One is moved to intense patriotism by their vivid accounts of the punch of our armed forces. But if only one knows that the same Pressmen who write these moving words are (with a few exceptions) moved to such eloquent emotion only by the liquor which flows freely on such briefs sponsored by the Defence Ministry.

One can understand politicians and private companies trying to strengthen their cases through Scotch. But it is unfortunate that journalists have to be supplied with liquor even to report about a subject like defence which concerns the country's integrity.

The PROs argue that the subject of defence is out of the normal and since this facility is available within the services, it is extended as a courtesy to the guests too.

The courtesy is understandable, if for example, a lunch or dinner is hosted in honour of a visiting Press party at the unidentified spot out there on the front. But journalists are given the run of the bar for entire evenings on such trips. The facility, in fact, has become a bargaining counter for coverage. Such have come to be the expectations of many a defence correspondent over the years that the PROs have themselves come to realise that stories do not get killed if the correspondents are well looked after.

## The Emergency

Emergency declared by Mrs. Indira Gandhi on June 25,1975, was the first test for the credibility of the Press. The history of the Press during the 19 months the Emergency lasted was one of cowardice. It is said that the Press was expected to bend, but it crawled and cringed before the government to the utter surprise of censors. The least that the Press could have done during the Emergency was to resist censors guidelines and play them down instead of blowing them beyond proportions. There have been brave journalists like K.R. Sunderajan (former Assistant Editor, *Times of India,* now a columnist) who was jailed for four, months for resisting Press censorship during the Emergency. He had the tenacity to expose the Indira Gandhi regime by writing articles in the foreign Press. Kuldip Nayar was another journalist who organised resistance against the Emergency and the Press censorship.

One of the well known columnist who waxed eloquence on the need to preserve democratic traditions described the Emergency as India's second liberation. Another top journalist who had hailed the Emergency, while deposing before the Shah Commission (a commission set up by the Janata Government to go into the crimes committed during the Emergency) decried Mrs. Gandhi. Such was the moral turpitude and degeneration of the journalists.

It is reliably learnt that when the government released Sanjay's guidelines, one of the editors of a leading paper woke up the News Editor at the dead of the night to arrange for the photograph of Mrs. Gandhi to be inset in the lead of Sanjay's 20 point programme. He even refused to publish the High Court judgements striking down certain censor's guidelines and giving explicit permission for its publication. This was the story of most of the editors except that of *The Statesman* and *The Indian Express.*

In contrast to the performance of the daily Press, the serious periodicals of the country displayed remarkable guts, and dragged the censor before the High Court. Minoo Masani, a public leader and editor of *Freedom First,* blazed the trail by challenging in the High Court the censor order against his journal. Ramesh Thapar would rather close down his prestigious monthly, *Seminar,* than submit to pre-censorship. Nikhil Chakravarty, Editor of *Mainstream* fought to the end for his right to express views freely.

The veteran A.D. Gorwala showed great ingenuity in keeping his *Opinion* in circulation until the Information and Broadcasting. Ministry got the Postal Department to refuse to carry the copies of his journal.

Rajmohan Gandhi's *Himmat* fought a plucky battle with the I & B Ministry until printing presses were forced by the government to close their doors to the journal.

The Marathi weeklies *Sadhana, Maanusand* and *Sobat* had a running battle with the government.

In the case of *Sadhana,* a highly respected weekly from Pune, the Bombay High Court pronounced the closing down of the press as a glaring instance of gross abuse of power. The judgement went on to say: 'as a citizen, the writer is entitled to criticise the policies and measures adopted by the government during the Emergency and also say that these are suggestive of fascist trends, and unless the criticism exceeds permissible limits...it cannot be regarded as offensive or objectionable.'

The exhortation was wasted on the daily newspapers. Such was the fear psychosis of journalists. Romesh Thapar, a veteran journalist, launched *Seminar* a monthly journal in 1959. It gave readers a wide range of views on a single topic of national interest.

Thapar refused to publish *Seminar* during the Emergency and submit to Press censorship. *Seminar* remained off the stand for seven months during 1976-77.

Similarly, the Bombay High Court struck down the censorship order on Minoo Masani's monthly *Freedom First* with a caustic comment: 'The objections urged are unrelated to any of the purposes or objects of the censorship order, most of the consequences contemplated are fanciful and far-fetched, and the view taken is such as no person acting rationally can ever possibly take. Logic rebels and reason revolts at inferences so devoid of any foundation in reality or basis in common sense.'

*Bhumiputra,* a Gujarati journal, edited by Chunibhai Vaidya and an organ of Gujarat Sarvodaya Mandal, dared to publish in its issue of October 25, 1975, an account of the speech delivered by former Chief Justice of the Bombay High Court and Union Cabinet Minister, M.C. Chagla, in the civil liberties conference held in Ahmedabad on October 12,1975.

Justice J.C. Shah, a former Chief Justice of the Supreme Court of India, presided over the conference. Justice Sheth, a judge of the Gujarat High Court, also attended the conference.

M.C. Chagla's speech was an assertion of the democratic right of dissent. Chagla criticised the proclamation of Emergency, groundless detention of political leaders and imposition of pre-censorship. The speech was delivered extempore with considerable warmth and feeling.

Excerpts of Chagla's speech are as follows:

> '. . . Prime Minister (Mrs. Gandhi) had been talking day-in and day-out against Jayaprakash Narayan. She says that Jayaprakashji had asked the soldiers and policemen not to obey illegal orders. This statement of Jayaprakashji is legally sound. International organisations have approved that it is not incumbent upon a police officer or any army officer to carry out an order which is illegal. All know that

> an American officer shot dead 50-60 innocent villagers in a Vietnam village and was tried in America. What J.P. said, therefore, is legally sound. But he never called upon the army to take up arms against the state.'
>
> '... I want you to endorse that conclusion that there was no conspiracy on the part of the opposition leaders. The conspiracy was by the Prime Minister to put the leaders in the jail, to have Press censorship and to deprive the people of India of their civil liberties. Now, the Prime Minister says almost everyday that India is a democracy and all that happens here is democratic. I am reminded of a story in "Alice in Wonderland", Humpty Dumpty told Alice "If I say that a word has a certain meaning, that word has that meaning. You cannot change it".

'So when the Prime Minister says that dictatorship is democracy, you must accept her word. She is Humpty Dumpty and she thinks all the nations are Alices. But, at least some of us who are here know what is democracy and what is dictatorship and cannot be fooled by her talks.

'And why does she get so angry with the Western Press? They are right in saying that they are sorry that we, the greatest democracy in the world, have adopted undemocratic system. What pains me most is the loss of freedom of Press. Democracy cannot function without a free Press. The Chief Justice of USA has said in his speech that the liberty which prevails in America is due to the combination of a free Press and an independent judiciary. These two concomitants are essential for liberty.

'What is the position today? Freedom of Press has two aspects. First, to get information and the second to purvey that information. Today both these channels are completely blocked. No paper or no news from outside can come into this country which contains any reference hostile to the Prime Minister or to her government. No article, letter or statement can be published in any newspaper which criticises the Prime Minister. As for instance, take Mohan

Dharia's speech, it was a first class speech but not a word of that speech was reported in any newspaper.

'Similarly, Kuldip Nayar was arrested and detained. The government realised it would lose the case, therefore, he was released before the judgement came. The court was told that it was not necessary to pronounce judgement. But it must be said to the credit of judges that they did deliver the judgement. In Maharashtra, nobody knows that Kuldip Nayar was ever arrested, nobody knows that the trial took place, nobody knows that he was released and nobody knows that judgement was delivered. I do not know about Gujarat. If you want to read the judgement you will have to read *London Times.* Therefore, even with regard to parliamentary proceedings which are privileged under the Constitution, even with regard to court proceedings which are a public trial, the censorship does not permit it to be reported.

But censorship, I can understand if it is related to a particular subject for a particular time under particular circumstances. We can understand censorship on the movement of troops or on our success or defeat if a war is on. But then that applies to all. But this is a unilateral censorship. You can sing hymns of glory to the Prime Minister, and they will be printed, not a word of criticism against her will be printed.

'Do you think that today's proceedings and speeches will be reported? It is running a serious risk of censorship. *The Times of India* has, of course, shown us the courtesy by reporting that today I shall inaugurate this conference.

'Now what are the reasons for this? Do you know the Article which provides for it? Emergency can be declared if there is a grave emergency which threatens the security of the state, by reason of war, foreign aggression, internal disturbance. Now do you find any war in the country or threat of aggression?

. . . then what is the justification of this Emergency? The Prime Minister says that the Emergency has taught people discipline. I do not know much about constitutional law but I did not know that in order to enforce discipline you can declare Emergency. No nation can be great without being disciplined. If the Prime

Minister's argument is correct then we must have Emergency in perpetuity.'

The government by its order on January 16, 1976, declared that every copy of *Bhumiputra* dated October 26,1975, along with the press be seized. Under Rule 48(2) on June 26, 1975, the Central Government had made the statutory order by which it subjected all news, comments, rumours and other reports to pre-censorship and prohibited their printing and publication without prior written permission of the censor or an authorised officer.

The management of *Bhumiputra* filed a petition in the Gujarat High Court against the government order on the grounds of violation of freedom of speech and expression. The petition was heard by a two-member bench consisting of Justice S.H. Sheth and Justice J.B. Mehta. The judgement was delivered on February 24,1976. The judges gave the verdict in favour of *Bhumiputra* and held the closure of the journal as invalid.

The judges said that the expression of non-violent and constructive criticism of the government does not amount to sedition. Such expression, far from disturbing public order preserves and maintains democratic public order. Therefore, pre-censorship cannot be applied to it under the present law.

The judgement may go down in history as a charter of the freedom of the Press even when the proclamation of Emergency is in force.

Before Justice Sheth delivered the judgement and the case was pending in his court, his son was threatened with dire consequences for opposing the government. Justice Sheth brought this to the notice of the Chief Justice of the Gujarat High Court. The latter talked to Gujarat Chief Minister Babubhai Patel (Janata Party) who immediately provided for a security guard at the judge's residence and for his son.

None of the daily newspapers in Ahmedabad except *Sandesh* and *Jansatta* carried the news of the High Court's judgement. Outside Ahmedabad, the *Janambhoomi* group of newspapers published from Bombay, Surat, Rajkot, and Bhuj reported a summary of the judgement. *Mumbai Samachar* a Gujarati daily from Bombay and *Gujaramitra* of Surat also reported it. But none of the big national dailies like *The Times of India, The Indian Express, The Hindustan Times, The Statesman* etc. thought it fit to inform their readers about the facts of the judgement.

The tenacity of the veteran journalist Y.D. Lokurkar was rewarded when the Bombay High Court struck down the action of Censor banning the publication of his two articles titled 'Pre-censorship: Nature and Scope' and 'Emergency Situation and Courts'. The judgement declared that the Censor had misdirected himself in law and had taken into consideration extraneous matters.

The Censor issued instructions to the editors of newspapers that the report on the Bombay High Court judgement on Lokurkar's petition was subject to pre-censorship. Lokurkar challenged the Censor's action with another petition in the High Court. The writ petition was admitted by the High Court and interim relief was granted, restraining the Bombay Censor from taking any steps or measures to prevent publication of any news or report about the dependency of the fresh writ petition filed by Lokurkur.

Thereupon the Chief Censor at Delhi issued instructions to all the news agencies to kill the news about the admission by the Bombay High Court of the fresh petition by Lokurkar. Lokurkar continued it with yet another application to the court to join the Chief Censor as a party to the writ petition and secured an ex-parte mandatory injunction, directing both the Censor at Bombay and the Chief Censor at Delhi to withdraw and countermand any instructions issued to any news agencies or newspapers preventing them from publishing any news or report about the admission of the fresh writ petition by Lokurkar.

Finally the counsel for censoring authorities made a statement in open court stating that the instructions have been withdrawn. An appeal was preferred by the Censor against the Bombay High Court judgement in Lokurkar's original case. The appeal was heard for about a week. Ultimately the Censor allowed the appeal to be dismissed with costs.

The Press, by and large, did not publish the High Court judgements. I would not like to go into greater details of what happened during the Emergency as much has already been written about it. But still attention must be drawn to the dark areas concerning the role of the journalists and Press as a whole during the aforesaid period.

The history of the Press during the post-independence period has been one of cowardice notwithstanding sparks of brightness under the editorships of Frank Moraes, B.G. Verghese, S. Mulgaokar, Arun Shourie and achievements of some other editors of regional papers and magazines whose names have already been mentioned earlier. But our achievements are peanuts as compared with our performance during the freedom struggle when we were fighting against a mighty empire. Now we have a democratic government, giving us an opportunity to expose many skeletons in the cupboard but we are reluctant to undertake the jobs because we have become a privileged class reluctant to forego patronage.

The journalists often defend themselves by saying that the overall decline in values has also affected them. I think this is not tenable. If journalists have to sit in judgement over others they have to present a clean image in order to be credible.

## Role of Press Council

The Press Council receives around 450 complaints every year from people who are affected by stories carried by newspapers and magazines. Such stories are published in newspapers at the district and the State level. In fifty per cent cases, the newspapers do not care to respond. An apology is published grudgingly.

It is extremely difficult to dwell on all these complaints. Some important complaints and the judgements have been mentioned. We would now describe briefly the nature of complaints and their disposal, to give an idea as to what should be avoided in a newspaper or a magazine.

The Council found a news item under the caption 'Krishna Theatre Den of Goondaism and Black-marketing' appearing in

*Lalit Awaz*, a Hindi Weekly of Lalitpur, U.P. It contained defamatory allegations aimed at character assassination of Mr. Lachhman Prasad Agarwal, the complainant. The Council upheld the complaint and directed the paper to publish contradiction promptly and also warned the paper not to indulge in unethical journalism.

The Council warned the editor of *Dharti-ka-Veer*, Bijnor, for carrying a defamatory news item against the Manager of Shri Gandhi Ashram, Bijnor. The paper had made allegations of embezzlement and the Council held that the editor should have cross-checked and verified the accuracy.

*Council Holds Reproduction from 'Verses Unethical* : This complaint was moved by Police Commissioner, Hyderabad, K.V.R. Rao, on May 3, 1989, against *Sunday* magazine. Certain contents of the banned book 'Satanic Verses' by Salman Rushdie reproduced verbatim in the *Sunday* an English weekly of Calcutta, in the issue dated February 26 March 4,1989, under the caption : 'What they find objectionable' caused concern. Whereas the Government of India had proscribed the said book, its reproduction in parts tended to disturb peace in Hyderabad city which is prone to communal disturbances, maintained the complaint. The publication also provoked protests from various prominent organisations and individuals. The respondent contended that the impugned publication was simply a reproduction of excerpts from an article published in a foreign magazine 'Impact International' (issue of October 28 November 10, 1988) brought out by a Muslim organisation in U.K. to enlighten the people as to what the Muslims in that country found objectionable in Salman Rushdie's book entitled : 'Satanic Verses'.

It was further emphasised that though the entry of this proscribed book into India had been banned under the Customs Act, that order did not prohibit import of the aforesaid magazine, or reproduction in India of the impugned excerpts therefrom.

It was claimed that in reproducing verbatim some excerpts from the said foreign magazine, run by a Muslim organisation, the respondents were exercising their fundamental right as also their moral and social duty to inform the people of India.

The respondents contended that they had no intention to 'promote enmity between religious groups and arouse communal feeling'. In sum, the respondents maintained that they had committed neither any offence under Section 153 A or Section 295 A, Indian Penal Code, nor any violation of journalistic ethics or good taste for which they would be proceeded against before the Press Council.

***Press Council's Objections***

1. Excepting the headline—'What they found objectionable'. The specific paragraphs of the verses which Muslim groups in Britain consider blasphemous'—The respondents have lifted and reproduced verbatim the impunged publication from the 23rd October 10th November edition of the magazine 'Impact International', published by a Muslim organisation in the United Kingdom.
2. The magazine 'Impact International' had published these original excerpts from Salman Rushdie's book 'Satanic Verses', under the caption 'Satanic Verses' to discount Rushdie's explanation that the book is not on prophet Mohammed but deals with a fictional character named 'Mahound' and to inform the readers that the Muslims in U.K. find these excerpts 'absolutely profane and blasphemous'.
3. In reproducing the impunged excerpts from the foreign magazine, the respondents were not actuated by any malicious intention requisite for the commission of a criminal offence under Section 153 A, or Section 295 A of the Indian Penal Code.

The above findings, in the Council's opinion, could not ipso facto exonerate the respondents of the charge of violating the norms of journalistic ethics.

The issue had to be considered in the contemporary context and the conditions prevailing in India. The mere fact that the publication of these excerpts in U.K. was not resented by the Muslims of that country would not be a correct criterion for gauging the likely effect of these reproductions on the religious susceptibilities of the Muslims in India.

One obvious reason as to why the Muslims in U.K. did not feel hurt by the publication of the excerpts was that these were parts of article, the tenor, tone and express object of which were directed to counter and demolish Rushdie's contention that the 'Satanic Verses' did not deal with Islam or Prophet Mohammed but with a fictional character.

Also by that article the aforesaid magazine was stoutly justifying the ban imposed by the Indian Government on the entry of this book. The quotaticn of those excerpts from 'Satanic Verses' in the context of that article, read as a whole, could not be construed by the Muslims in U.K. as an attempt to outrage or wound their religious feelings.

In the impugned publication the respondents have culled out only the excerpts of the proscribed book from that article without reproducing the context and the setting in which they were quoted. The bare reproduction of these excerpts sans the context of the article as it appeared in 'Impact International' did not exonerate the impugned publication of the propensity of producing an adverse effect on the religious feelings of the Muslims in India.

Furthermore, the conditions prevailing and the intercommunal relations obtaining in India are naturally different from those in U.K. Several regions and towns of India are plagued by recurring communal strife. The communal ethos in India is such that even innocuous criticism of the practices of a religion or its founder may touch off serious communal trouble or inflame communal feelings.

***'Surya India' Warned :*** *Surya India*, a monthly magazine, published from New Delhi, carried in its issue of August 1989, an article captioned: 'Youth Congress—Have Libido will Travel' relating to the participation of Indian Youth Congress (I) in the youth festival held at Pyongyang, D.P.R. Korea in the first week of July, 1989. The article purported to have been based on the report of its correspondent Suresh Kumar. The article contained the following passage attributing reprehensible conduct to the complainant under the influence of drink at a Sino-Indian function.

'Pavan Kumar Bansal, a hot favourite with Rajiv Gandhi and a member of the Rajya Sabha from Chandigarh, won laurels for India when, while addressing an august gathering on Sino-Indian relations, he suddenly collapsed on the floor and had to be removed on a stretcher. As the delegates from all over the world watched the stretcher being carried out of the hall in hushed silence, an Indian delegate whispered into the ears of his Czechoslovakian neighbour: 'No, he does not suffer from a serious ailment. It is just that he is piss drunk.' The news spread like wild fire and some of the delegates later recollected how Bansal found it extremely difficult to keep his balance when he mounted the dias and literally grabbed for the mike.

By means of a letter to the Editor of *Surya India,* the complainant contradicted the above-quoted report characterising it as 'wholly baseless', 'utterly false', 'mischievously derogatory' and 'concoction of a story about me at a function which I did not attend to defame me in the public eye.'

In the last paragraph of that letter, the complainant expressed the hope that the Editor of *'Surya India* would enquire into and publish an apology.'

The Editor of *Surya India* published an edited version of the complainant's letter in its issue of November 1989, but added a footnote: *'Surya* stands by the reportage.'

The Press Council held that it is evident from the story that the reporter made derogatory statement on mere hearsay. This is clear from the sentence: 'The news spread like wild fire and some of the delegates later recollected how Bansal found it extremely difficult to keep his balance when he mounted the dias and literally grabbed for the mike.' Professional prudence required the editor to verify and cross-check the facts from the complainant and other authentic sources.

## The Confirmation

For the guidance of editors when they are called upon to handle reports /articles containing libellous statements, the Press Council reiterated the principle as follows:

> Whenever a newspaper or a magazine receives a report or article containing imputations per se defamatory to any person or organisation, the editor should before getting it published, verify its truth (apart from other authentic sources), from the person or the organisation whose reputation is likely to be harmed by its publication and elicit his/its counter version or clarification and publish that also along with the report or article.

Provided that after carefully considering the totality of information elicited by enquiries from various sources, the editor has reasonable grounds to believe that the report is true and its publication will be in the public interest.

The editor in this case made no effort whatever to contact the complainant and check the facts with him, though the latter could be easily available at Delhi.

In the Council's opinion and in the facts and circumstances of the case, the respondent's act in adding the footnote: 'Surya stands by the reportage', was not in consonance with the norms of responsible journalism. The respondent's conduct in publishing the impugned story in excising and omitting from publication, the crucial portion of the complainant's contradiction, and in adding the footnote to the truncated contradiction, was violative of journalistic ethics for which a warning should be administered to the respondent.

## The Justification

Seldom had the Press Council voted contrary to the recommendation of its Inquiry Committee which goes into the merits of complaints against the fourth estate received by this statutory body. The case filed by former Lok Sabha Speaker Balram Jakhar against *The Illustrated Weekly of India*, was one such notable instance.

Jhakar had alleged that the photograph which *Weekly* had carried of him with Ram Swarup, the alleged spy, in November

17-23, 1985 issue was fake and its publication was violative of journalistic norms.

But the Press Council ruled otherwise, even though the Inquiry Committee had observed that the *Weekly* should placate the Speaker by publishing the correspondence between it and him detailing reasons for publication of the picture.

In fact, some members of the Press Council were so exercised in the matter that they wanted the Speaker to apologise to the *Weekly*, or withdraw his complaint altogether.

The Press Council ruled: 'We are of the view that *The Illustrated Weekly of India* was justified in publishing the photograph which was noteworthy. *The Illustrated Weekly*, therefore, did not violate journalistic norms and ethics by publishing the photograph.'

This case has evoked wide interest and for the first time the Press Council threw open its hearing to the public.

***Details of the Case :*** On November 17,1985, *The Illustrated Weekly of India* published a photograph of Jakhar with Ram Swarup in illustration of Swarup's interview, denying the charges of violation of Official Secret Act and Foreign Exchange Regulation Act (FERA). The text contained no reference to Jakhar at all. The best course would have been to deny any relation with Swarup and leave it at that. Everyone knew that Swarup used to circulate freely at public functions.

S.D. Bali, Jakhar's Secretary, who filed the complaint, noted later in the correspondence that people 'get themselves photographed with VIPs at different functions. The photographs do not imply that these people are connected or known to the VIP.'

Instead of adopting this dignified stand, Bali shot off two letters on November 18, one to the *Weekly* and other to the Chairman, Press Council. The letter did not challenge the genuineness of the photograph but only the intent behind its publication since Swarup is not known personally to Jakhar.

The *Weekly* replied on November 22,1985, disowning any intent to implicate Jakhar with Swarup and expressing an apology if any wrong impression has been conveyed. The apology was deemed inadequate by Bali.

He wrote on November 29, 1985, asking the *Weekly* to intimate the source from which the photograph in question had been procured so that his office was able to trace the background for the whole mischief.

The Weekly's reminder that journalists do not reveal their sources of information was brushed aside by Jakhar's Secretary. However, out of respect for the Speaker, the Weekly informed the Speaker that the photograph was taken at Parliament Annexe when a delegation had come to India. Bali denied that the photograph was ever taken there.

On March 2, 1986, the Weekly published an interview with Jakhar so that he could give his version. On March 22, it published an editorial note denying that it had sought to imply any links between Jakhar and Swarup. Neither satisfied Bali or Jakhar.

When the matter was heard by the Press Council Inquiry Committee, neither Jakhar nor Bali cared to appear, to depose to and justify the grave charges they had levelled against the Weekly persistently.

The Inquiry Committee gave the finding that the publication of photograph, though genuine, was likely to tarnish Jakhar's reputation. Accordingly the publication was not justified, although the Committee is satisfied that there was no mala-fide intention on the part of the Weekly. It directed the Weekly to make further amends.

This recommendation was rejected by the majority of the Council. The Council ruled that the publication was justified because it was 'noteworthy'.

***Right to Reply :*** A newspaper reports news and events of public interest every day and seeks to place them in perspective by adding its own analysis and comment. Such reporting and comment affect individuals and groups in different ways.

It should be the newsmen's effort to report facts accurately and completely and to give balanced coverage to different viewpoints as far as practicable.

However carefully this is done, individuals and groups directly affected often feel aggrieved that the facts are wrong or incomplete, that their particular viewpoint is left out or that unfair comments have been made. The fair and accepted thing to do in such cases is to grant them the right to reply.

It has been observed that there is an inadequate understanding among both editorial staff and readers as to what this right of reply is and what it is not and when it is warranted and when not.

Some of the cases dealt with by The Times of India Ombudsman, former Chief Justice of the Supreme Court, P.N. Bhagwati, which throw light on these issues are given below:

> In a report headlined 'Austerity is for lesser mortals', there was an allegation that a minister had not taken kindly to an official pointing out to him that he was not entitled to an extra air-conditioner, and that things were made so difficult for the officer concerned that he sought voluntary retirement.

The officer, who had been named, wrote a letter clarifying that he had taken voluntary retirement 'not on account of what has been mentioned in the report but for purely personal reasons.'

There could not be a clearer case in which the right of reply should have been immediately recognised: The writer had been named in the paper, he was denying a specific allegation made in the report, and his letter was short and to the point. The letter was published only after my intervention, and so late that the readers might have missed the link. The editorial staff should be more alert in such cases and carry the reply promptly.

*Clear Distinction :* In another case, the 'Pune-Plus' edition had carried a straight report of a representation by a citizens' body demanding a probe into alleged irregularities in the award of contracts to a firm of engineers and civil contractors. The firm's proprietor complained to The Times Ombudsman stating that similar allegations had earlier been dismissed by the High Court and, therefore, the report should not have been published.

After looking into the matter carefully Justice Bhagwati ruled that not to publish such reports without checking the truth of every allegation would really amount to shutting them out, since the newspaper is really not competent to carry out conclusive investigations on all manner of subjects.

The reporter, however, has the duty and obligation, to keep a clear distinction between facts and allegations, and not to allow misimpressions to form in the minds of readers that what is merely alleged is a fact. I believe that the 'Pune-Plus' report passes this clear test of;

(i) clear public interest, and (ii) careful reporting.

But since it was clear that the complainant's interests were affected, he was asked to submit a short, darificatory reply for publication.

A businessman had complained that his reputation had been affected by a news report that his business and residential premises had been raided during the investigation of a 'hawala ring'. As nothing incriminating had been found, he demanded an unconditional apology by the paper. The Editor promptly published a correction that 'we do not know if the documents seized were incriminating', but the complainant was not satisfied.

Justice Bhagwati looked into the matter and found that the report was based on firm information from reliable sources in the enforcement directorate and that its publication was justified keeping in view that it was a matter of clear and evident public interest. However, as the report affected the complainant's personal reputation and public standing, he was entitled to a right of reply giving his side of the story.

*Conscience Keepers* : The director of a national level medical institution complained that there were distortions in a report on the issues underlying the agitation by a section of doctors. He submitted extensive documentation in support of his contentions and invited the paper, as the 'conscience keeper of the nation', to conduct a detailed enquiry and publish its conclusions. While asking him to submit a brief reply clarifying specific points, Justice

Bhagwati felt it necessary to explain to him the limited role of the Press in matters such as that of his institution.

Justice Bhagwati wrote : 'It would be highly presumptuous and wrong for journalists to see themselves as the conscience keepers of the nation. They do not have the competence to conduct open-ended enquiries and resolve the internal disputes of institutions such as yours, and it would be unfair to expect them to perform such a role.

If any person directly concerned feels that the facts have been incompletely reported or that the opinions aired are one-sided, the newspaper should give him the opportunity of placing those specific points before the readers.

The right of reply applies not only to news reports but also to comments. *The Times of India* Ombudsman got a large number of letters from persons objecting strongly to particular views expressed in the editorials or opinion articles in the paper, and claiming the right of reply.

There can be no such blanket right, the newspaper is bound to afford the opportunity of reply only to those persons or institutions who are clearly and directly affected by what is written in the paper. Letters discussing and controverting the editorial stance and opinions expressed in the paper are welcome and many of them are published.

A reporter had done a story on unhealthy speculation in the stock markets and discussed the case of the scrips of two companies which were showing steady but inordinate increases in price, unjustified by 'the fundamentals'. He had quoted many market observers to say that this was due to excessive speculation in the scrips.

A shareholder of one of the companies wrote a letter arguing that the company's performance justified the share movement and that the report, based on the biased remarks of a few brokers, might harm the interest of the shareholders.

The letter was published. Justice Bhagwati pointed out to the complainant that if the reporter was wrong (that the share price was ruling high because of speculation and was not justified by fundamentals) the shareholder had nothing to worry about, he ought to be concerned only if the report was right.

## Role of Language

Throughout the month of March 1990, the national Press particularly *The Indian Express*, under the editorship of Arun Shourie lambasted Deputy Prime Minister Devi Lal and his son Haryana Chief Minister O.P. Chautala for abuse of power and violence in Meham from where the later sought election to Haryana Assembly.

*The Indian Express* carried an editorial on March 28, 1990, on Chautala's horrors in Meham with a caption: 'Throw Him Out'. This infuriated Devi Lal. He rang up Arun Shourie, intimidated and abused him. Shourie tap-recorded the conversation which was reproduced in *The Indian Express* dated March 29, 1990 as follows:

*Arey, tujhe patta nahin hai tujhe aise nahin likhna chahiye?*— it was Devi Lal on the phone. '*Arey*, don't you know you should not be writing like this?'

It was past ten at night on March 28 and that was his opening sentence.

We had published an editorial that morning about Chautala's horrors in Meham. 'Throw him out', we had counselled. And Devi Lal was reacting.

*'Tu jaanta nahin hai, apna fayade ke liye yeh poonjipati kuch bhi kara sakte hain?'* ("Don't you know for their gain these capitalists can do anything?')

*'Toone pichli boar se sabak nahin sekha?'*—'Haven't you learnt a lesson from the last time?'

Nothing had happened in Meham, he said, just a few reporters had cooked up stories to sell their papers. The photographers too? I asked. *'Sab ek hi to hain'* — 'All of them are one'.

*'Tujhe pataa nahin, yeh Deputy Prime Ministry main joote per rakhta hoon?*—'Do you not know, I wear the Deputy Prime Ministership on my joota?' *'Mujhe Deputy Prime ministry chahiye?'*—'Do I need the Deputy Prime Ministership ?'

It is all a conspiracy of you Pressmen, he said. What more could I have done ? he asked. I said count all the votes in those booths to that man... I ordered a judicial enquiry.

*'Main to aur bhi badaa khel khelnejaa rahaa hoon'* — 'I am about to play an even bigger game,' he concluded.

Next morning I narrated the call to my colleagues. Some felt that we should publish the text at once. Others said that doing so would be premature. We should continue our work on Meham and ignore the call.

We continued our work.

Devi Lal phoned Mr. R.N. Goenka in Bombay, Mr. Goenka was not well that day. And so he was succinct. 'If you want me to do something about something written in the paper, the answer is "No"', he said. 'If you want me to do something else, the answer is "yes"'. And he handed the phone to his nurse and secretary.

Devi Lal bombarded her with fulsome abuse of me and, I understand, a colleague.

## A Visit

On Friday, March 16, the man resigned his Deputy Prime Ministership and all. So Gurumurthy and we met him for an hour that night. He was fuming. *'Woh behan(. . . )'* — about a fellow editor, about Arun Nehru. *'Inki aukaat kya hai'* — 'What do they count for'. *'Dekhne log mujhe aate hain'* — 'It is me that the people come to see'. *'Maine behan(. . . . .) ko kameti mein dala, aur maalik ban gaen hain'* - 'I am the one who put the behan(. . .) in the committee, and they have become the owners'. He ranted about everyone—Kapil Sibal, some Ram Pujan Patel, up to NTR, Hegde and all. But the foulest abuse was for one of my colleagues and for Arun Nehru.

*'Yeh saaraa kuch Arun Nehru likhwa rahaa hai'*, he insisted. (This is all being done at the instance of Arun Nehru.)

We were conciliatory. We tried to cajole him to let him blow off steam.

I assured him that the young girl who had written the accounts for *The Indian Express* was not the sort who would be meeting Arun Nehru, who would be influenced by him. It so happened that she had already resigned and left for another paper.....

*'Paanchon* Chief Minister *mere aadmi hai*—Biju, Chautala, Laloo Prasad, Mulayam Singh, Chimanbhai' — 'All the five Chief Ministers are my men he claimed.

Twenty-four hours had not to pass that Chimanbhai, Laloo Prasad and Mulayam Singh realised that were Devi Lal to force the issue, their governments would be the first to fall. On Sunday they were therefore the most energetic in making him see sense.

We commented on his withdrawing the resignations in another editorial. 'The next two-steps', urging that now that the first thing was done, the Janata Dal should be compelled to field Chautala from Meham again and that the man should be made to lose his deposit there.

***'Pitwa doonga' :*** Later that day, Devi Lal accosted a senior officer of the Government just after the budget proceedings.

'Have you seen what the *Express* has written? Do you know what the next two steps are ...?' he fumed.

He wanted Mr. Goenka to be talked to and our mouth shut.

*'Main baniya to hoon nahin'* — 'I am not a baniya'. *'Main to aadmi bhej ke pitwa doonga'* — 'I will send the men and have them beaten up.'

The officer did not trouble Mr. Goenka. He narrated the ire to me.

Others came and reported Devi Lal's thunder and abuse— the 'behan( ......... )' it seemed were now reserved for me.

'Shourie told me that he has dismissed the fellow who was writing his azaariyas (the editorials)', he complained, 'but die damned editorials are still appearing......

He had mixed things up. I couldn't have dismissed the writer as I had been writing the editorials myself.

In public, of course, he was making a distinction:

'I have nothing against you Pressmen', he has been saying.

'It is a conspiracy of the capitalists — Goenka, Ambani, Birla, Jain. . . .' Bereft as I am of a rural background, I presume the subtlety would do a buffalo proud.

Our Sunday edition carried two articles—one on the Meham episode and one on his fulminations. Monday's editorial, 'A tantrum a week', dealt with his dismissal of Ajit Singh from the secretaryship of the Dal's Parliamentary Board. Tuesday's editorial began with reference to him.

***His Call Yesterday*** : His mouthpiece was on the phone early. 'These things have been happening in Bengal. . . in Bihar. . . .' As I shouted, there was a sudden switch to the same bovine subtlety: 'Nahin, nahin, yeh jo Hindustan Times wale campaign kar rahen hain, main uske bare mein....' 'No. no It is about this campaign that The Hindustan Times people are conducting that I......'

And lo and behold the wonders of rural advancement—prerecorded chimes struck up a tune as I waited.

'Arey, tera akhbaar to aise hi chal rahaa hai—'Arey, your paper going on the same way, said Devi Lal for openers.

'Ji haan', I said. 'Aur aise hi chalega'—And it shall go on the same way.

'Kyon?' — 'Why?'

It is an issue of public importance, I said. And in any case, you have taken to abusing us morning and evening. I said curtly.

'Gaali na doon to aur tujhe kya karun?' he growled.

'Aap jo marzi kar leejiye'—'You do what you like', I explained.

'To achcha....' he -put the phone down.

Mercifully.

I would not have been able to feign deference much longer. Arun Shourie raised the following questions on this issue. Several questions arise:

How does this intimidation square with the Janata Dal's professions?

How much time do you think this man has spent on affairs of state—on Kashmir, on Punjab—since his son's depredations in Meham, and how much on his son? Is that the scale of priorities for which the people placed this government in office?

Should the government remain mortgaged to a man who just to shield his son from the consequences of the tatter's criminality rocks the government every week?

Is there any issue, any principle involved in what he is doing? O yes, he did attempt the day after his resignation to endow his shove with some intellectual content. A grouse about the selection of candidates for the Assembly elections; it was foolish, for it was he who had presided over every meeting and had his way at every meeting at which the candidates were selected. V.P. Singh had not even attended the meetings. And of course, there was that great formulation— fifty per cent of ambassadors, governors, judges should be persons of a rural background: that was not just foolish, it was laughable. Should a man with such mental capacities and notions be entrusted with the affairs of the country ?

Is what he is doing to the government anything but blackmail?

Can a government which submits to this man's blackmail stand up to blackmail by others? By the terrorists in Kashmir? In Punjab?

Should everyone else sit back, wondering how V.P. Singh will react? Should all this be seen at all as a private contest between V.P. Singh and Devi Lal? Should everyone else in the Janata Dal not rise and call a halt to this bully? Should parties which support the government—the BJP, the CPM— which see the problems that beset our country which see how much more feeble these jolts leave the government for dealing with the problems, should they not step forth and call a halt to him?

## The Complaint

Against reproduction of this conversation by Arun Shourie, S.L. Kalra, Editor, *University Today*, filed a complaint to the Press Council of India on the grounds of violation of journalistic ethics.

Mr. Kalra emphatically stated that the impugned news item was a text book example of everything that is to be branded as undesirable journalism and goes against the norms, prudents and adjudications of the Press Council of India. The complainant found it absolutely embarrassing that four letter words be printed and read by his children of impressionable age and they too pick up this kind of vocabulary.

The complainant further submitted that the expletive used by the respondent-editor with impugned story in such a blatant manner is more to demonstrate his clout that the country's Deputy Prime Minister calls and cares for him, than any other major public interest of information or in the legitimate exercise of his right of free speech.

In a further communication dated May 4, 1990, the complainant added that, in fact, the respondent-editor had misused his position as an editor of the newspaper on whose columns he has unfettered control to show his clout, his influence and his personal importance. In his view the impugned news item was an example of sheer journalistic terrorism.

The complainant was asked about his *locus standi* in the case, keeping in view that something very personal was said in the impugned article about the Deputy Prime Minister who had not come to the Council with any complaint. He responded that the newspaper *Indian Express* with the objectionable vocabulary had travelled to his house and he had found it absolutely embarrassing that four letter words be read by his children of impressionable age. Had he known, he would have asked the hawker not to drop the paper at his house at least on that day.

The respondent in this case quoted Press Council decision in the complaint dated January 19, 1988, filed by Mr. Harbhajan Singh against *The Sunday Observer* of Bombay pertaining to the publication of a news item under the captions : 'Who gains from Riyasti's murder?' in the January 17-23,1988 issue of the English Weekly enquiring whether the then Home Minister, Mr. Buta Singh was in any way connected with the mysterious murder of Tarlochan Singh Riyasti, Congress-I, General Secretary.

In its decision rendered on January 23, 1989, the Press Council had found that Mr. Buta Singh had not denied the allegation against him. He did not appear to have taken any exception, nor had he asked for contradiction to be published. He had also not filed a complaint with the Council, nor had he appeared before the Council, nor had he otherwise any interest in the complaint.

The allegation in the news item were all made against Mr. Buta Singh and there could be no justifiable reasons for his not lodging a complaint, if he had felt aggrieved by the allegations. He had, however, not chosen to do so and Mr. Harbhajan Singh, who had lodged the complaint, could not have any knowledge of the correctness or otherwise of the allegations made.

In the absence of any denial from Mr. Buta Singh, the Council could not hold that the allegations were false and baseless. The complaint was accordingly dismissed.

While citing the decision of the Council mentioned above, the respondent pleaded that in the present case, also, the complainants had no *locus standi* to make this complaint as it was for the Deputy Prime Minister (Devi Lal) to make a complaint to the Council if he had felt aggrieved by the publication of the article in question.

The complainant, on the other hand, pleaded that if a matter of public interest is there any person should be allowed to make a complaint and *locus standi* could not be questioned.

The Press Council has to establish a Principle whether a journalist can reproduce such abuses in his writings in a newspaper. If so, can the complainant be permitted to reproduce such abuses of local *thanedar* or local vice-chancellor.

The complainant further said that he was not challenging the factual accuracy of the impugned publication; what he was objecting to was the reproduction of the four letter words. The use of such filthy words was not in public good taste, nor of public interest.

The respondent (Arun Shourie) submitted that telephonic conversation of the Deputy Prime Minister with him was not personal. How was the Deputy Prime Minister bullying the Editor and reminding him whether he had forgotten he had been dismissed by the owner of the same newspaper.

He was threatening the editor and tried his best to intimidate and silence him and the newspaper. The example of a *thanedar* using abuses may be similar but we have to have a sense of proportion. The respondent agreed that the words were horrible but these were- used by the Deputy Prime Minister of India.

These words had to be reproduced in the article. Language is an index of mind. The respondent further submitted that this is not a matter where Council can lay down absolute rules and guidelines.

There are a number of judgements that absolute rules cannot be laid down. Besides, if the physical health of a Minister is of public interest his mental health is also of public interest.

In regard to the point that the children of impressionable age are affected by such writings, the respondent denied the charge that the complainant's children might conclude that probably it is quite an accepted norm and practice in journalism to use obscenities.

The respondent submitted that on the contrary, the fact that these words are not used by newspapers and were used in the impugned article alone, must lead his children to conclude that using such words is not an accepted norm and practice in journalism.

On being asked whether Devi Lal had used such foul language in any of his earlier conversations with him, the respondent replied in the negative. He added that in reproducing the entire conversation verbatim including these filthy words actually used by Devi Lal, his objective was not only to expose the former's misconduct which was unbecoming of the holder of the high public office of Deputy Prime Minister, but also to seek redress against the venegal threat wrapped in that obscene language, at the bar of public opinion.

As against the above, the complainant, Mr. Kalra submitted that the whole impugned publication had been deliberately punctuated with these loathsome epithets more with a view to sensationalise rather than to seek redress or serve any higher purpose. Mr. Kalra urged that the limited point for the consideration of the committee was whether or not the act of the respondent in repeatedly reproducing these obscene words, was in conformity with the high standards of journalistic ethics and decency?

**The Judgement**

While dealing with this point, the committee invoked by way of analogy, the test: If abusive, 'unparliamentary language' is used by some members of Parliament, should that be allowed to pass on as 'Parliamentary' in the media ?

While noting that the standards and notions as to what is 'Parliamentary language' and what is not changing all over the world, and expunction of words from parliamentary records is becoming a rare phenomenon, the committee felt that in the facts and circumstances of this case, the respondent should have, in deference to high standard of the profession and public good taste, avoided reproduction of these abusive words in his article.

Thus, the Council observed that even without reproducing these offensive words, the respondent could have written the article in a way so as to have the same impact on the minds of the readers, which the faithful reproduction of the conversation could produce.

# 10

# Reorganisation Process

Regretfully, All India Radio (AIR) performance in informing, educating and entertaining its listeners has not been impressive and it has failed to come up to its promise as an instrument of mass communication. Its failure has been twofold: it has failed to provide a broadcasting service satisfactory to the community and it has failed to fulfil the purpose of the state to inform and educate the masses, to enthuse them with plans of social and economic progress and to enlist their cooperation in fulfilling them. This failure is attributable to many factors; basically they arise from organisational deficiencies and inadequate financial resources.

According to the Indian Telegraphs Act of 1885, as amended, the Government of India has the exclusive privilege of establishing, maintaining and working a broadcasting service. The Act provides that a licence may be granted to others also. This permissive provision was used when in 1926 the Indian Broadcasting Company Ltd., was granted a licence for the two stations at Calcutta and Bombay. Since 1930, when the broadcasting service was taken over by government as 'The Indian State Broadcasting Service' no licences have been issued except for small agricultural stations at Allahabad and Dehra Dun, both since defunct, and to the Madras Corporation for a restricted city service until the Madras station came on the air in 1938. AIR thus enjoys a monopoly in the field.

## A Government Department

Since its inception AIR has been a department of the government. At present, its status is that of an attached office of the Ministry of Information and Broadcasting. The minister is responsible to the Cabinet and accountable to Parliament for all broadcasting activity. Except for short spells during the period 1947-65, the minister has not been a member of the Cabinet. Since January 1966, the ministry once again is put under a minister of state. It is unfortunate that it has been so. Effective mass communication in a developing country is essential for its economic and social regeneration. The minister at the helm should have suitable authority and status for the purpose. It is equally unfortunate that the Cabinet Committee on Information and Broadcasting has been recently discontinued. This again makes the link between the minister and the Cabinet tenuous.

The Director General is responsible to the ministry for the working of AIR as its executive head. He is appointed by the government in consultation with the Union Public Service Commission. It is usual to appoint an officer of the programme cadre of AIR to be the Director General, though the post is not specifically reserved for the cadre. There have been occasions when officers of the Indian Civil Service were drafted to be Director General.

Though the pay of the Director General is the same as that allowed to a Joint Secretary, he has not been equated in status to a Joint Secretary nor does he exercise any powers of government. The heads of two other similar organisations, namely, the Director General, Posts and Telegraphs, and the Director General Tourism, both have ex-officio Secretariat status and the former is remunerated by a higher salary.

The Director General is supported by a Chief Engineer ranking next only to him and three Deputy Directors General, one each for Programmes, Inspection and Administration.

The Deputy Director General (Programmes) is in charge of the preparation of programme schedules and recruitment and utilisation of staff artistes, their emoluments etc. He is assisted by eight Directors, in the rank of Station Directors, nine Chief Producers, two Deputy Chief Producers and other staff.

The Station Directors of AIR administer the various stations on behalf of the Director General. Similarly, there are Directors in charge of Units such as the Staff Training School, the TV Service, the Transcription and Programme Exchange Service, the External Services, and the News Services. They are assisted by Station Engineers/Assistant Station Engineers, Assistant Station Directors and Producers or Assistant Producers.

Like all other departments of government, the entire expenditure of AIR is met by appropriations made by Parliament. In theory, the licence fee on receivers is levied to sustain the broadcasting service. But in practice, revenue derived from licence fees, after deducting collection charges, is credited to the Consolidated Fund and both the capital and revenue budgets of AIR are debated and voted upon annually by Parliament. There is thus no direct link between licence fees collected and amounts appropriated. In many countries the entire collection of fees reduced by the cost of collection is placed at the disposal of the broadcasting organisation either directly or through a vote of Parliament without a detailed control over its activities.

## The Procedure

We should now consider whether organised as it is today as an attached office of a ministry with concomitant financing arrangements, AIR can develop as a national organisation and provide a countrywide service of quality and excellence.

In the first place, a theme of centralisation runs through the fabric of India's administration. It is more marked in the field of financial administration. This by itself is a deterrent to the growth of departmental initiative and expeditious transaction of business. Even the ministries of government do not enjoy full financial powers over the appropriations made to them for purposes embodied in the estimates as approved by Parliament. They derive financial authority by delegations made from time to time by the Finance Ministry. The principle that all executive levels should have administrative authority and financial power commensurate with their responsibilities and functions has yet to find acceptance. There is also a general disinclination to part with power and the Director General in his turn has been chary in delegating powers to the Station Directors.

A government department is subject to the discipline of rules and regulations both in regard to its employment policy and utilisation of resources allocated. These rules and regulations framed for administrative purposes are not wholly suitable for the commercial activities of government or for a creative medium like AIR. It is on this consideration that industrial and commercial activities of government have been entrusted to statutory corporations on companies. In the case of AIR no such dispensation has yet been made. The purpose of adopting the corporate form was to free the commercial activities of the state from inappropriate rules and regulations and to place them on a comparable footing with private enterprise.

We do not wish to overload this report with details but would refer to a few major limitations which impinge on the efficiency of AIR's administration. In the administrative field the Director General's powers for creation of posts only extend to minor posts of clerks and peons. Similarly, he can order transfers of only junior officials, not of Directors and not even of Assistant Station Directors if they hold independent charge of a station. His disciplinary powers are also extremely limited and hemmed in by archaic regulations. In this situation, it is difficult for him to administer the department efficiently nor can he command the respect of his subordinates.

His financial powers are even more limited. He cannot send out any officer on tour for more than ten days at a time and he cannot authorise air journeys where necessary. Even his powers in regard to programme planning do not allow him to make worthwhile adjustments. One might well say that he has responsibility without the authority necessary to fulfil it.

We now consider whether basic requirements of AIR would be met by enlarging the powers of the Director General.

First, he has to work within the limits of funds appropriated by Parliament In the framing of estimates AIR's proposals are first scrutinised and usually pruned down by the Ministry and the process is repeated in the Finance Ministry. Thus, it is seldom that the reductions are made in a constructive way keeping in view the main purpose for which funds were demanded. Secondly, the Director General cannot spend the amounts voted according to his requirements without adhering to detailed allocations to different activities. He has hardly any powers of re-appropriation.

Thirdly, the capital grant is determined by the Planning Commission's decision regarding the rate of development and the priorities in this development. As we have mentioned earlier, broadcasting does not figure in the list of priorities drawn up by the Planning Commission. We were informed that AIR's plan has just undergone a fifth revision to accord with the Commission's proposed total allocation of resources in the Fourth Plan. This has at one stroke nullified AIR's earlier intention to provide a medium-wave network to serve 95 per cent of the people by the end of the Fourth Plan.

Fourthly, the Director General is not competent to engage the type of people he needs and offer them salaries they are worth, as all recruitment has to be made through prescribed government channels and remunerations paid according to scales laid down by government. There is thus little flexibility in the selection of staff and in determining the terms and conditions of service'. And the Director General has no authority to dispense with the services of unsuitable staff.

We say all this to pinpoint the present disabilities of AIR, but we do not for a moment suggest that the Director General should be allowed to function without control and guidance or that he should be given all the resources he demands. He should, however, be brought into closer collaboration in the shaping of policy and programmes and given greater flexibility in their fulfilment.

Before we discuss what would be the most suitable organisation for AIR, we should make one point of substance and that is that the stations and other units of AIR must be given greater autonomy than they enjoy at present. It is the stations which are actually concerned with broadcasts and the test of a broadcasting organisation is the quality of its programmes. The need for speedy decisions and initiative at the stations is indisputable but cannot be met if their Directors have to obtain the Director General's approval for every little thing that they need or propose to do. Their status in the organisation has been progressively whittled down over the years.

For reasons we have developed earlier, it is not possible in the Indian context for a creative medium like broadcasting to flourish under a regiment of departmental rules and regulations. It is only by an *institutional chance* that AIR can be liberated from the present rigid financial and administrative procedures of government.

We first explored the possibility of adopting the form of one or other governmental agency which has greater freedom in movement than departments of government. The Railway Board, the Atomic Energy Commission, the Council of Scientific and Industrial Research, were suggested by some as a possible model for AIR.

Anxious as we were to limit structural changes to the minimum, we studied these organisations but came to the conclusion that none of the patterns would meet the needs of AIR. The reasons for our conclusions are as follows: There is a clear division of functions in Railway operations and it is not so in broadcasting. Secondly, the Railway Board is not engaged in creative activity. And thirdly, as a ministry of government, the Board has to work within the limitation of rules and regulations framed for recruitment, promotion, etc. On all these counts, the Railway Board pattern would not meet the needs of AIR.

Similarly, both the Atomic Energy Commission and the Council of Scientific and Industrial Research are engaged in specialised activities which do not make it necessary for them to be in constant touch with political, cultural and social developments with which Radio is intimately involved.

We, therefore, proceed to consider whether it would not be best to give AIR the corporate form which has been successfully adopted by broadcasting organisations in countries with a democratic constitution. In this consideration it would be relevant to examine the policy resolution which led to the acceptance of the corporate form for state industrial enterprises.

It was acknowledged that subject to the observance of certain general principles, the organisation of management suitable for each undertaking must necessarily be determined with reference to its particular requirements. The method of recruitment, the regulation of scales of pay, conditions of service and discipline of employees, the procedure for financial control, the system of accounting applicable to the normal activities of government could not obviously be adopted for the efficient administration of industrial enterprises. We feel that the same considerations apply with equal force in the case of AIR.

Experience has shown that the corporate form by itself has not brought about a psychological transformation nor given flexibility in operation because the Boards as constituted do not ensure independence implicit in the form. It is necessary to safeguard this position by making AIR a *national authority* in which major national interests would be represented to give it balance, quality, poise and purpose. Secondly, even with such a constitution the autonomy of the corporation would not be real unless it is financially independent and viable.

We have carefully studied in detail the major types of broadcasting organisations in different parts of the world. Major broadcasting systems are either in private hands largely exploited for profit, or they are owned by the state but entrusted to autonomous corporations subject to specified control over policies and programmes.

It is necessary at the outset to make the point that all radio and television organisations are subject to control and regulations by the state. First there is the international obligation in the use of wave lengths and frequencies. This requires the issue of a licence to operate as prescribed by the International

Telecommunication Union. The grant of licence is subject to certain legal formalities and regulations framed by each government. Apart from legal requirements, no state can allow unrestricted authority to a broadcasting organisation to embark on programmes which offend against social and moral values.

These media have a tremendous potential in moulding public opinion; they can equally enslave or liberate the human mind. The state has to safeguard the public interest through its regulatory power. It is largely on this consideration that the Supreme Court of the United States of America had declared: 'Unlike other modes of expression, radio inherently is not available to all. That is its unique characteristic. That is why unlike other modes of expression it is subject to government regulations.'

The outstanding example of private ownership and management is provided by the United States of America where licences to operate Radio and Television Stations are issued by the Federal Communication Commission subject to certain laws and regulations. This system also operates in many other countries, notably, Japan, Canada and Australia. All the three countries have each a public corporation owned wholly by the state, but they have also licensed private stations which operate in competition.

There is a variation of this form which provides for joint state and private collaboration. The best examples of blending of public and private ownership are provided by the Italian and Swedish organisation. RAI, the Italian organisation, is a private limited company which has been granted a monopoly of Radio and Television and wire distribution. The majority of its shares are held by the Institute of Industrial Reconstruction which is a government agency. Although RAI enjoys a considerable measure of independence, it is subject to obligations and inspections by the state. The Board of Management and the Board of Auditors have government members.

In Sweden, programming rights are vested since 1925 solely in a company known as Sveriges Radio. The state owns the transmitting network and is responsible for its maintenance and operation. The programme company is privately owned; the state has no financial interest in it. Two-fifths of the shares are held by the Press, another two-fifths by large national organisations and popular movements and one-fifth by business and industrial interests. The government, however, reserves the right to appoint the Chairman and one half of the members of the Board of Governors; the other half being elected by the shareholders.

In the other category are public corporations constituted by Royal Charter of Statute. They are run independently by a body specifically set up for the purpose and are largely independent of government financially. All governments, however, retain overriding control by prescribing regulations under which the corporations must operate and also have discretion to alter the regulations from time to time. Theoretically the supervisory powers vested in the governments are extensive but in practice they are invoked only if the corporations tend to behave in an irresponsible manner or offend against the public interest.

Unlike privately owned corporations, they are not actuated by the profit motive. They are under an obligation to utilise their income to promote denned objectives. The best known examples of this type of broadcasting organisation are the corporations and commissions in the United Kingdom, Canada, Japan, Australia, France and West Germany.

We reproduce below an extract from the Beveridge Report on Broadcasting in the United Kingdom as an example to show how autonomy has been reconciled with control:

The formal power of the government over the British Broadcasting Corporation is absolute. The Governors who constitute the Corporation can be removed at any time by order in Council and can be replaced by others. The licence can be revoked by the Postmaster General, if at any time the Corporation in his opinion is failing in its duties. The Postmaster General can veto any proposed broadcast or class of broadcast, and in doing so can require the Corporation to refrain from announcing that a veto has been imposed. Any government department can require the Corporation to broadcast any announcement or other matter desired by it.

In practice it has become the agreed policy of successive governments, accepted by Parliament, that the Corporation should be independent of the government in the day-to-day conduct of its business, including both the making of programmes for broadcasting and general administration.

We now discuss the suitability or otherwise of the two forms we have outlined. On many consideration we are not attracted to the idea of entrusting radio and television to commercial interests. First, there is the consideration that no commercial interest would be able to undertake the enormous capital outlay involved in setting up a radio and television organisation, unless it were given unfettered discretion to earn revenue from advertisements. They might not also provide requisite time and resources for programmes of educative value, and indulge in sensationalism, sacrificing objectivity and integrity in presenting news. We must, therefore, turn our face against this form of organisation.

The most important consideration on which we have rejected this form, however, is that radio and television have a purposeful role to fulfil in our developing economy. They have to mobilise public opinion to support the plans of development, they have to educate and inform the people and strive to better their social and economic life. That should be the major role and purpose of radio and television in India.

Several witnesses including some Union and state ministers and officials were in favour of allowing private stations to operate side by side with the national network. They felt that the national network should be supplemented by private endeavour to meet the requirements of the local communities. They also felt that independent private stations would be able to provide programmes which would give greater satisfaction to the listening public. This in our view is a danger. It may lead to a lowering of standards. We, therefore, are unable to subscribe to this view and would retain for the national network a monopoly in the field of broadcasting.

*Need for an Autonomous Public Corporation:* We are also averse to the system in which these two media are used primarily for purposes of propagating a particular ideology and regimentation of its citizens. We are thus left with the only alternative of entrusting the broadcasting services to an autonomous corporation set up by statute which would clearly define the authority and control which government would exercise over its activities. We found overwhelming support for this idea from the officials of AIR, distinguished witnesses whose advice we sought and from others who either sent in written memoranda or gave evidence in addition. The Press also largely supported the transformation of AIR into a Corporation.

There are other valid considerations which influence us in making this recommendation. AIR must not be considered by the people as an instrument of the government of the day as it is widely regarded today. If its organisation were to be made autonomous and its programmes based on the concept of social responsibility, its value and effectiveness would be considerably enhanced. It would create public confidence and lead to the acceptance of its programmes as objective and unbiased and consequently their impact would be far greater.

**Political Consideration**

There is also a political consideration which cannot be lightly dismissed, more so in a federal state. If some of the states come to be controlled by parties other than the one in power at he Centre, AIR would be exposed to stresses and strains which are best avoided.

We now turn to the nature of the Corporation we recommend. The Corporation should be set up by an Act of Parliament in which its objectives should also be clearly defined and be free of ambiguity. The right to require the Corporation to broadcast certain programmes as also the right to veto broadcasts in certain subjects may be reserved to government. It must be understood that such powers must be sparingly used and only when the national interest so demands. These reservations would automatically define the accountability of the minister to Parliament. We also consider that the Act itself should lay down the authority and powers of the Governors to prevent possible encroachment.

*The Board of Governors:* The constitution and composition of the governing body are all-important. The Chairman of the Corporation should be a *public figure* with a national reputation for his integrity, ability and independence. The members, the number of whom we consider should not exceed seven, should similarly be drawn from diverse fields of national life, each enjoying a reputation in his particular field.

One of the complaints in the functioning of autonomous corporations, here as elsewhere, had been that the ministers are able to influence their policies without issuing directives, thus escaping parliamentary accountability. This position can be safeguarded only when the composition of the Board is such that it will not be amenable to undue and unreasonable pressure.

The people who constitute the Board must understand fully the purposes of broadcasting and see that they are fulfilled. They must also take note of public opinion and ensure that the programmes respond to it.

Various suggestions for ensuring independence have been made. One is that appointments should be made by the President, the other that they should be made by him on the recommendation of the Chief Justice, a third is that public organisations and associations with related activities should each submit a panel and selections should be confined to the names included.

We do not favour any of these suggestions. A responsible government is expected to function in a responsible way and we would much rather leave selections to government indicating only the broad principles to be observed. Secondly, experience has shown that once selected to such autonomous bodies people act independently and do not sacrifice the interest of the organisation to outside pressure.

It now remains to consider whether members of Parliament and service personnel should be categories specifically excluded as suggested by some. We are against such a blanket ban and would not demur if, by reason of eminence and specialisation, one or two were drawn from these sources.

The term of office of the Chairman and Governors should, we feel, be six years and it should be provided mat for the sake of continuity two members should retire every other year in rotation.

The Director-General: The selection of the Director General requires equally careful consideration. As Chief Executive, on him will devolve the responsibility for maintaining objectivity, ensuring efficiency and economy and building up an attractive image of the organisation. He has undoubtedly to be a person with a dynamic personality endowed with drive, imagination and initiative, capable of creating a well knit team of devoted workers and giving it resolute leadership. It is difficult anywhere to find one with all these attributes.

It will be more so in India, particularly if according to present practice the selection is confined to government servants. The net will have to be cast much wider. It may even become necessary to persuade an outstanding personality in the fields of journalism, advertising, the film industry and the academic world to accept this assignment in a spirit of dedication and service. If a civil servant is selected by the Board of Governors, there should be a stipulation, as in the case of the Reserve Bank, that he should resign from service.

The question of the status of the Director General was also mooted by some, it being suggested that in a protocol-ridden society it is important that the Director General should be accorded a high rank commensurate with his responsibilities. We, however, do not attach importance to mis suggestion. The status of the Board and its Chief Executive would automatically come to be determined by the place the organisation comes to occupy in our national life and the public esteem it is able to command by its independence, integrity and excellence.

Though the details of the organisation and the rules or business should be drawn up by the Board, we should suggest certain broad principles so mat in inheriting the organisation it does not inherit the deficiencies.

Even at the risk of being repetitive, we should stress once again the need for decentralisation of authority and functions. This is necessary in the interests of efficiency in any organisation, it is more so in a broadcasting organisation. For example, in a country so vast as ours with a multiplicity of languages and cultural patterns and with, regions in different stages of development, central control of programme planning and the imposition of uniformity in their contents and presentation would not only be inappropriate but would defeat the basic purposes of the broadcasting system. We would, therefore, give the Station Directors complete freedom in the matter and subject them only to policy directions as to the types of broadcasts which should be discouraged.

We do not suggest that this decentralisation should be absolute. It should be obligatory to relay the national news bulletins and other national programmes of interest. It is necessary though that determination of themes of broadcasts as national should be made with circumspection and discretion.

Another way to achieve decentralisation is to have several channels of broadcasting, one of which would provide the national programme, the other regional programmes and the third a local service on local transmitters which we have recommended earlier. The only practical way as we have stressed, is through such local stations.

The establishment of competitive channel of broadcasting was advocated by several witnesses. They argued that a monopolist enterprise tends to become complacent, stale and ineffective. It needs the stimulus of competition to make its staff more alert and enterprising and the programmes more lively. It was said that the establishment of the Independent Television Authority in Britain had a tonic effect on the BBC's TV Services.

We have considered this question carefully. We have come to the conclusion that having regard to the availability of resources both in manpower and in funds, and the role we envisage for broadcasting, we should not at this stage bring in considerations which might well come in the way of the development of radio.

We should, however, encourage universities to instal closed circuit radio and television services, or the state governments and major municipal corporations to set up local transmitters for agricultural, social and educational purposes to meet the needs of local communities which cannot be effectively served by the national network.

*Finance:* It is necessary to consider how the Corporation we have proposed should be financed. The question falls into two parts: capital expenditure to add to the network by installing additional transmitters, studios and other equipment; revenue expenditure for sustaining and improving the service.

We now turn to the question how future capital expenditure should be financed and how best the revenue of AIR should be augmented. In the case of state enterprises, government have provided both equity capital and loans to maintain a proper ratio between the two. While interest is chargeable on the loan (there has been a period of moratorium in many cases), the return on equity investment depends on the profits, if any earned. This is the policy adopted in the case of commercial activities. Similarly, government meet the capital expenditure on welfare measures, on education, health and activities necessary to increase agricultural production.

Broadcasting is not a commercial activity, though a monopoly, it cannot, unlike other monopolies, adjust prices, rates and fees to meet interest liability on capital expended. On all considerations and having regard to its primary role as a medium of education and information, we consider that capital expenditure is a legitimate charge on public revenues.

We propose, therefore, that the assets of AIR should be transferred to the Corporation without any interest or any other financial liability. Similarly, the allocation in the Fourth Plan should be made available to the Corporation free of charge. We consider that thereafter the proposals we make on revenue account, would make the Corporation fully viable, able to expand with its own resources taking resource to borrowing, if necessary, on its own financial standing.

We have one important observation to make in regard to capital expenditure. We find that organisationally AIR is geared to an expenditure of about Rs 2 crores a year. To enlarge its spending capacity efficiently, it would be necessary to bring about a reorganisation and the sooner it is undertaken the better it would be. The allocation in the Fourth Plan is bound to be larger and we have recommended certain priorities for providing local transmitters and the reorientation of the external services.

To fulfil this plan, AIR needs organisation and effort which should be preplanned.

*Licence Fees:* There has been a suggestion that licence fees should be discontinued. We do not accept this suggestion. It would be unfair to burden the community at large to support a service when the beneficiaries are small in number. The fee should continue to be recovered from users of the service. (Licence fee has since been abolished).

We consider that considerable improvement in the recovery of licence fees is possible. It is common knowledge that a number of sets in the country are unlicensed; some suggest that it is as high as sixty per cent.

*Advertising:* The steps we have recommended would give elbow room to AIR but would not make it fully viable nor enable it to finance.

By far the most fruitful source of additional revenue would be the acceptance of advertisement in programmes. In dealing with Television we have marshalled the arguments in favour of its acceptance with certain safeguards and restrictions. We do not feel that there are any special considerations which would justify making a distinction on this question between television and sound broadcasting. Consistent with our thinking on this subject, we would limit advertisements to the Vividh Bharati channel alone. By timing the spot advertisements suitably there need be no interference with a programme or its continuity. Vividh Bharati is a light programme predominantly of film music and the inclusion of advertisements is not likely to infringe on its quality or appeal.

***Television Organisation :*** Television is a comparatively new medium far more sophisticated than radio. There are basic differences between radio and television in important matters of technique and financing of operators and planning and execution of programmes. Television also presents other problems infinitely more complicated.

Even so, many countries with well-established broadcasting systems found it convenient to entrust the development of television to their existing organisations. This arrangement soon proved to be little more than a marriage of convenience. The rapid growth of television, the remarkable advances in its technology and programme planning, and its versatility in use, brought new responsibilities which could be hardly fulfilled within the resources of existing organisations. This difficulty has been sought to be met by investing the television wing with virtual autonomy. In the United Kingdom, the Union of Soviet Socialist Republics and in Italy, the television centre has now become a distinct, separate and powerful entity with tenuous links with the parent organisation.

In the light of these developments, it has to be considered whether it will be possible or wise to place television under the aegis of AIR. This possibility has to be ruled out as AIR is not organisationally and financially equipped to shoulder this responsibility. It would also be unfair to tag on television to AIR and expose it at its birth to prejudices which exist against AIR. On all these considerations, we would strongly advise against the development and management of this new medium, requiring a dynamic and imaginative approach and ample resources, being linked as an ancillary to an organisation which itself needs a major overhaul and refurbishing.

The question still remains whether the new organisation should follow the pattern of AIR and become an attached office of a ministry or whether it should be made an autonomous corporation, created by a special statute of Parliament. Having carefully considered the question in all its aspects, we have come to the conclusion that to develop on correct lines television must not be hampered by the limitations of a department; it should have a broader outlook, greater flexibility and freedom of action which the corporate form alone can give.

While discussing the future organisation of AIR we have already stated in detail the reasons for our recommendation that an autonomous statutory corporation would be the best form of organisation for providing a broadcasting service. These consideration apply with equal, if not greater force, in case of television.

We consider that to give shape to our recommendations immediate steps should be taken to invite a competent agency to prepare the project report. An officer of the status of a Chief Engineer, should be associated with their team in its preparatory work, who could later be selected to head the technical wing.

To ensure that the two processes of project study and operation planning go hand in hand, it would be necessary to form the Television Corporation with the nucleus of staff necessary to access the ultimate requirements of staff, organise training, draw up the programme policy and prepare an estimate of the finances required. It should also initiate negotiations with potential collaborators but keep government closely informed of developments. The agreements reached should naturally be subject to government approval.

We have already given our views on the staffing of AIR and suggested reorganisation. The staffing pattern and employment policy of the Television Corporation we propose will have to be differently conceived and designed.

As mentioned earlier, television is basically a different medium from radio and cannot be given the same treatment. Being, however, a part of AIR, the Delhi Television Centre has unfortunately the same organisation as a radio unit and has developed unsuitable trends and nuances. For one thing, it has tended to become a top-heavy organisation in which the more expensive technical staff was until recently being incorrectly employed; for another, its programmes being produced on the basis of radio techniques and experience, are indifferent and even colourless. It is essential that the two activities should be separated at the large scale inception of television, to give it a fair wind.

We are in agreement with our Consultant mat 'television needs a lively, decisive, imaginative, adventurous yet responsible staff. This implies that its control and operations should be in the hands of those who have these attributes.

Taking a look at the Delhi Centre, the first point that struck us was the strength of the staff deployed for its limited output. It appeared that there had not been a proper assessment of the staff required in different categories and that as problems arose they were sought to be met by hurriedly transferring whoever was conveniently available in the radio wing. As a consequence of this haphazard and irrational staffing, the sanctioned strength has been raised to 271 to allow for the recent extension of the service.

The Centre provides a one-hour evening programnme of news and entertainment of which only about a third is produced at the Centre itself, the rest being films or recorded material obtained locally or from abroad. It also provides three twenty-minute school lessons a day for six days a week for each of the two shifts in the schools, giving a total broadcast time of about 120 minutes a day. But of these lessons one or two a week are repetitions of old lessons already recorded and telecast, thus reducing the output of the studio to about eight hours a week.

In the opinion of our Consultant, the Centre is grossly overstaffed. Our Sub-Committee concurs in this assessment on the basis of its study abroad. 'Telescuola' in Italy, running school and adult literacy programmes, is on the air for 41-1 /2 hours a week but it employs a total of 128 people only including 27 technicians and 16 teachers, e.g. Admittedly, its telecasts do not require certain categories of staff which an inclusive service of information, education and entertainment would need, but even so the contrast is striking.

Our Consultant also informed us that a firm International Television Consultants had recommended a total staff of approximately 50 for certain African countries embarking on television with a daily programme output of four hours. Similarly, a UNESCO Mission, which advised Israel on the introduction of television, recommended a total staff of 226 distributed between the three organisations of the Central Administration (the equivalent of the directorategeneral of AIR), the Jerusalem and the Tel Aviv Studio Centres. This requirement was based on a suggested output of 23 hours of programmes a week of which over 12 hours were to originate in the two Studio Centres.

The second point that struck us was that at its inception the Television Centre was manned largely if not entirely by people drawn from sound broadcasting without a mature consideration whether this arrangement was suitable either for the installation or the development of this medium.

Training is essential for the success of all human endeavour. The more difficult the objective, the greater is the need for training for its attainment. Yet the necessity of advance training of the required number of people in the difficult and varied techniques of television had been ignored before the Delhi pilot project was launched in 1959.

It was only after six years, in 1965, that a producer was obtained on loan from the BBC to give a course of training to a small number of selected production staff. We consider that this is totally inadequate even to sustain the extended programmes of the Centre and to improve their quality, leave alone to handle the expansion we recommend.

We have earlier mentioned that the installation of a television network needs massive financial outlay, a large part of it in foreign exchange. On both these counts, some acceptable form of foreign collaboration will have to be considered. Financing of the television service is another matter; it needs a different treatment.

Because of the low priority given to broadcasting, the allocation of Plan resources has so far been minuscule. We have already adduced many considerations why television should receive equal priority with industrial and agricultural schemes of development. Even so, the competing demands of other nation-building activities might make it difficult to allocate to television all the money it needs for developing a country-wide network by the end of the Fifth Plan. We have perforce to consider alternatives which would ensure adequate financial support.

We have made as detailed a study as is possible, in the absence of complete documentation, of developments elsewhere and the manner in which countries similarly situated have set about to bring the benefits of television to their people.

Foreign collaboration in two different forms has been adopted to cover fully the foreign exchange component of the project for the supply of capital goods such as transmitters, studio equipment, installation of links and other ancillary facilities. It has either taken the shape of participation in the equity issue of the corporation or it has been a straight loan with a period of moratorium before repayment commences. Some countries have adopted the former method in which a consortium of industrialists has a minority financial interest, the controlling interest being retained by government. Some others have preferred the latter method but have not encountered any lack of response because of this choice. We also consider that we must not have any foreign equity participation in the proposed Television Corporation. It is needles to add that the provision of a loan must not give any voice to the donors in deciding the policy of the Corporation.

In addition, it has been arranged either separately or as a part of the same scheme that the foreign exchange requirements of manufacturing television sets and the essential equipment would be provided by the foreign associates, the inducement being that they would themselves supply the television sets until, manufacture has been established but without an appreciable outflow of foreign exchange.

It is found impractical for a single county to provide the required financial support, the formation of a consortium might become necessary. The idea of forming a consortium has caught on even in the matter of international aid to developing countries. It should not, therefore, be difficult to bring about the formation of a consortium to assist our project should this become necessary.

We contemplate a package deal in which the collaborator would also accept responsibility for the manufacture of television sets and other equipment. It may be necessary to set up a separate manufacturing unit.

The willingness to collaborate with technical assistance and a loan will naturally depend on the viability of the project and its ability to generate enough resources to be able to repay the loan in agreed instalments. Under the plan we later discuss, we have no doubts that the revenues of the Corporation will be ample to meet all its commitments. We are confident that foreign collaborator would feel equally reassured.

The question will still remain how the rupee finance of the project can best be found. The allocation of a high priority for television together with the realisation that the acceptance of the plan we later unfold would make television a viable and even a productive venture should make it possible for the Planning Commission to release necessary resources. The expectation that television would become self-financing within a short time, if not at its inception, and that it would not, therefore, make annual demands for its running expenses should be a weighty consideration in the allocation of resources. It would imply that the initial investment needed would be little more than a capitalisation of a few years recurring expenses, provision for which would have to be made otherwise, being inherent in the acceptance of a television scheme, however, unambitious it may be.

There is another aspect developed earlier, that is the extensive use of television for educational, agriculture, health and other socioeconomic purposes. On a long term view, it may be found more economical, yet more effective to invest in television than, for example, to build schools for which teacher cannot be found, or equipment provided, or build health centres which can only be manned by indifferent and unimaginative people. Similarly, recurring expenditure on publicity to give an impetus to programmes for self-sufficiency in the production of foodgrains and other expenditure now incurred for popularising the introduction of improved strains of seeds, the use of fertilisers and pesticides, the rotation of crops, etc., could be considerably minimised by visual presentation which television alone can provide.

These savings would be a recurring annual feature and should give welcome relief to the budgets of these departments. Once mis important aspect of television is realised, there should be no difficulty in either increasing the allocation for television by corresponding reduction in the capital budgets of the ministries concerned; alternatively, they should invest a part, albeit a small part, of their capital grants in building up a countrywide television network. A small advisory body of the participants in programme planning should ensure the allocation of adequate time to each.

The cost of operating the network depends on its output, the standard of the producers and artistes it employs, the level of remuneration it pays, and the type and quality of programmes it provides. It must obviously be the aim to give the optimum output within the capability of the network and to plan and produce programmes of the highest quality employing first class artistes. This implies that there must be resources available for establishing and sustaining a high professional standard comparable to other television services.

The method evolved by the British Broadcasting Corporation, and followed by some other broadcasting systems, is to levy a licence fee from the owners of receiving sets and to allocate the proceeds, after deducting the cost of collection, to broadcasting. The yield is thus directly related to the number of receiving sets held and licensed. The limitation of this arrangement is that the rate of levy cannot be easily adjusted to accord with the needs of the service. There are many factors including public resistance which have to be taken into account in a revision of the fee.

When the British Broadcasting Corporation entered the field of television, a separate and higher scale of levy was designed to finance its programmes and other operating costs. This levy has been adjusted upwards from time to time to sustain an expansion of programmes, to improve their quality and to neutralise rising costs. The public had gone along with these increases. More recently an Independent Television Authority was created by statute and was given freedom to run its services with advertising revenues without sharing with the British Broadcasting Corroboration the licence fees collected. This brought a new concept of financing television in tradition-bound and conventional Britain.

The programmes controlled by the Independent Television Authority not only proved attractive but were made available without any payment by the viewing audiences. We shall refer to the ITA later in the narration but mention it at this stage because of its indirect impact on the recent demand of the British Broadcasting Corporation for a substantial increase in licence fees both for existing services and for opening up a fourth channel which has become available. Government considered the increase demanded unreasonable and also unfair to licence-holders and conceded a smaller increase. This has left the British Broadcasting Corporation in a quandary.

It has to be appreciated that in a country like India the licence fees have to be kept reasonably low to accord with the people's capacity to pay. On the one hand, the number of sets in private hands in the initial stages will be small and the yield of licence fees negligible, on the other, there will be the need for a wide network to bring the social programmes within the reach of the community which needs them most. It will thus become necessary to accept commercial advertisements to supplement the revenue derived from licence fees.

We are aware of the opinion which still persists against the acceptance of commercial broadcasts. There is the apprehension that were commercial advertisements to be accepted television would become largely dependent on revenues derived from commercial interests and this might well lead to the political, economic and social policies of the organisation being influenced and even indirectly controlled by these interests. There is also the apprehension that the advertisements to have a popular appeal, might tend to become somewhat vulgar and demoralising.

Experience elsewhere has shown that the acceptance of advertisements to accord with the programme policy of a television organisation does not bring it even remotely under the control of commercial interests nor does it lead to the presentation of material which is in questionable taste.

It is necessary to review in a brief compass, the policy adopted by different organisations, discussing later their merits and demerits. In the United States of America and Latin American countries as also in Iran, Lebanon, Thailand and the Philippines, television is in the hands of private interests who finance their operations, including the setting up and expansion of their existing networks, from revenues derived entirely from the sale of time to advertisers. In the United States of America and most of these countries, the advertisers not only buy time but also provide programmes of their choice which go with the advertisements.

In Australia, Japan and Canada this system has been adopted by a number of comparatively small television stations which operate in competition with the national organisations which are maintained out of licence revenues. The acceptance of commercial programmes, known as 'sponsored programme' has resulted in the largest and most prosperous television network in the world being built up in the United States of America and it has also given impetus to the growth of television in the countries mentioned and in Latin America and some countries of Asia. The major undesirable feature of this system is that the television organisation has very little control over the programmes put on the air with the result that they are often in questionable taste and have a demoralising effect on impressionable and immature minds. It has been suggested that the increase in the rate of child delinquency in the United States of America is attributable to these programmes.

Benefiting by the experience of the United States of America, countries which entered the television field later, more particularly the European countries, evolved a new system. While accepting commercial advertisements as inescapable for supporting the growth of a sound television system and also the U.S. practice of selling time, they safeguarded the quality and standard to the programmes by refusing to allow the advertisers to produce them or even to have a say in the programmes which would include their advertisement material. By this method commonly known as 'spot advertising' or 'spot announcements', the organisations retained full control over their programme policy. An additional safeguard was also introduced, by stature where necessary, but mainly by a code of conduct voluntarily agreed upon by the organisations and the advertisers, to control the make-up of the advertisements. Italy went a step further and set up a corporation to handle and produce all advertisement shots.

Television stations in West Germany, Ireland, Italy, Spain, the United Arab Republic, Iraq, Pakistan, to mention a few countries, have adopted this system of spot advertising to raise resources to supplement revenues from licence fees. Some countries such as Italy and West Germany have introduced the practice of presenting in a single special programme all advertisements within an allocated period of time, usually 20 to 30 minutes, at an excellent viewing hour, between eight and nine o'clock in the evening. Other countries intersperse the spots, not exceeding five or six minutes in an hour, in their daily programmes.

It is necessary to discuss the two practices, their merits and demerits and their revenue potential. The practice of concentrating all advertisements in one programme has two attractive features: First, it enables the viewers who are not interested in commercials to switch off at the hour when they are on the air; secondly, by not breaking into a programme, it preserves the continuity and entertainment value of the programme and also the atmosphere it creates. The advertisers, however, do not consider this method as attractive as spots in regular programmes. They also consider that a spot should be repeated in a number of programmes in any one day to have worthwhile advertisement value.

The latter practice has undoubtedly greater advertisement value, as it provides a captive audience and a repeated presentation of the same spots in different programmes at different viewing hours. The irritation caused by the spots breaking into a programme has been sought to be removed by putting the advertisements at the beginning, the intermission and the end of the programmes. This is an improvement from the viewers point and meets the advertisers' demands to a certain extent. The revenue potential of this practice is undoubtedly greater.

We have very carefully considered which of the two systems, the U.S. one of sponsored programnmes or the European one of spot advertisement to recommend, or whether a combination of the two would be more suitable. We do not feel that one need be squeamish about sponsored programmes as such so long as they have an educative and cultural value and do not include any advertisement material except to mention at their commencement or conclusion that they were presented by the courtesy of so and so (naming the sponsors). Such programmes do not have the connotation or implications of sponsored programmes in the United States of America and should even be welcome as being useful and valuable additions to the repertoire of the television organisation. Such programmes are not uncommon elsewhere and have been viewed and appreciated by some of us abroad. These 'prestige' programmes are presented by sponsors who are inspired to contribute to the growth of the television system and incidentally bring their names and contributions to the notice of the viewing public. However, the revenues from this type of sponsored programmes will not be substantial but that should be no reason for excluding them.

The acceptance of advertisements should be considered only if it brings significant financial support to the growth of television. There is nothing non-ethical in accepting advertisements prepared in good taste provided that they do not affect the quality of the telecasts or make excessive demands. If the educational, social and children's programmes do not carry spots and they are confined to the entertainment programmes, there should not be any objection in adopting a practice which has now become more or less universal.

***Verghese Committee :*** A 12-Member Working Group headed by B.G. Verghese was set up on August 17, 1977, to go into the working of AIR and Doordarshan and suggest changes. The following were the other members of mis Group: V.G. Rajadhyaksha, Dr. Malcolm S. Adiseshiah, Chanchal Sarkar, P.L. Deshpande, Umashankar Joshi, A.G. Noorani, G.R. Subramanian, Mrs. Nayantara Sehgal and Dr. Ishwar Das (Member Secretary).

The group made wide-ranging recommendations to transform All-India Radio and Television into a more responsive organisation from a mere government department.

The two-volume report running into 405 pages was presented to Parliament on March 9, 1978. In its unanimous report, the working group suggested that the national broadcasting services should be vested exclusively in an independent impartial and autonomous organization established by law to act as a trustee for the national interest.

The legal framework of the autonomous national trust, as envisaged by the working group, was that the establishment of the corporation should not await a constitutional amendment. The law establishing the corporation could be enacted and the organisation brought into being to be followed subsequently by an amendment of the Constitution.

The autonomy of the corporation and its independence from government control should be entrenched in the Constitution itself and the idea of a trust woven into it.

In making recommendations, the working group was guided by a factor that mass media, radio and television must fit into a wider perspective of national communication policy or philosophy.

It rejected a proposal to create two separate corporations for All-India Radio and Television. However, it conceded the need to recognize the distinctive identity of radio and television within the ambit of a new integrated structure.

The group also did not favour the creation of autonomous regional corporations or even a federation of State Government corporations.

While rejecting the proposal to create two separate corporations or set up autonomous regional corporations, the working group argued that there would be a large measure of power delegated to the regional and local level.

This was kept to the fore so that the organisation enjoyed the advantages of quick decision making, sensitivity to local problems and tasks, and close linkages with various governments and institutions.

In recommending the new set-up, the working group did not apparently follow any model operating in any other country.

At the apex of NBT, the working group suggested a board of trustees consisting of 12 persons, and not exceeding 21 persons. The trustees would be guardians of the charter given to the NBT by statute.

The Controller-General of Broadcasting (CGB), heading the central executive board, was conceived by the working group as a link between the trustees and the entire broadcasting organisation. He would be ex-officio secretary to the board of trustees so as to provide an organic link between these two tiers.

Apart from the Chairman, the board of trustees would have three other full-time members to devote themselves to the fields of current affairs, extension and culture. They will operate through the CGB.

In addition to the Chairman and the three full-time trustees, the board would have two part-time trustees—one highly experienced in the field of finance and management and the other an eminent scientist or engineer familiar with the technology of broadcasting.

For the first time in the history of over half-a-century of broadcasting in India, there would be a complaints board comprising persons selected by the Chief Justice of India.

The recommendation of the working group for constituting a complaint board assumed significance in the light of the experience gained during the Emergency when the broadcasting system was blatantly used by the previous regime to further partisan ends.

***Board of Trustees :*** According to the report, the board of trustees would be responsible to Parliament through its budget and an annual report. Together with accounts and auditor's comments, reports of the complaints board, among other things, would also figure in the annual report.

The complaints board would deal with complaints from the public relating to charges of unjust or unfair treatment including unwarranted invasion of privacy and misrepresentation, provided the right of resources to court was waived. The findings should be published by NBT in the programme 'Journal' and broadcast in special programmes..

In order to ensure the independence of the proposed NBT, the report recommended that the trustees, with six-year terms of office, would be appointed by the President on the recommendation of the Prime Minister from a list of names forwarded to him by a nominating panel.

The nominating panel for trustees would consist of the Chief Justice of India, the Lokpal and the Chairman of the UPSC. It would be a healthy convention if the Prime Minister consulted the leader of the Opposition before submitting the list of names to the President.

The trustees would enjoy the status of Supreme Court judges.

***Financial Autonomy :*** In regard to financial autonomy, the report recommended several measures. Initially, the government should make up the revenue deficit for a period of five years, after transferring the existing assets of All-India Radio and TV.

Later, NBT should be expected to stand on its own feet or raise additional resources by charging for broadcast time, made available by it to various users, including the Central and state governments.

It also felt that the Trust should undertake a comprehensive review of commercial broadcasting rates and procedures. The group also recommended an increase in broadcast receiver licences for certain categories of radio and TV sets.

The report comprehensively surveyed the entire scene of broadcasting and television network since the Chanda Committee submitted its report on radio more than 12 years ago. The Chanda Committee had also recommended an autonomous set-up for AIR.

According to the report, there were now some 20 million radio receivers and 600,000 TV sets. 'With population rising to say, 950 million by 2000 AD and 'an end to destitution' and fuller employment, at least 80 to 90 per cent of all households should possess radios,' the report added.

In a perspective study for 2000 AD there would be 160 to 180 million radio sets and between 12 to 15 million TV sets by the turn of the century.

In the opinion of the working group, AIR and TV combined in themselves the characteristics of the marketplace, newspaper, university, national extension agency and cultural academy. As such a unique institution must enjoy a unique autonomy.

The report called upon the National Broadcast Trust to bridge the urban-rural divide and combine modernity with relevant tradition.

It recommended the establishment of a strong audience research division. It noted that the audience research unit had a very limited staff and budget. It was, therefore, impossible to conduct any regular audience surveys or to operate on more than very small samples.

The audience research reports should be made available simultaneously and directly to the board of trustees, since these reports would constitute one of the most important antenna of the broadcasting organisation.

## Prasar Bharati Bill

The Prasar Bharati Bill was introduced in the Lok Sabha on December 30, 1989, by the National Front Government led by V.P. Singh. The purpose of this Bill was to grant autonomy to the electronic media, that is AIR and Doordarshan.

The Lok Sabha passed the Bill on August 30, 1990 and the Rajya Sabha approved it on September 6, 1990. The President accorded assent to the Bill soon after.

The changes in the original Bill ran as follows:

The autonomous Prasar Bharati or Broadcasting Corporation of India will be directly answerable to three authorities—a Parliamentary Committee, the Central Government and the proposed Broadcasting Council.

The original draft of the Prasar Bharati Bill introduced in the Lok Sabha did not contain any provision for the Parliamentary Committee. The government inserted this provision on August 29,1990, as one of the 65 amendments proposed by an all-party consensus. Members of the committee will be elected by proportional representation and will ensure that the Corporation functions in the manner set out in the Bill.

There was no opposition in Parliament to this particular provision as it was only intended to make the autonomous body accountable. Besides being answerable to the Committee, the corporation has to submit annual reports of its activities to Parliament.

The powers envisaged for the Central government, however, have given rise to immense misgivings. The initial draft said the Central government could give directions to make or not to make a certain broadcast only when 'the security of the state or preservation of public order' was at stake. But the August 29 changes widened the ambit by saying that the Central government can also issue directions 'in the interest of sovereignty, unity and integrity of India'. These concepts are very subjective and have been left undefined, tremendously increasing the scope for abuse of power.

Further, the Central government has been empowered to demand any information from the corporation. This means, for instance, that it can order Doordarshan to divulge the source of a news report. If the corporation 'persistently' refuses to comply with any direction, the Central government has been empowered to recommend to Parliament any action, including supersession of the Prasar Bharati Board. The government's recommendation has been given such weight that a ratification by a simple majority will be enough to supersede the board.

The only constraint is that the President, before issuing the notification of supersession, will have to give 'a reasonable opportunity to the board to show cause as to why it should not be superseded'.

The maximum permissible period of supersession is six months. The powers and functions of the board during that period will be discharged by 'such person or persons as the President may direct.'

The third authority which will be vested with some power over the corporation is the Broadcasting Council, which corresponds to the Press Council. The original draft of the Bill, envisaged as a watchdog to protect the interests of the citizens, empowered the Broadcasting Council to decide complaints against the corporation and recommend appropriate remedial action to it. What happens when the corporation rejects the Broadcasting Council's recommendation? An amendment provides for such a contingency: The Broadcasting Council will have the authority to force the corporation to broadcast the recommendation. This, in fact, is the only form of vindication the Bill offers to a citizen aggrieved by the corporation.

If Doordarshan or Akashvani, after they are unfettered, broadcast a programme or news report defamatory to somebody, he cannot sue or initiate criminal proceedings against the corporation or anybody in it. This is due to a clause granting immunity against all legal action to the corporation and its employees.

Thus, on the one hand, the proposed corporation is sought to be given the freedom enjoyed by newspapers, on the other, the producers and reporters in the broadcasting field will not be liable for their mistakes as their counterparts in the print media.

The relevant section (24) in the initial draft grants the legal immunity 'for anything which is in good faith done or intended to be done in pursuance of this act or of any rules or regulations made thereunder.' The language is general enough to enable anybody in the corporation to take refuge under this clause for any error committed by him. Yet this section has surprisingly managed to survive the radical amendments made in the Lok Sabha to the original draft.

The Prasar Bharati Board which forms the core of the legislation has also undergone many changes. In the first place, its name was 'Board of Governors'. But the high sounding 'governor' has been replaced by the simple 'member'. The strength of the board has been increased by the inclusion of two ex-officio members—the Director-General of Akashvani and Doordarshan and two elected members from among the employees of the Corporation. The whole-time chairman has been made a part-time one.

All the whole-time members of the board have been made employees of the Corporation.

Among other amendments are: the inclusion of four MPs (two from each House) in the Broadcasting Council, the stipulation on the Broadcasting Council present an annual report to Parliament, deletion of the power to dismiss an employee without being given an opportunity to defend himself and the bar on the Corporation from ceiling its assets.

The Verghese Committee which also advocated autonomy to the electronic media wanted the Ministry of Information and Broadcasting to shed its control over Broadcasting. But the Prasar Bharati Bill puts a representative of the Ministry on the Board of the Corporation.

The most controversial clause as stated earlier is Parliament's power to supersede the Prasar Bharati Board.

In the original version of the bill, this power was sought to be vested in the government.

The present dispensation is an improvement but the effect is the same to ensure that the Prasar Bharati behaves. BJP leader, L.K. Advani sought to soften the blow by suggesting during the discussion of the Bill, an amendment that would have required any resolution on supersession to be passed by two-thirds majority instead of a simple majority. But surprisingly except for one member, nobody supported his suggestion. Strangely, the CPI(M) appeared particularly averse to Mr. Advani's plea.

Voting in Parliament is on strictly party lines and it is unimaginable that if an official resolution is moved for supersession of board of governors, the ruling party members would vote against the resolution.

The official justification for such sweeping Parliamentary control is that if the Prasar Bharati were to be left completely to its devices there was a danger of its being taken over by big business. According to P. Upendra, all autonomous corporations are accountable to Parliament and their functioning is supervised by the Committee on Public Undertakings. This according to him, has not led to interference in their day-to-day affairs, so why should there be fears about such interference in the case of Prasar Bharati.

The fact is that no political party, especially the Left and the Congress wanted an absolutely free Prasar Bharati. They wanted to avoid a situation when the corporation could go 'amuck' in the name of autonomy.

The Congress party also opposed the decision to transfer the assets of AIR and Doordarshan to Prasar Bharati. It is on the insistence of the Congress party that the Bill was amended to say that the new corporation would use the assets in accordance with the terms and conditions prescribed by the government.

Commenting on the question of how autonomous would be the electronic media under the new set up, B.G. Verghese said that the concept is to de-governmentalise broadcasting, both radio as well as television, by placing it under an autonomous corporation—as against where it is now as a subordinate department of the government. Its autonomy would be safeguarded by two or three things.

One is that, according to the Bill, the corporation's accountability is not to the Information & Broadcasting Ministry, but to Parliament. Secondly, the appointment of its top board will be done by a selection committee consisting of the Chairman of Rajya Sabha, the Chairman of the Press Council and a third member to be selected by the President and their decision will be final. This prevents the body from being packed by government favourites.

The third safeguard is that if these people are to be removed it will have to be by a special procedure which is applicable to the members and chairman of the UPSC. They cannot be sacked. And now, they have also added the clause that if the board collectively misbehaves by persistently defying the government directives, then the ministry can make a report to Parliament in which it could recommend supersession, and following a decision of Parliament, supersession can take place. According to Mr. Verghese, Parliamentary control is unnecessary and he feels that the contingencies in which these powers would be used are extreme. They are theoretically possible but in practical terms, they are unlikely to be used.

According to Mr. Khushwant Singh, the well-known journalist, freeing the electronic media from government control deserves to be applauded as the National Front government's biggest achievement of its nine-month rule. All our past Prime Ministers and Ministers of Information and Broadcasting paid lip-services to the principle of freedom of expression for Press, Radio and Television, but everyone of them meddled with their free functioning when they found themselves at the receiving end of criticism.

Jawaharlal Nehru was no exception. He was riled by what Durga Das (father of Inderjit, Member of the Lok Sabha) wrote about him and did his best to damage his career. His Minister of Information and Broadcasting, Keskar, had Nirad Chaudhuri dismissed from AIR and then blacklisted for eulogising the British in the dedication of his autobiography of an unknown Indian. Keskar had not bothered to read the book.

Mrs. Gandhi had scant respect for Press freedom and blatantly misused Radio and Television to propagate herself and denigrate rivals like Jayaprakash Narayan. She pressurised proprietors of newspapers to remove editors she did not like. Her sycophantic ministers like N.K.P. Salve and H.K.L. Bhagat (Vasant Sathe was one exception) went a step ahead to cancel programmes like 'The World of Nature' which had nothing whatsoever to do with politics for the sole reason that it was written by someone who Mrs. Gandhi regarded as her critic.

It was the same during the short regimes of Morarji Desai and Charan Singh: editors were fired, broadcasters, they did not approve, removed. Blacklists continued to be maintained by AIR and Doordarshan throughout Rajiv Gandhi's tenure as Prime Minister. Who is the Congress (I) to talk about freedom of speech and expression? For Messrs Salve, Bhagat and their likes to extol them is like harlots extolling the virtues of chastity.

It is still not clear how free from political meddling will be the board that will control Radio and Doordarshan. However, a very bold and significant step has been taken. Full credit for this must go to P. Upendra and V.P. Singh.

This is what Mr. Nikhil Chakarvarty, a columnist, said about the electronic media's autonomy. He said there was little consultation even with the media circles before the Bill was drafted, but the criticism was more than negated by two things. First, the speech made by Information and Broadcasting Minister, P. Upendra, while introducing the Bill had a ring of sincerity that reassured many that the present government was earnest about autonomy for the government owned media.

Second, the Minister, on his own, announced that there would be free and wide-ranging national debate on the proposed legislation and the criticisms, suggestions and comments to be made in such discussions would be taken into consideration in amending the bill before it was taken up by Parliament. Not only that, his ministry promoted such discussions all over the country. But after the much publicised computerisation of proposals and suggestions, the amendments which the government announced came as a big shock. These were largely retrogressive.

Meanwhile, the government has been remiss on another count. Upendra had promised that there would be a non-official committee to oversee the functioning of the Akashvani and Doordarshan in the interim period until the proposed Prasar Bharati Corporation took over. It was stated that within a couple of weeks this interim set-up would start functioning. Nothing of this kind happened.

Looking at the amendments so far tabled in the Lok Sabha, I for one cannot be optimistic about our setting up a genuinely autonomous corporation. For instance, there is an amendment seeking to establish a Parliamentary Committee to control the set-up. This sounds very impressive as evidence of democratic control but in practice it would have meant not the autonomy of the media but its domination by the party bosses in Parliament.

Vasant Sathe, one of the more competent among the long line of Information Ministers, has been harping on behalf of the Congress, on the need for functional autonomy instead of a new autonomous set-up as envisaged in the Bill. Functional autonomy would mean that the functionaries of the Radio and Television set-up would be ensured autonomy irrespective of ownership-government or a corporation.

In fact, such functional autonomy would be needed even if and when the Prasar Bharati is set up.

***The Implementation :*** The Prasar Bharati Bill was supported by the Congress under Rajiv Gandhi and received the President's assent on September 12, 1990. The election manifesto of the Congress party issued in April, 1991, contained a pledge to implement the Act. But the Congress government has now developed cold feet towards its implementation.

In March 1992, the Information and Broadcasting Ministry, in a note to Prime Minister P.V. Narasimha Rao, observed that the 'circumstances have changed' since the time when the idea of autonomy to the electronic media was mooted.

The note cites some of the fruits of the government's recent liberalisation policy on media, including the advent of satellite broadcasting, video news cassettes and cable TV networks as evidence of the fact that the government no longer holds a monopoly over the electronic media.

The ministry wanted the Prime Minister to consider whether the notification on Prasar Bharati should be deferred.

The note also sought the Prime Minister's opinion on whether second Doordarshan channels in the four metropolitan cities should be simultaneously leased out to one or more entities who may share time among themselves.

With regard to cable television, the I&B Ministry note solicited the Prime Minister's opinion on whether permission should be given for the cables to operate with or without dish antennae. It has asked whether such permission, if given, should be through a system of licensing, or a mere registration with a local authority would suffice.

***Varadan Committee :*** The government constituted an interdepartmental committee on September 3, 1991, under the Chairmanship of K.A. Varadan, Additional Secretary, Ministry of Information and Broadcasting, to suggest options available for implementation of the scheme for offering broadcasting rights to public corporations. The committee submitted its report in October 1991.

A major recommendation of the Varadan Committee relates to leasing out the second channel of Doordarshan in the four metropolitan cities to suitable licencees. At the same time, additional radio channels including FM stations wherever available, could also be leased out.

The government proposed to set up a Broadcasting Council of India. The Council could, among other things, serve as the agency for redressal of complaints emanating from individuals or institutions in regard to any programme broadcast by a new channel.

The Varadan Committee's Report on leasing out broadcasting rights of Doordarshan and Radio channels has offered a way out to the Congress government dilemma of liberalising the media without upsetting the existing power structure or losing its propaganda advantage.

It has achieved this by watering down and moderating many of the radical reforms that the government had earlier proposed.

The government has refused to give broadcasting rights to individuals and private firms. Instead, it has recommended that the government would lease out parts of Doordarshan's second channel and extra channel of AIR to potential licences.

In addition, the Varadan panel has recommended that the so-called 'public limited companies' to which such broadcasting rights are to be granted are to be decided by a single statutory or autonomous body known as the Broadcasting Council of India.

By adopting a more cautious approach towards privatisation, the Committee has done well to ensure that the autonomy does not mean replacement of state control with market ownership.

In a developing society like India, privatisation would only succeed in promoting elitism and consumerism which could be socially disastrous. It would help prevent perpetuation of monopoly by industrial houses running the newspapers.

Unfortunately, the Varadan Committee does not effectively tackle the two most important questions before it—the threat of foreign TV networks' invasion and the related issue of improving Doordarshans' fallen credibility.

While cognisant of and cautioning against the evil design of media Multinational Corporations (MNCs) which subject newly freed countries to cultural imperialism, the Committee pleads that nothing can be done to stop these transmissions or ban their receptions. The government must establish some kind of regulatory mechanism to monitor the programmes being beamed into the country from outside.,

At the same time the government must implement the Prasar Bharati Act at the earliest. It is only by injecting professionalism and credibility into Doordarshan that the government can hope to wean away Indian audiences who are getting hooked to alien broadcasting networks.

# 11

# Freedom of Expression

The expression 'freedom of the Press' as such has not been defined or referred to in the Indian Constitution. However, Article 19(1)(a) of the Constitution dealing with one of the fundamental rights says: "All citizens shall have the right to freedom of speech and expression."

## Constitutional Guarantee

This freedom is referred to in general terms, and includes not only freedom of speech which manifests itself through oral utterance, but also freedom of expression, whether such expression is by written or printed matter.

The original Article 19(1) and Article 19(2) of the Constitution (before amendment of the latter in June 1951) read as follows:

"19(1) All citizens shall have the right :

(a) to freedom of speech and expression;

(b) to assemble peaceably and without arms;

(c) to form associations or unions;

(d) to move freely throughout the territory of India;

(e) to reside and settle in any part of the territory of India;

(f) to acquire, hold and dispose of property;

(g) to practise any profession, or to carry on any occupation, trade or business.

"(2) Nothing in sub-clause (a) of clause (1) shall affect the operation of any existing law insofar as it relates to, or prevent the State from making any law relating to libel, slander, defamation, contempt of court or any matter which offends against decency or morality or which undermines the security of, or tends to overthrow, the State."

By the Constitution (First Amendment) Act of 1951, sub-section 3 of Article 19(2) of the Constitution was replaced in the form in which it exists at present. Clause (2) of Article 19, as it stands now, reads as follows:

"Nothing in sub-clause (a) of Clause (1) shall affect the operation of any existing law, or prevent the State from making any law, insofar as such law imposes reasonable restrictions on the exercise of the right conferred by the said sub-clause in the interests of the security of the State, friendly relations with foreign states, public order, decency or morality or in relation to contempt of court, defamation or incitement to an offence."

As compared with Article 19(2) as it originally stood, the additional subjects with respect to which legislative restrictions could be imposed on the right of the freedom of speech and expression were (1) friendly relations with foreign states, (2) public order, and (3) incitement to an offence. The amended Article 19(2), however, stated that the restrictions were to be "reasonable". The courts were given power to decide in any particular case whether the restrictions in respect of the various subjects were "reasonable" or not. The restrictions under Article 19(2) thus became a justiciable matter, just as other restrictions enumerated in clauses (3), (4), (5) and (6) of Article 19 were justiciable issues from the very beginning.

***Press Laws Enquiry Committee :*** Long before the Constitution (First Amendment) Act was placed on the statute book (18 June

1951), the Government of India had set up the Press Laws Enquiry Committee to:

(a) examine and report to the Government on laws regulating the Press in the principal countries of the world, including India;

(b) review the Press Laws of India with a view to examine if they were in accordance with fundamental rights formulated by the Constituent Assembly; and

(c) recommend to Government any measures of reforms in the Press Laws considered expedient upon such review.

The Committee, which submitted its report on 21 March 1948, considered comprehensively the Indian Penal Code, the Criminal Procedure Code, the Sea Customs Act, the Indian Telegraph Act, and the Indian Post Offices Act. It discussed the Press and Registration of Books Act, the Indian States (Protection Against Disaffection) Act, the Indian Press (Emergency Powers) Act, the Foreign Relations Act, and the Indian States (Protection) Act. It reviewed the working of ten Provincial Acts adopted between 1947 and 1948 in the interest of public security.

The recommendations of the Committee, generally, favoured the abolition of laws specially concerning the press, and the incorporation of its major provisions in the ordinary laws of the land.

The Committee, however, supported the provisions of the Indian Telegraph Act, the Post Offices Act, and the Sea Customs Act which provided the right of interception of messages and literature. It recommended the retention of the Official Secrets Act, and the three sections of the Indian Penal Code dealing with disaffection, communal hatred, and tampering with the loyalty of the armed forces. It suggested that suitable alterations should be made to exclude peaceful agitation for social and economic change.

***The Press (Objectionable Matters) Act :*** Introduced in Parliament on 31 August 1951, the Bill attempted to give effect to only some of the recommendations of the Committee. The Bill, its statement of objects and reasons said, was directed against encouragement of violence or sabotage and certain other grave offences, and against the publication of scurrilous matter. Under the Bill, the following laws were repealed:

1. The Indian States (Protection against Disaffection) Act, 1922
2. The Press (Emergency Powers) Act, 1931
3. Foreign Relations Act, 1932
4. The Indian States (Protection) Act, 1934
5. Five Press Acts in force in the acceding states of Hyderabad, Madhya Bharat, Mysore, PEPSU and Rajasthan.

The provisions contained in 13 Acts, referred to in the second schedule to the Bill, were repealed.

The government had the power, under the Act, of demanding and forfeiting security on a judicial decision, of declaring certain publications confiscated or seizing and forfeiting undeclared printing presses producing unauthorized news-sheets, of detaining imported packages containing, certain documents, of prohibiting postal transmission of certain publications and messages, and of seizing and destroying unauthorized news-sheets and newspapers.

The right of trial by jury was conceded to persons proceeded against under these rules. The Press (Objectionable Matters) Act was severely criticised. It came to be known as the "Black Act". Eventually in 1957, the Act was repealed.

***Parliamentary Proceedings (Protection of Publication) Act :*** In 1956, the Parliamentary Proceedings (Protection of Publication) Act was passed, at the initiative of late Feroze Gandhi, husband of Indira Gandhi. It gave immunity to the press in regard to faithful reporting of parliamentary proceedings. The Act conferred an immunity from any liability in respect of the publication in a newspaper of a substantially correct report of any proceedings of either House of Parliament, unless the publication is proved to have been made with malice. The Act permits the press to report defamatory statements in Parliament without committing a breach of privilege of Parliament, and by implication no libel action for the publication of any such statement referring to any outsider would lie. This Act applies only to the proceedings of Parliament and not of State legislatures, which are left free to enact its own legislation in that respect.

Three ordinances were proclaimed, after the promulgation of Emergency on 25 June 1975, to effect changes in certain press laws. The government armed itself with special powers to restrain the individual's freedom of expression. One of these ordinances provided for the repeal of the Press Council Act, 1965. The second one was the Prevention of Publication of Objectionable Matter Ordinance. The third ordinance repealed the Parliamentary Proceedings (Protection of Publication) Act, 1956 (popularly known as the Feroze Gandhi Act, since he had initiated it).

The Press Council was established in 1966 with the aim of evolving a code of conduct for the press and bringing about a fusion of rights and responsibilities on the part of the press. Since the objective had not been served in the then government's view, it repealed the Press Council Act of 1965 and abolished the institution with effect from 1 January 1976.

The repeal of the Parliamentary Proceedings (Protection of Publication) Act of 1956 was officially held to be a natural consequence of the decision to promulgate the ordinance to prevent publication of objectionable matter. According to the then government, the immunity conferred on the press by this legislation had been 'largely misused', bringing about a lowering of the standards of journalism.

The Prevention of Publication of Objectionable Matter Ordinance, 1975 provided "for action mainly against publications which are likely to excite disaffection against the constitutionally established government, incite interference with production, supply or distribution of essential commodities or services, create disharmony amongst different sections of the society and indecent or scurrilous or obscene writings".

The ordinance provided for security to be demanded from the printer, publisher, or editor responsible for the publication of an objectionable matter as defined. Any words, signs, or visible representations, which were defamatory of the President, Vice-President, Prime Minister or any other member of the Council of Ministers, the Speaker of Lok Sabha, or the Governor of a State became an offence, punishable under the Prevention of Publication of Objectionable Matter Ordinance.

### The Dark Days and After

With the imposition of Emergency in the country on 25 June 1975, an elaborate censorship apparatus was set up, and the press: came virtually under total censorship the country had never known before.

The DAVP's jurisdiction was expanded not only to include nationalized concerns, such as banks and the railways but also the public sector undertakings. The DAVP also prescribed for them where to place advertisements and at what rates.

The government also tightened its control over newsprint supply through state monopoly, i.e., State Trading Corporation.

The four privately-owned news agencies were 'coerced' to merge into 'Samachar' on 1 February 1976, initiating an organized process of thought control. The merger was effected through veiled armtwisting, and a variety of overt and covert governmental pressures.

According to the White Paper *Misuse of Mass Media,* issued by the Ministry of Information and Broadcasting in August 1976, as many as 258 journalists were detained during the Emergency (110 under MISA, 66 under Defence of India Rules, 83 for other reasons); 43 correspondents, 2 cartoonists, and 6 cameramen were disaccredited; 7 foreign correspondents were expelled out of the country; and the entry of 29 was banned.

Government advertisements were withheld to nearly 100 newspapers and periodicals, while requests for advertisements in respect of a number of newspapers and periodicals were rejected; 28 newspapers and periodicals were put on the banned list. The housing pool for pressmen was wound up. Those whose accreditation had been cancelled, and Indian correspondents representing foreign news organizations were ordered to vacate the government houses within two months.

The information and publicity budget excluding AIR and Doordarshan rose to Rs.18.70 crores in 1976-77 as compared to Rs.11.90 crores in the pre-Emergency year 1974-75.

After the new government came to power at the Centre in March 1977, the Prevention of Publication of Objectionable Matters Act was repealed, and the Parliamentary Proceedings (Protection of Publication) Act was re-enacted. The censorship on newspapers was abolished.

The Constitution (45th Amendment) Act, 1978 passed by the Parliament provides constitutional authority to Feroze Gandhi Act. It also extends the protection to journalists in respect of publication in newspapers of proceedings of State legislatures as well. The new Article 361-A, to be inserted in the Constitution, provides that no person shall be liable to any proceedings, civil or criminal, in any court in respect of publication in newspapers of a substantially true report of any proceedings of either house of Parliament, or either house of the State legislature, unless the publication is proved to have been made with malice. This provision cannot be suspended even during an Emergency. The immunity, however, does not extend to secret sittings of legislative bodies. A few legislatures have conferred this immunity on the press by separate Acts.

The government announced on 14 November 1977 its decision to dismantle the Samachar and restore the status quo ante in respect of four news agencies.

The Indian Press once again came into its own enjoying full freedom after passing through 19 months of arbitrary press control.

The advocates of press freedom argue that all subtle forms of influence over the press should come to an end. They are of the view that subsidized housing facilities and other perquisites enjoyed by correspondents including sponsored tours, reprehensible practice of fixing advertisement rates for newspapers, and disallowing newspapers to directly import the newsprint they require should be done away with.

They also like the government to make a constitutional provision to ensure that the press freedom was not interfered with in the future. They concede that the institution of Press Council is necessary, but are of the view that the government should have nothing to do with it. They suggest that cess should be collected on newsprint and distributed to the press to finance the Press Council and the news agencies. The press, they argue, is one of the four pillars on which the mansion of democracy stands. If one pillar collapses, the whole structure would crumble. However, all freedoms are relative and are subordinate to the freedom of society. The press should, therefore, evolve a code of conduct to regulate itself. Any kind of external regulation or interference is neither desirable nor called for.

Criticism and dissent are essential in democracy. The press, however, has to ensure that these are objective and unbiased and not influenced by favours, money, or the bottle. Only then the press can play the vital role of mobilizing public opinion, and also act as the 'watch-dog' in safeguarding peoples' liberties.

No freedom, however sacred it may be, can be absolute. This is also true of press freedom. Not only the freedom of the press is subject to the laws of the land, such as law of contempt and libel, but also to the privileges of Parliament and State Legislatures.

The stress should be not so much on the freedom of the press but on 'free and responsible press'. The press should be, no doubt, free but should also be responsible to the society it serves. It should accept certain responsibilities in the discharge of its functions.

The press has an obligation-voluntary and self-imposed-that in presentation of truthful news and fair comment it adheres to certain norms of decency and decorum, and that it does not indulge in vulgarity, obscenity, character assassination, violation of citizens' privacy and incitement to violence, disorder and disintegration of the country.

The role of press in India should neither be that of an 'adversary' in the West nor that of an 'unquestioning ally' as in the socialist countries. It has to adopt a middle course and help in the development process.

## Press in Democracy

A seven-point 'Declaration on Press Freedom in India and Democracy' has been evolved by a group of Indian newspapermen. The declaration followed the discussions held under the auspices of the International Press Institute and the Friedrich Naumann Stigtung (26 November 1977).

The following is the text of the Declaration:

1. Freedom of the press is at the heart of all liberty. Where there is no free exchange of information and thought, no other liberty is secure. Freedom of the press is one of the pillars of a free society and a means of extending the frontiers of liberty.
2. In a democracy, a free press has an inalienable right to an adversary role. It should be free to criticize authority at all levels in the general public interest, and to function as a watch-dog over the government's handling of the problems of the people and the country. The press should always be responsive to society as a whole, and act as a channel of communication to purvey facts and give fair and considered information on all issues. A free press should always be conscious of its responsibility to present to the public news without fear or favour or distortion, suppression of censorship.
3. Citizens should be able to publish and read newspapers and journals of their choice. The relationship between the management and the editor should be one of cooperation. Within a newspaper's broad policy framework, the editor should be left free to function without interference.
4. A free press must enjoy the confidence of its readers. There is need for self-regulation by the press, and this is

best achieved by a press council set up by the press representing professional and lay opinion.

5. It is essential to have more than one news agency. News agencies should be competitive and free of government control.

6. A free press can be strangled through economic pressures. For instance, the government has no right to fix advertisement rates for individual newspapers or to use government advertising as a form of patronage or to canalize newsprint supplies through a state monopoly.

7. The flow of information entails not only a free press but also free and competitive radio and television services, which should be regulated by genuinely autonomous agencies.

***Professional Secrecy and the Law :*** The press in almost all the free countries of the world has, of late, demanded a legal recognition of its right to professional secrecy as an essential aspect of the freedom of press.

The reasons for and against such extension have been succinctly summarized in the excellent study *Professional Secrecy and the Journalist* published by the International Press Institute, Zurich in 1962.

The reasons for, in part, include:

1. That the journalist has a moral and ethical duty to protect the anonymity of an individual who gives him information with the understanding that it is to be regarded as confidential as to source.

2. That the journalist must protect his sources as a practical assurance that he will continue to receive information in confidence, if need be, and make it possible for the newspaper to publish information that should be made known to the public.

3. That the press contributes to the public welfare and performs an essential public service in presenting information that should be made known to the public.

4. That the journalist, serving the public welfare, is as much entitled to special privilege under the law as is the doctor or clergyman or lawyer.
5. That, if a journalist can obtain information, the public agencies-including the police and the courts-should be able to obtain the same information without putting pressure upon the individual journalist to do their work for them and, in the process, betray a trust.

Arguments against, include the following points:

1. That the function of the courts in the preservation of law and order must take precedence over any claim of privilege by the journalist.
2. That the journalist receives information with the specific understanding that it is to be made known, whereas the doctor, lawyer, clergyman receive it with the express understanding that it is not to be made known.
3. That a journalist, given a legal right to withhold source, could publish any sort of assertion or charge actually made up by the journalist to serve some purpose contrary to the public interest, or be used for that purpose.
4. That there is no evidence to show that the press performs any better or any worse, whether or not it operates under law granting protection.

In spite of the demand for legal protection to professional secrecy, few countries have provided it, and in varying measure. Although the press in India does not enjoy any legal protection to professional secrecy, the cases in which the journalists have been compelled by the courts to disclose the sources of their information, or where the journalists have been penalised for non-disclosure, are very few indeed, if any at all.

## Ethical Code

It was expected from the earlier Press Council that it would draw up a code of ethics for journalists and newspapers, so as to ensure maintenance of high professional standards in Indian journalism. This was, however, not done. It was hoped that the rulings of the Council would help build up a body of case law, which would serve as a code of ethics for the press. Since the Council dealt only with minor cases, this expectation remained unfulfilled.

The code of ethics for the press can either be drawn up by the revived Press Council or by some representative body of newspapers, such as All India Newspapers Editors' Conference. A code acceptable to all concerned has not emerged so far. A code was drawn during the Emergency by a committee of editors.

The press is a public service and, therefore, accountable to the community as a whole. Press freedom means not only freedom from unnecessary restraints, but also freedom for the purpose of advancing certain basic concepts enshrined in the Constitution.

It is agreed by all that press is an essential organ of the democratic set-up, an important vehicle of communication and a vital instrument in the creation of public opinion. As such, it is necessary that journalists should regard their profession as a trust to serve public interest.

Any code, to be drawn up in the future, should provide that the press must "present a truthful, comprehensive and reliable account of the events in a context which gives them meaning, project a representative picture of constituent groups in society, regard itself as a forum for comment and criticism and discharge its social responsibilities by clarifying the goals and values of society".

Also, in presentation of news as well as comments, the press should avoid sensationalism and vulgarity. It should eschew publication of reports tending to incite violence which may lead to civil disorder, mutiny or rebellion. Anything obscene, or tending to encourage the crime or unlawful activities should be kept out of both news and advertisement columns. Rumours, gossips, and scurrilous reports concerning the private life of an individual should be avoided.

Any future code of ethics for the press should also lay down that journalists should not use their position to secure personal favours, or seek information for non journalistic purposes.

The editor of the paper, vis-a-vis the government and proprietor, should be left free in the discharge of his responsibilities as long as he adheres to the paper's policy. The editor's decision should be treated as final in all editorial matters.

A free press can only flourish in a democratic environment. As such, it should be the duty of the press to use its freedom so as to strengthen the democratic foundation of the state. The press can guard its freedom best by exercising self-regulation through enforcing voluntarily a code of ethics drawn by it.

Since the basis of a code of conduct is the acceptance of its voluntary enforcement, it is not necessary or proper to enact the code of ethics into law.

## The Guidelines

In 1966, the Press Council evolved certain guidelines for the conduct of newspapers. These were circulated to over 10,000 newspapers and periodicals in the country. These guidelines can form the basis of any future code of ethics for the press.

Explaining the rationale behind these guidelines, the Council stated that "while it is the legitimate function of the press to draw attention to the genuine and legitimate grievances of any community with a view to having the same redressed by peaceful, legal and legitimate means, it is improper and a breach of journalistic ethics to invent grievances or to exaggerate real grievances, as these tend to promote a communal ill-feeling and accentuate the discord".

According to these guidelines, the Press should avoid:

— exaggeration or distortion of facts or incidents in relation to communal matters or giving currency to unverified rumours, suspicions or inferences, as if they were facts and base their comments on them;

— employment of intemperate and unrestrained language in the presentation of news or views, even as a piece of literary flourish or for the purposes of rhetoric or emphasis;

— encouraging or condoning violence even in the face of provocation as a means of obtaining redress of grievances, whether the same be genuine or not;

— scurrilous and untrue attacks on communities or individuals, particularly when they are accompanied by charges attributing misconduct to them, due to their being members of a particular community or caste;

— falsely giving a communal colour to incidents in which members of different communities happen to be involved;

— emphasising matters that are apt to produce communal hatred or ill-will or fostering feelings of distrust between communities;

— publishing alarming news which are in substance untrue or making provocative comments on such news or views, which are otherwise calculated to embitter relations between different communities or regional or linguistic groups;

— exaggerating actual happenings to achieve sensationalism, and publication of news which adversely affect communal harmony with banner headlines or in distinctive types; and

— making disrespectful, derogatory or insulting remarks on, or reference to, the different religions or faiths or their founders.

While the press, in a democratic country like India, has a primary duty to report events objectively and faithfully, it has also a larger obligation to the nation to defend and preserve the democratic way of life. It is, therefore, necessary for the press to voluntarily adopt a policy not to play up or give undue publicity or to give 'celebrity' treatment to news, which tend to promote authoritarian and dictatorial trends or to aggravate communal or regional tensions. In defending democracy and rule of law, the press, in fact, is defending its very existence, as freedom of the press can survive only in a democratic set-up.

### The Restraints

Every daily newspaper ought to print a disclaimer in each issue. It would read something like this:

This paper, and the hundreds of thousands of words it contains, has been produced in about 15 hours by a group of fallible human beings, working out of cramped offices while trying to find out what happened in the world from people who are sometimes reluctant to tell us and, at other times, positively obstructive.

*The Limitation :* There are limits to the process of journalism. Shortage of time and the frequent unavailability of information are two which are endemic. So too are the errors that journalists make when working under pressure. There are also limitations on good journalism which are created by journalists themselves and by those who control or own newspapers. One of this trade's great myths is that coverage of events is shaped by a paper's style and news values. Would that it was all as simple as that. Instead, the quality and nature of a paper's journalism is also shaped by the owners' priorities, the prevailing journalistic culture and what readers' values are perceived to be. And there is often conflict between these factors.

*Lip Service :* Owners may pay lip service to concepts of truth, light and the virtuous way, but they are generally in the business to make money or propaganda or both. The way those who control newspapers' purse strings use them for propaganda is so well attested that it does not need re-stating with all its gory details here. Promotion of their own views, exclusion of opposing ones, slanting coverage to fit a point of view or commercial interests and pursuing personal vendettas are major themes of press history.

One example will suffice. It involves William Randolph Hearst, the American newspaper magnate who behaved all his life as if he and honesty had never been properly introduced. He it was who, when a film called *Citizen Kane* was made patently based on his life, offered money to the studio to have the master and all prints destroyed before distribution. When that failed he had his gossip columnist, Louella Parsons, ring studio executives and distributors and threaten them with the exposure of personal details. She told them: 'Mr Hearst says that if you boys want private lives, he'll give you private lives.'

Nothing, however, better illustrates Hearst's attitude towards journalism, and that of many other proprietors down the years, than one exchange of cables from 1898. Hearst was very anxious, for personal political reasons and circulation purposes, that there should be a Spanish-American war over Cuba. His main paper, the *New York journal*, ran slanted, jingoistic stories with lurid, distorted headlines ('Feeding Prisoners To The Sharks' and 'The Worst Insult to the United States In Its History', etc.). He also sent his staff on all kinds of escapades to find evidence of Spanish 'atrocities'. The honest ones filed nothing (and found their careers suffering), others used their imaginations. One of the former was an artist called Frederic Remington. Finding all quiet and no bloodshed, he cabled Hearst: 'There will be no war. I wish to return.' Hearst replied: 'Please remain. You furnish pictures. I will furnish war.' And, by running a series of distorted and invented stories, he duly did.

(Eccentricity was also often a hallmark of the single proprietor. Colonel Robert McCormick, owner of the *Chicago Tribune*, once ordered his Paris correspondent William Shirer to the French countryside to try to locate a pair of binoculars he had left in a barn nine years before. The champion lulu, however, was James Gordon Bennett Jnr. Not only did he insist his *International Herald Tribune* print the same weather report for 24 years, but also once marched into its offices and dismissed all the men standing on the right hand side of the room, sacked a music critic for the length of his hair and celebrated New Year's Day 1877 at the home of his fiancee's parents by urinating in the fireplace and then fighting a duel with her brother.)

**New Trends**

Now-a-days owners are far more likely to be a corporation and their propaganda requirements are likely to be confined to supporting a known political party, stroking politicians able to favour them (or kicking those who can't) and urging stories that aid and abet their business interests. As a general rule, corporate owners are less active propagandists than individual proprietors and some show very little interest in editorials until it frightens the advertisers. What they are supremely focussed on is maximising profit margins and urgently so if their debt is being financed by outsiders. This has meant, in the last two decades of the twentieth century, a concentration on lowering costs and, especially in monopoly situations, a fierce reduction of editorial staff. The experience of the regional weekly I once edited, which has seen its newsroom cut from 21 reporters to less than ten, is common.

The result, in terms of coverage and of scrutinising officialdom, has been devastating. In the case of covering local authorities, for instance, the former practice of assigning a reporter to track each department (education, leisure, environmental health, social services, etc.), has now been widely abandoned. Add the proliferation of public relations departments at local councils, health authorities, etc., and you have the recipe for coverage that is haphazard at best and spoon-fed at worst. These staff cuts, and the expectation of more stories per reporter than was once the case (often formalised into half-baked schemes to measure reporters' output'), has meant that many reporters who now pass their days glued to a telephone behind a desk would not recognise the experiences of their predecessors, only a generation ago, who routinely tramped the streets meeting contacts (and readers) in search of stories. If that sounds like nostalgia, look around your newsroom, imagine its staff doubled and think how your coverage (and your own working life) would be changed. Owners' priorities have probably imposed more limitations on how journalism is practised than any other factor in the last 20 years.

Journalistic culture sets what editors and their executives regard as a good story or dismiss as 'boring' and determines the subjects they think of as 'sexy' and those that are not. It also creates the moral atmosphere of a paper and is thus far more responsible for the ethics that are in daily use on a paper than any theoretical commandments.

In this culture, one of the most admired skills is 'a nose for a story'. This can either be a genuine ability to see meaning and interest in what others might overlook, or, in its degenerate form, the artful technique of presenting the mundane as the unusual. This journalistic conjuring trick is normally performed by excluding context, as when, in the early 1980s, the editor of the *New York Daily Post* filled the front page on a slow news day by asking reporters to collect details of every little crime committed in the city and then wrote them together in one breathless story under the headline 'Mayhem On Our Streets'.

A feature of such dishonest ingenuity is that a broadly accurate series of parts add up to a totally inaccurate whole. And it is not just admired on the tabloid papers where it originated. It has a wide influence on what is thought to be smart, slick behaviour everywhere. Sleight of hand with the facts and judiciously selecting information that is then presented out of its true setting is often copied, albeit in a milder form, throughout journalism. Part of this is unavoidable because any reality, which by its very nature is messy and complicated, has to be simplified, or at least have language and coherence imposed upon it, when it is related in words. A lot of journalism, however, wilfully omits context and unduly magnifies this effect for the sake of rendering reality in a more dramatic way. After a while the process is barely a conscious one.

## Mass-market Culture

The culture of mass-market papers also prizes the writing of facile narratives. What is involved here is certainly some talent, but also, far more, a stretching of facts and the meaning of words to give an arresting construct. Its most common form is where the story is given a false intro by deducing from some of the elements some spuriously dramatic (but probably far-fetched) possibility.

The giveaway is often the words 'could', ,may' or 'claims'. As with the conjuring tricks referred to above, the sneakiness is in the way in which some sort of plausible defence of each component can be mounted. The finished article, however, still amounts to a lie. Neither is the writing and editing process on more serious, 'quality' papers free of this corruption. There it originates with the desk editors who talk of 'running the story through their machines' to 'beef it up'. Often stories do benefit from such attentions, but frequently this amounts to, and is openly acknowledged as, putting a synthetic gloss on a story, stretching the implications of each fact to the utmost and thus producing a misleading overall picture.

And what is done in the editing process today is liable to be done at the reporting stage tomorrow. Reporters competing to get their stories published anticipate executive values and are prepared (or feel obliged) to adopt practices which are at odds with their private values. This professional schizophrenia is at its most chronic where the prevailing culture is known to favour stories that are composed of vivid blacks or whites and not the messy greys and ambiguous mid-tones of reality.

To an extent all journalism favours such stories. A story where A cheats B with provably false documents and then uses the ill-gotten gains to live it up in the Caribbean, is obviously more immediately interesting to all of us than one where A and B are in dispute over a deal, both are claiming to be cheated and the trip to warmer climes turns out to be a business visit to service off-shore accounts. In any language, for any paper, the first version of that story would be preferred to the second. It is more unusual and it patently has greater news value. The problem is that such preferences get understandably formalised into the journalistic culture. Reporters and editors, knowing that simplistic stories of black and white are the most attractive to editors, can then look for these to the exclusion of more subtle, and certainly more realistic, tales. Worse is the way that this view of what constitutes a 'good, hard story' can affect the research and writing and rob a story of balance. There is an unconscious tendency to stop asking questions at the nice and simple, clear-cut stage. 'Don't check it out too closely' is the cynical, snickering advice of too many news editors.

It is not a very large step from this to regarding news as something to be packaged to conform to a pre-conceived recipe, or formula. On mass-market papers in particular, editors are determined to have stories of certain types-light, frothy ones or breathless, dramatic ones. Executives hear of a story in the early stages, decide the kind of headline or treatment they want and then they (or the reporter) organise the facts or the treatment of them to force the story into the formula. It is journalism by headline. It presents to readers a world where the extraordinary always happens, there are only certainties and simplicities, rights and wrongs, and only stereotypes exist.

These are the limitations of the journalistic process seen at their most extreme. Many papers do not go this far, but those that do, and those journalists on other papers who have absorbed some of this culture, have one standard answer to objections: the readers. No group of people are more often invoked to defend the otherwise indefensible. No group of people have their appetites more regularly or wilfully taken for granted, nor their vocabularies and intelligence more patronisingly underestimated. 'Time to go and write my 200 words for people who move their lips when they read', as one British tabloid correspondent always used to say.

Readers are the ones in whose names stories and subjects are selected, treatments applied, intros written and re-written, and presentation and design carried out. Yet, of all the conflicting elements in journalism — those who supply potential information (sources), those who process it (reporters, editors, owners or controllers) and those who consume it (readers) — the latter are the only ones who are not actually present during its creation. Their tastes have to be anticipated.

Newspapers in established, sophisticated markets do this in a variety of ways. They and their journalists build up over the years, through responses they have had to stories, readers' letters, telephone calls, complaints and so forth, an anecdotal 'knowledge' of what their readers want. Or rather what they believe their readers want. This internal folklore may or may not be successful and it may or may not be accurate. Unless it is put to the test with some serious research, no one will ever know.

## Personalised Idea

Often it is not. It is instead combined with the prejudices of journalists, executives and owners to produce a highly personalised idea of what readers want, or what they think they ought to want. Times without number one hears in editorial conferences the phrase, 'What the reader wants is ...'. Too often this is based on the speaker's own preferences and tastes, or those of friends; or, even worse, those he or she wants to impress.

A danger here is that journalists often inhabit circles and have life-styles, habits and tastes that are far removed from those of their readers. They might, if they are a 'serious' journalist, mix constantly with figures in authority and officials and so absorb some of their values. In many developed countries the payment of relatively fancy salaries on many papers has meant that journalists breathe a different air, eat different meat and live a life far removed from that experienced by their readers. It takes more imagination than most such journalists have to appreciate that the restaurants they dine at, the clothes they buy and the holidays they take are not pleasures enjoyed by their readers. And if they do use their imagination, they run the risk of conjuring up a patronising pastiche of their readers' tastes.

Research, if scientifically done, is part of the answer. Some papers rightly use research companies to find out as much as they can about readers: ages, male/female ratio, incomes, occupations, education, interests, concerns, tastes, how they spend their leisure time, spending patterns, etc. They then know, for instance, how many of their readers aged 35-50 take holidays in France, or how many aged 25-35 own a mobile phone. The only problem is that this information is collected for the benefit of the advertising department and is only rarely passed to journalists.

The research normally initiated by the editorial department is into reader attitudes, both to the paper and to the issues and subjects they might cover. This can either be simple surveys via a form printed in the paper, 'readers' panels', or by research companies whose structured questioning finds out what people do read (or, rather, what they claim to read). Surveys are, however, strung about with trip-wires for the unwary. They should ask very specific questions on detailed points of the paper's coverage. It is no good asking people if they want more news — of course they do, but what kind? And what would they like less of to make room for it? Then there is the problem of respondents telling researchers what they think they want to hear, or, even worse, stating preferences that they would like to be thought of as having, rather than their real ones.

Just after 1945, the British *News of the World* was the largest-selling paper in the world. Each Sunday some 7,000,000 copies were sold to people who lapped up its diet of murders and sex cases. A few 'respectable' features were mixed in. Then the editor had a hunch that morals and tastes were changing and so commissioned a survey. Men were hired to visit readers' homes and quiz them about what they liked and did not like in the paper. Since this work was done during the day, it was mainly women who answered the door. None, understandably, was prepared to say to their male inquisitors: 'Yes, I like the rape cases and the indecency and my husband is very fond of stories about priests and small boys.' Instead, respondents assured the researchers that they only took the paper for the respectable features. The editor read the results and immediately dropped all mention of sex from the paper. After just two weeks, circulation had fallen by 500,000. By the third week, the paper had a new editor, the content returned to its seedy normality and sales eventually reached 8,500,000.

Readers do have a disorientating tendency to say they like one thing while preferring another and publicly disdain some forms of journalism while consuming them avidly in private.

That is why some researchers use two-way mirrors to observe a focus group reading a paper or uninhibitedly discussing its contents. There are even visor-like devices which fit on to people's heads, monitor their eye movement and so give a precise record of what they read, merely glance at, or ignore. If the technology or money is not available for those black arts, there is an alternative which, for journalists, is probably more effective than any research. That is to spend as much time as possible with readers and observing them. How many journalists have ever stood and watched people as they select a paper at the news stands? Or studied them in bars or on trains and seen how they read papers? This is all part of the unquenchable curiosity that journalists should have about readers. It should make them want to talk to them at every opportunity, meet them and get to know as much as they can about them.

Advertisers are the other element in the paper's audience and for smaller circulation papers they are economically more important than readers. This commercial power is what makes many think that advertisers are continuously exercising this muscle to intimidate papers into tailoring their coverage to suit them. The surprise is that the instances of this, and there are many, are not even more frequent. Of course large advertisers have sometimes withdrawn advertising in protest of a paper's coverage (or lack of it), many have threatened to do so and even more have tried a chummy phone call to an editor or publisher to get their way. And some have succeeded.

The dangers of this are greatest when papers, normally provincial ones, are inordinately dependent on one advertiser or group of advertisers. But far more common than this overt pressure is the influence of potential advertisers on feature coverage. Editors are often under enormous pressure from the commercial side of the paper to run features on certain subjects because it is known, or anticipated, that this will generate advertising. This can result in some subjects getting more attention than they otherwise would. A lot of this is relatively harmless in itself, but then proves to be the precursor of more demanding attentions.

These limitations on the journalistic process — the ones endemic to information gathering and those imposed by owners' priorities, editorial culture and readers' tastes-mean that perhaps the disclaimer suggested for most papers at the opening of this chapter should be a little longer. This paper, and the hundreds of thousands of words it contains, has been produced in about 15 hours by a group of fallible human beings, working out of cramped offices while trying to find out about what happened in the world from people who are sometimes reluctant to tell us and, at other times, positively obstructive.

Its content has been determined by a series of subjective judgements made by reporters and executives, tempered by what they know to be the editor's, owner's and readers' prejudices. Some stories appear here without essential context as this would make them less dramatic or coherent and some of the language employed has been deliberately chosen for its emotional impact, rather than its accuracy. Some features are printed solely to attract certain advertisers.

These limitations have all the inevitability of recurring bad dreams. In the end, journalists have only one answer to them: to develop universal standards and skills and act upon them. They are our only protection. If journalists do that, they can beat the limitations. It can be done; for every day, somewhere on this planet, it is being done. Reporters are exposing corruption, uncovering negligence, revealing dangers, unmasking criminals and reporting hard facts that someone wanted kept secret. Papers are publishing information and, to paraphrase *The Times'* editor of a century ago, making it the common property of the people. Even bad newspapers do more good than harm — and you can't say that about governments.

12

# Law and Journalism

Very few reporters specialise in legal reporting and there are fewer newspapers who hire them on a full-time basis. Most newspapers are content with hiring lawyers on a part-time basis. Invariably these lawyer-reporters string their reports with legal jargon that is rarely understood by the lay reader. It would seem to be largely a case of lawyers writing for lawyers. Take the following examples culled from two of Bombay's leading dailies and mark the words underlined.

## Select Cases

***Writ Petitions against Bombay Varsity Admitted :*** Mr. Justice Ashok N. Mody at the Bombay High Court admitted three *writ petitions* filed by St. Xavier's College, Sophia College and the Wilson College against the University of Bombay, Vice Chancellor, University of Bombay, Slate of Maharashtra and the Director of Education, Maharashtra and pending the hearing and final disposal of the petition *restrained* the *respondents* from applying clauses (ii) and (iii) of Appendix II of the Vice Chancellor's Order dated 7th June 1978 which provides for constitution of selection committees for the appointment of principals and teachers in colleges affiliated to the University of Bombay.

The State of Maharashtra and Director of Education, Maharashtra, were also restrained from withholding or curtailing the Grant-in-aid to the said Colleges on the ground of *non compliance* with the said clauses.

A *Division Bench* consisting of Mr. Justice S.K. Desai and Mr. Justice B. Lentin had earlier admitted a petition by an Ahmednagar College involving similar question.

Thereafter, the managements of the above three colleges through their advocates addressed a letter to the State of Maharashtra and also called upon the Vice Chancellor to withdraw the said clauses (ii) and (iii) of Appendix II to his order dated 7th June 1978, which refer to the constitution of selection committees for the appointment of principals and teachers.

However, the University did not comply with the said request. The colleges, therefore, challenged the said order.

Mr. R.A. Dada, instructed by Mr. M.S. Bodhanwalla of Messers Smetham, Byrne Lambart & Dubash appeared on behalf of the Petititions.

Mr. Deshpande appeared on behalf of the University of Bombay and the Vice Chancellor.

Mr. V.N. Lokur, Government Pleader, appeared on behalf of the State of Maharashtra and the Director of Education, Maharashtra.

***Court Injunction against Wholesale Trade :*** On a *writ petition* filed by Mr. M.P. Ghule, President, Shri Chatrapati Shivaji Market Yard Adate Association, Pune, Mr. Justice Deshpande and Mr. Justice Mehta of the Bombay High Court *issued a rule* and granted *interim injunction* against the Municipal Corporation, Pune, directing them to prevent the members of the Bhumata Seva Sanghatana, Pune, from carrying on wholesale trade at Phule Market, Pune, subject to the order dated May 25, 1979 passed by the High Court in Civil Revision Application No. 382 of 1979.

The Court further granted interim injunction against the Commissioner of Police, Pune, directing him to prevent the entry of goods trucks in the streets adjoining the Phule Market and also to prevent parking of goods trucks in the streets adjacent to the Phule Market.

The petitioner alleged ....

Mr. C.R. Dalvi appeared for the Petitioner.

Mr. K.K.Singhavi, Mr. A.M. Malik and Mr. A.V. Sawant appeared for the Respondents.

The presumption in all daily reporting in newspapers is that the average reader understands such key words as petitioner, respondent, restraint, writ petition, non-compliance, division bench, interim injunction, certiorari etc. In most law reporting in India, no effort is made to explain these terms; this is due in part because the law reporter assumes that what he knows the reader ought to know as well and partly because the news editor does not take the trouble to tell his reporter that he ought to write for the layman and not for lawyers. Mental laziness on the part of both results in unreadable copy.

There is also the fear that simplifying law reporting might make it susceptible to the charge of incorrect reporting. The law reporter, therefore, takes no risk. He is more comfortable with jargon; the news editor does not complain and neither, apparently, does the average reader.

*Nurse Gets Damages for Unnecessary Operation* : Mrs Blondell Maynard was subjected to an "unnecessary, undesirable and unreasonable" diagnostic operation at Hast Birmingham Hospital in 1970, Mr Justice Comyn ruled in the High Court yesterday.

He held that Mrs Maynard, aged 41, a staff nurse, of South Yardley, Birmingham, was entitled to damages against West Midlands Regional Health Authority.

In a second medical negligence action the judge ruled that Mrs Maynard was entitled to damages against Mr Herman Nohl-

Oser, a consultant surgeon who examined her when she visited him in 1973 to see if he would be a witness in her claim against the hospital authority.

In both cases the amount of damages will be decided later, and the rulings may be subject to appeal.

The judge said the operation on Mrs Maynard, who came to Britain from the West Indies in 1963, had paralysed one of her vocal chords. She suffered difficulties in breathing and speaking.

The first paragraph gives the gist of the court's judgement. The second paragraph identifies the person in whose favour the judgement was given. It mentions her age, her occupation and her address.

The third paragraph gives further information on the judgement.

The fourth paragraph mentions whether the court's ruling was subject to appeal.

The final paragraph gives adequate detail about the plaintiff's complaint.

***Children Denied Stepfather's Name :*** Before Lord Justice Lawton, Lord Justice Bridge and Lord Justice Dunn (Judgements delivered on July 24)

The Court of Appeal dismissed an appeal by a mother, divorced and remarried, against an order that she must continue the use by the children of their father's surname. Their Lordships considered two lines of cases and decided that changing the children's surnames after the divorce of the parents was important matter so far as their welfare and interests were concerned, and that it was not merely a peripheral matter. Mr. Lester Boothma for the mother. The father did not appear. Lord Justice Dunn said that the order, by Judge Hutton in chambers, was in effect that the two children of the marriage should continue to use the father's surname. Although the father was not represented on appeal, it was clear from his solicitor's letter that he opposed a variation of the order. The mother had applied to the judge to be released from an undertaking that she had given not to change the name as a condition of taking the children to live in Australia. The only matter in issue was whether she should be allowed to change the children's name to her own new surname. The parties were married in 1966, the children were born in 1968 and 1970. The marriage was dissolved in 1974, joint custody being granted to the parents and care and control to the mother. Both parents having remarried, the father now had two sons by his second marriage and the mother a daughter born in 1978. The mother's new husband, an Australian, wished to return to live in Australia.

Concerning the change of name, the judge was faced with a dilemma because there were two lines of apparently conflicting authority. The first was that the change of name was an important matter, the second that it was comparatively unimportant. The judge chose the first approach and the ground of appeal was that he had erred in so doing. Mr Boothman had conducted the appeal with great ability and responsibility. In *In re WG (1976)* 6 Fam Law 210, the issue was the same as that before the court. The Court of Appeal reversed the judge's decision permitting a change of name, Lord Justice Cairns saying that the courts recognised the importance of maintaining a link between the father and the child.

Mr. Boothman relied on two authorities for the mother. In *R v R* (1977) I WLR 1256, a mother left home with her four children and went to live with a soldier. The youngest child returned to live with the father. The issue was whether custody should go to the mother or whether it should remain with the father. It was held by Lord Justice Stamp and Lord Justice Ormrod that the fact that the children were known in the army camp by the soldier's name and not by the father's name had no significance in regard to the characters of the soldier or the mother. The observations of Lord Justice Ormrod that too much attention was paid to names on some occasions and that the issue of names was peripheral should be read in their context and not as a general proposition. In *D v B* (1979) Fam 38, another decision of Lord Justice Stamp and Lord

Justice Ormrod, it was clear that, in the course of the appeal, the father consented to the child being known by the mother's new surname so that the question of change of name was not the issue. Their Lordships upheld the judge's order as to access, but varied the order after construing technical regulations.

Lord Justice Ormrod made some general comments on applications to change a child's name. "What is real is that the father and the child should know one another, that the child should in course of time come to recognise the fact that D is his natural father and so long as that is understood, names are really of little importance and they only become important when they become a casus belli between the parents." The last sentence was not necessary on the issue and was obiter. Even if it were necessary, his Lordship would go farther and say that he did not agree with those remarks. In *L* v *F*, Mr. Justice Latey said that those two cases were in direct contradiction of a series of decisions of the Court of Appeal and the High Court which had held that a change of name was important so far as the children's interests and welfare were concerned. His Lordship agreed with every word of that statement. Further, in that case, a distinguished psychiatric had given evidence that children, when they grew older, were often greatly concerned with their biological origin. It could not be said that a change of name was of little importance to children. *In re WG*, Lord Justice Cairns said, correctly, that it was important that it should be realized that the mere fact that there had been a divorce and that the mother had remarried, and had custody of the child, was not a sufficient reason for changing the child's name.

How then did the law stand? The welfare of the children was the first and paramount consideration, as provided by Section 1 of the Guardianship of Infants Act, 1925. It was a matter of discretion for the judge, after hearing the case, seeing the witnesses and parents, and possibly the children, to decide whether such a change was in the interests of the children. All the facts should be taken into account, including the possible embarrassment of the child at school, his long term interests, the importance of his links with the father's family and the stability of the mother's new marriage. The judge had preferred *In re WG* to the other two decisions, and he was right in taking that course.

Should the judge have taken the children's wishes into account? He said: "I have seen the children. I think they are too young to express a view on what is a fairly drastic step. I pay little regard to their views that largely reflect the mother's views. I mean no disrespect to the mother in saying this." Their Lordships could not go beyond that. Children were naturally suggestible and had spent their whole lives with the mother and would be anxious not to offend her. The judge was entirely right not to attach decisive importance to the views of children aged 10 and 12.

It had been said that there were advantage in changing the children's names as they would be making a fresh start in Australia and would go as a united family, and that the children could change their names back later if they wished The judge must have had all those matters in mind. He was entirely right, and his Lordship would have reached the same conclusion.

Lord Justice Lawton and Lord Justice Bridge agreed.

Solicitors: Sharpies & Co.

The case reported is a case that went up to the Court of Appeal. The case was heard by three judges who are named at the beginning of the report. The introduction gives the gist of the judgement. The very next paragraph states who appeared for the mother. Then the views of the judges are given in the context of the arguments advanced by counsel for the mother. It will be noticed that very little legal jargon appears in the report which is largely given in indirect language. At the end the report names the solicitors.

## Legal Terms

It is, however, important, that the reporter is acquainted with legal terms. In the following instances, no attempt is made to define words in strict legalese, but to give a general idea of what the words mean. The purpose is to acquaint the reporter with a sense of the words, not to turn him into a lawyer.

*Abatement of nuisance.* This means summary removal of a nuisance by the persons injured, without having recourse to legal proceedings. If the branches of trees on a neighbour's land overhang on a person's land and thereby cause nuisance, he is entitled to top off those branches.

*Abduction.* This means the unlawful carrying away of a woman for marriage or immoral intercourse.

*Abetment.* A person abets the doing of a thing who, first, instigates any person to do a thing, second, engages with one or more other person in any conspiracy for the doing of that thing and third, intentionally aids, by any act or illegal omission, the doing of that thing.

*Abide the event.* The expression "costs shall abide the event" means that the successful party in a court case must get the costs.

*Abortive trial.* This is a trial where the case has gone off and no verdict has been pronounced without the fault or management of the parties.

*Abrogation.* This means the annulment of a law or its repeal by competent authority.

*Abscond.* Absconding is to hide oneself in order to escape arrest for a crime. The absconder need not necessarily be away from his residence; he may stay in his own home as long as he is in hiding.

*Absoluta sententia expositore non indiget.* Latin for "plain words require no explanation".

*Accessory.* Something contributing in subordinate degree to a general result or effect. If a citizen harbours a prisoner or deserter or receives stolen property he is dealt in England under the head "accessory after the fact".

*Accomplice.* An accomplice is a guilty associate in crime; he is present when a crime is committed but is not interested in disclosing it.

*Account payee.* A cheque marked "Account Payee" makes it incumbent on the collecting bank to place the proceeds of the cheque to the credit of the account of the payee.

*Accusare nemo se debet.* No one is bound to accuse himself.

*Acquittal.* If a magistrate, upon taking the evidence, finds the accused not guilty, he shall record an order of acquittal.

*Ad idem.* Negotiating parties are *ad idem* when they are totally agreed upon the same thing in the same sense.

*Ad interim.* During the intervening period; temporarily.

*Adjourn sine die.* Adjournment to a date, that is not, at the present time, fixed.

*Administration durante minori actate.* That which is granted when the executor is a minor and which continues until the minor attains the lawful age to act.

*Adverse witness.* This is a witness whose mind discloses that he is hostile to the party calling him.

*Affidavit.* This is a sworn statement in writing made especially under oath or on affirmation before an authorized magistrate or officer.

*Affirmanti non neganti incumbit probatio.* The burden of proof lies upon him who affirms, not upon him who denies.

*A fortiori.* By a stronger reason, all the more.

*Agnate.* A relative whose kinship is traceable exclusively through males.

*Alibi.* Elsewhere. When a person provides an alibi, he shows that at the time of the commission of an act he was elsewhere at that time.

*Alimony.* An allowance made to a woman for her support by a man, pending or after her legal separation or divorce from him.

*Amicus curiae.* A friend of the court, usually a member of the bar who informs the court when it is doubtful of any fact. The Supreme Court may hear any person who is not a party to the case where the nature and importance of the question before the court would require the assistance of such a person.

*Anathema.* A denunciation pronounced with religious solemnity by ecclesiastical authority, involving excommunication.

*Anuloma* (Sanskrit). The form of marriage between a high caste man and a woman of inferior caste.

*A posteriori.* An argument based on observation or experiment. From the effect to the cause.

*Appellant.* One who prefers appeal.

*Appellate.* Relating to or taking cognizance of appeals; a superior tribunal having the power under law to sit in judgement over another tribunal.

*A priori.* From the antecedent to the consequence.

*Attest.* Affirm to be true or genuine; bear witness.

*Audi alterant partem.* Hear the other side. Condemn no man unheard.

*Autrefois acquit.* This is a plea in criminal cases. When a person is indicted for an offence and acquitted, he cannot then be indicted for the same offence, provided that the first indictment was such that he could have been lawfully convicted on it.

*Autrefois convict.* No person shall be prosecuted and punished for the same offence more than once.

*Bail.* Security given for the due appearance of a prisoner in order to obtain his release from imprisonment.

*Barratry.* A wrongful act wilfully committed by the master or crew of a ship to the prejudice of the shipowner or charterer without his knowledge or connivance, like sinking the ship or stealing the cargo.

*Bequest.* A gift of personal property by will. A legacy.

*Cause calibre.* A legal case that excites widespread interest.

*C.A.V. (Curia Advisari Vult.)* The court wishes to consider the matter.

*Caveat.* A warning; a legal warning to a judicial officer to suspend a proceeding until the opposition has a hearing.

*Caveat emptor.* Let the buyer beware. It does not mean in law that the buyer must take a chance; it merely means that he must take care. The principle applies to court sale of immoveable property.

*Certiorari.* This is a prerogative writ of superior court to call for the records of an inferior court or a body acting in judicial or quasi-judicial capacity. The order of certiorari requires that the record of the proceedings in some cause or matter pending before the inferior court shall be transmitted into the High Court to be there dealt with, in order to ensure that the applicant for the order may have the more sure and speedy justice.

*Codicil.* A supplement to a will already made or something of a similar nature to a will as regards both its purpose and the formalities relating to it. A codicil is capable of independent existence in that the revocation of a will does not necessarily effect the revocation of a codicil thereto.

*Cognate.* Related by blood; related on mother's side. One person is said to be cognate of another if the two are related by blood or adoption but not wholly through males.

*Cognizable offence.* An offence in which a police officer may, in accordance with the First Schedule of the Code of Criminal Procedure or under any law for the time being in force, arrest without warrant.

*Collateral.* Accompanying as secondary or subordinate; relating to an obligation or security attached to another to secure its performance.

*Collateral consanguinity.* The relationship between persons who are descended from the same ancestor (brothers, cousins etc.) as opposed to *linear consanguinity* which means persons of whom one is descended from the other (father and son, grandfather and grandson).

*Conjugal rights.* Rights which husband and wife have to each other's society.

*Connivance.* A petitioner for divorce or judicial separation must satisfy the court that he has not been accessory to or connived at the respondent's adultery. Connivance of adultery bars a decree for judicial separation or divorce.

*Consuetudo est altera lex.* A custom has the force of law.

*Consummation.* The completion of a thing; the completion of marriage between affianced persons by cohabitation or sexual intercourse.

*Coparcenary.* This is a form of tenancy when two or more persons get property on the death of the owner.

*Co-respondent.* Where a husband files a petition for divorce against his wife on the ground of adultery, the alleged adulterer must be made party to the petition as a co-respondent.

*Corpus delicti.* The body or gist of the offence.

*Criminal breach of trust.* If a person entrusted with property dishonestly misappropriates or converts to his own use that property, he is guilty of criminal breach of trust.

*Culpable homicide.* Whoever causes death by doing an act with the intention of causing death or with the intention of causing such bodily injury as is likely to cause death, commits the offence of culpable homicide.

*Dayabhaga.* Hindu law, of supreme authority in Bengal.

*Decree nisi.* A provisional decree which, on the proper steps being taken, will be made absolute or final, unless cause is shown to the contrary.

*Dehors.* Outside the scope of; irrelevant.

*Demurrer.* A form of pleading by which a party objected that his opponent's pleading disclosed no cause of action or ground of defence. Demurrer is an objection to the form of substance of the indictment.

*Double jeopardy.* No person shall be prosecuted and punished for the same offence more than once but for this rule to be applied, a person should first have to be both prosecuted and punished.

*Due process of law.* What is just and proper according to the circumstances of each particular case.

*En ventre sa mere.* In its mother's womb. In Hindu law a child in his mother's womb is equal in many respects to a child actually in existence.

*Ex facto jus oritur.* The law arises out of the fact.

*Ex gratia.* As a matter of favour or grace.

*Ex post facto.* From a later act or event.

*Fait accompli.* Thing done and no longer worth arguing against.

*F.C.S.* Free of capture and seizure, in a policy of marine insurance.

*Felo de se.* A felon with respect to himself: a suicide.

*Flagrante delicto.* In the very act of committing the crime.

*F.O.R.* Free on railway; the seller is to put the goods into the wagons free of all costs.

*Force majeure.* Some physical or material restraint.

*Grievous hurt.* Permanent privation of the sight of either eye, hearing of either ear, any member or joint, disfiguration of head or face or any hurt which endangers life.

*Habeas Corpus, writ of.* A prerogative process for securing the liberty of a person by affording an effective means of immediate release from unlawful or unjustified detention whether in prison or in private custody. By it the court commands the production of the person and inquire into the cause of his imprisonment. The object of the writ of habeas corpus is to bring up prisoners who are detained in custody under civil or criminal process before magistrates for trial or examination on any charge.

*Hearsay evidence.* This is what a witness is merely reporting and not what he himself saw or heard and not what has come under the immediate observation of his own bodily senses.

*Homicide.* The killing of a human being by a human being.

*Hypothecation.* The act of pledging a thing as security for a debt.

*In flagrante delicto.* Caught in the act of adultery.

*Injunction.* A judicial process whereby a party is ordered to refrain from doing a particular act.

*In loco parentis.* In the place of a parent. A person taking upon himself the duty of a father of a child.

*Innuendo.* Oblique hint or allusive remark, that, if depreciatory, may amount to defamation.

*In pari passu.* On equal footing.

*Inter alia.* Among other things.

*Intestate.* When a person has died without making a testamentary disposition capable of taking effect in respect of property, he is deemed to die intestate.

*Intra vires.* Within the power of as against *ultra vires* which means beyond the scope, power or authority of any statutory body.

*Joint family.* A Hindu joint family consists of all persons lineally descended from a common ancestor and includes their wives and unmarried daughters.

*Justiciable.* Liable to be examined in a court of justice.

*Kabin-nama.* A deed of dower in a Muslim marriage; a marriage settlement.

*Karnavan.* The eldest male member and the manager of the joint, undivided Marimakkathayam family in Malabar, consisting of all the descendants in the female line of one common female ancestor.

*Karta.* A coparcener who manages the family property either under an express or implied authority of other coparceners.

*Legatee.* One to whom a legacy is bequeathed.

*Libel. A* false and defamatory statement made or conveyed by written or printed words without lawful justification or excuse. Libel is a criminal offence.

*Lien.* The right of a man to retain that which is rightfully and continuously in his position, belonging to another until the present and accrued claims of the person in possession are satisfied.

*Loco parentis.* A person taking upon himself the duty of a father of a child.

*Locus in quo.* The place where it is alleged a thing has been done or happened.

*Locus standi.* The right of a party to an action to appear and be heard on the question before any tribunal.

*Mala in se.* Acts wrong in themselves.

*Malfeasance.* Wrongful conduct, especially by a public official.

*Mandamus.* A command. The order of mandamus is an order of a most extensive remedial nature and is practically a command issuing from the High Court of Justice, directed to any person, corporation of lower tribunal requiring him or them to do some particular thing and is in the nature of a public duty. The grant of an order of mandamus, generally speaking, is a matter of discretion of the court. It is not an order granted as of right and is not issued as a matter of course.

*Misdemeanour.* All those crimes and offences for which the law has not provided a particular name and which act punishable by fine or imprisonment.

*Misfeasance.* The improper performance of a lawful act; the doing of a lawful act in an unlawful manner.

*Mitakshara.* A true digest of Smriti law. It is of supreme authority in India except in Bengal where the Dayabhaga is given paramount importance. According to Mitakshara law, each son acquires at his birth an equal interest with his father and on the death of the father, the son takes the property not as his heir, but by survivorship.

*Mutatis mutandis.* With the necessary changes.

*Obiter dictum.* An incidental opinion of a judge which is not binding.

*Plaintiff.* One who commences a law suit; the complaining party in any litigation.

*Prima facie case.* When it is clear that a case can be made out on the evidence available.

*Primogeniture.* The exclusive right of the eldest son or nearest male relative to inherit.

*Privileged communication.* A communication made to a witness which he cannot be compelled to disclose.

*Probate.* A copy of a will certified under the seal of a court of competent jurisdiction with a grant of administration to the estate of the testator.

*Pro forma.* For the sake of mere form.

*Pro rata.* In proportion.

*Pro tern.* For the time being.

*Puisne judge.* One of the judges of the High Court other than the Chief Justice.

*Putative.* Supposed, reputed, commonly accepted.

*Re.* In the matter of; relating to.

*Res ipsa loquitur.* The thing speaks for itself.

*Respondent.* The defendant in an appeal. The defendant in a matrimonial suit.

*Search warrant.* An authority given by a competent person to an officer to search the house or any other place mentioned therein for anything or person.

*Seduction.* The inducing of a girl or woman to part with her virtue for the first time.

*Solatium.* A sum paid to a person as compensation or consolation for injured feelings.

*Sub judice.* In course of trial; pending decision of a competent court.

*Sui juris.* Of his own right. A person under no legal disability.

*Taccavi.* Advances of money made by the government to cultivators for agricultural purposes.

*Talak.* Divorce; dissolution or annulment of marriage by a Mahommedan husband.

*Tort. A* civil wrong, like assault, trespass.

*Vis major.* Irresistible violence; inevitable accident; act of God.

*Waiver.* The abandonment of a right.

### *Not an Amateur's Job*

A law reporter, it should go without saying, should be well acquainted with the law, should know the elements of good reporting (clear, unbiassed, accurate, interesting, thorough) which would suggest that he has studied law and journalism as well.

Far too often, the reporting of legal news is left to an impecunious lawyer, which is bad in practice and detrimental to good reporting. He may be good at law but poor in reporting. And in trying to bring out the legal issues involved, miss the essential drama of a case. It cannot adequately be stressed that a law report has to be *accurate.* That, in any event, is the essence of any good reporting. It should contain the minimum of legal jargon that can put off the reader. A reporter who is well acquainted with law and its provisions would be in a sound position to comment on it as well. Once a trial is over, newspapers enjoy the privilege of *fair* comment, fairness implying that criticism is based on actual facts. Newspapers may review the facts of the law and express their opinions even if they be contrary to the decisions of the court. But this implies considerable knowledge of the law, which is why it is always advisable that an editorial writer entrusted with writing an editorial on a celebrated case has knowledge of the law at the tip of his fingers. Editorial writing on law is definitely not for amateurs.

# 13

# The Legislation

## Press and Law

Those engaged in journalistic profession should be familiar with the laws which affect them in their day-today work. The most important among them are law of libel and defamation, contempt of court and legislatures, copyright, etc.

*Libel* **:** It is a writing tending to injure and degrade the character of a person, who is the object of it. It is a defamatory statement published in the press or otherwise, while slander is oral defamation. Libel is the publication of a false and defamatory statement, expressed in writing, printing, or by signs, pictures or in some form which is permanent, published without lawful justification or excuse concerning a person and which injures his reputation.

Libellous statements are divided into the following 4 categories:

1. Exciting hatred, contempt, scorn or ridicule.
2. To be shunned or avoided by society.

3. Affecting profession, calling or office.

4. Affecting trade or business.

For instance, calling a person a liar, a villain, a jackal or swine or making dishonourable comparison with the persons to the characters in history, fiction or mythology or making erroneous announcements are libellous statements.

The defence usually put up are justification, privilege, fair comment and innocent dissemination. To impute a truth about a person for public good, or to express in good faith any opinion respecting the conduct of public servant in discharge of his public function, or of any person touching any public question is not libel. Similarly, to publish a substantially true report of the proceedings of a court of justice, or to comment in good faith on merits on civil and criminal cases is not considered defamatory.

A reporter, in good faith, can express any opinion on the merits of the case, which has been decided, or the merits of any performance which its author has submitted to the judgement of the public. He can also make an imputation on the character of another person in good faith, if it is for the protection of the person making it or of any other or for the public good. Similarly, he can convey a caution to one person against another, or prefer an accusation or censor the conduct in good faith of a person over whom he has authority.

The acceptance of defence as indicated above depends upon the interpretation of the statement made and the appreciation of evidence by the court.

The remedies available to the aggrieved person in India are of two kinds-civil action under the common law, or criminal proceedings for defamation. In the first, the claim is essentially for damages by monetary compensation. In criminal proceedings, it is punishment with fine and/or imprisonment.

***Parliamentary Privilege :*** Journalists have to take care while reporting proceedings of Parliament or State legislatures. The Parliamentary Proceedings (Protection of Publication) Act, 1956, which is popularly known as Feroze Gandhi Act, provides that no person should be liable to any proceedings-civil or criminal, in respect of a publication in a newspaper of a substantially true report of any proceedings of either House of Parliament. This Act was repealed during the Emergency, but has now been re-enacted. All State legislatures, however, have not enacted such Acts.

While reporting the proceedings of Parliament or Assemblies, care should be taken that the writings do not constitute breach of privilege or contempt of the House. The general principle is that the writings which tend to destroy the image of the House and its members in the performance of their functions and duties by diminishing the respect due to them and by bringing them into odium, contempt and ridicule would constitute a breach of privilege and contempt of the House. There is no legislation enacted, so far, defining precisely the circumstances in which the publication may constitute a breach of privilege. However, action has been taken in the following types of cases:

1. Inaccurate reporting.
2. Distorted, unfair, wilful, mendacious rendering of proceedings, or a wilful suppression of an account.
3. Publicizing the expunged proceedings, and publication of reports or proceedings of subcommittees of the House or resolutions or questions or motions, etc. before they are brought before the House.

The Constitution (45th Amendment) Act, 1978, passed by Parliament, provides constitutional authority to 'Feroze Gandhi Act' and extends protection to publication of State legislatures' proceedings.

***Contempt of Court :*** Any act done or writing published, calculated to bring a court of law into contempt or lower its authority or to obstruct or interfere with due course of justice or lawful process of the court, amounts to contempt of court. For instance, publication of proceedings of a case being heard in camera, false and grossly inaccurate reporting of court proceedings, publication that may tend to interfere with orderly administration of justice, or publication that scandalizes the court, the judges, counsels, parties or witnesses fall in this category. Also, no comment should be made, and proper care should be taken in reporting, when the case is sub judice.

The press does enjoy the privilege of fair comment, but personal attacks on judges attributing incompetency, corruption, partiality, judicial dishonesty, political bias, improper motives or 'other considerations' in the court amount to contempt of court.

The Contempt of Court Act XXXII of 1952 says: "Save as otherwise expressly provided by any law for the time being in force, the contempt of court may be punished with simple imprisonment for a term which may extend to six months or with fine which may extend to Rs.2,000 or both. It is provided that the accused may be discharged or the punishment awarded may be remitted on an apology being made to the satisfaction of the Court."

***Copyright :*** Copyright is a right accruing to a person in respect of a work produced by him as a result of exercise of skill, judgement and labour. Under the Copyright Act, protection is afforded to literary, dramatic, musical, artistic, archaeological or any work relating to craftsmanship, engraving and also to films, television, broadcasting diffusion. In such cases, the author has exclusive right for publication, production, reproduction, performance in public, translation, etc. However, a fair dealing with literary, musical, artistic work for the purpose of research, criticism, review, reporting current events in a newspaper or magazine or for judicial proceedings, etc. do not constitute an infringement of copyright. Under the Copyright Act, 1957 registration of any work in which copyright exists is entirely voluntary. In the absence of registration, redress for infringement is under common law.

Copyright Act, 1957 is meant to consolidate the law relating to copyright. It protects the right of the authors of (a) original literary, dramatic, musical and artistic works; (b) Cinematography films; and (c) Record Advertisements to be protected under the Act must be original.

Copyright (Amendment) Rule, 1984 provides details of compulsory licence for publications of unpublished works, translations and reproduction of such works.

***Press and Registration of Books Act, 1867 :*** The Press and Registration of Books Act regulates printing presses, newspapers, registration of books and newspapers printed in India. It places a duty on the publishers of any newspaper to furnish annual statement, etc. to the Registrar of Newspapers along with returns and reports.

Under the Act, one copy of newspaper published in English, Hindi, and Urdu is required to be sent to the Press Registrar, New Delhi. The offices of the RIB receive the copies, on behalf of the Press Registrar of India, in other languages as under:

| | | |
|---|---|---|
| Calcutta | : | Bengali, Oriya and Assamese |
| Madras | : | Tamil and Telugu |
| Ernakulam | : | Malayalam |
| Bombay | : | Marathi and Gujarati |
| Bangalore | : | Kannada |
| Delhi | : | Any other languages. |

***Delivery of Books and Newspapers (Public Library) Act, 1954 :*** Under the Delivery of Books and Newspapers (Public Library) Act, 1954, books and copies of newspapers are to be delivered free to the four national libraries: National Library, Calcutta; Connamera Public Library, Madras; National Central Library, Delhi; and Central Library, Bombay.

## Other Laws

*The Cinematograph Act, 1952* is an Act to make provision for the certification of cinematograph films for exhibition and for regulating exhibitions by means of cinematographs.

*Code of Criminal Procedure* enables the Government to forfeit every issue of a newspaper or a book, whenever it appears to them that it contains matter that brings hatred or contempt, or excites disaffection towards the Government. It extends to the whole of India except the State of Jammu & Kashmir. The Act came in force on April 1, 1974.

*Customs Act, 1962* consolidates the law relating to customs and replaces the Sea Customs Act, 1878. The Act contains provisions for the prohibition of the importation and exportation of objectionable goods. The Government by a notification may prohibit the importation of goods like obscene literature, or particular book or journal as specified in the notification. The Act also contains provisions for search, seizure and confiscation of prohibited goods.

*The Drugs and Cosmetics Act, 1940* enables the Government to regulate the import, manufacture, distribution and sale of drugs and cosmetics. It authorizes the Central Government to constitute the Drugs Technical Board, the Central Drugs Laboratory and the Drugs Consultative Committee to carry out the provisions of the Act. The Government can prohibit the import of any drug or cosmetic which is not of standard quality or which is misbranded or adulterated or prohibited under the rules. It can also prohibit the manufacture for sale, or sell or stock or exhibit for sale or distribute any drug or cosmetic. The Act provides punishment for use for Government Analyst's report for advertising. The Act provides separate provision for Ayurvedic (including Sidha) and Unani Drugs.

*Drug and Magic Remedies (Objectionable Advertisements) Act,* 1954 is to check the increase in number of objectionable advertisements published in newspapers or magazines or otherwise relating to alleged cures for venereal diseases, sexual stimulants and alleged cures for diseases and conditions peculiar to women. These advertisements tend to cause the ignorant and unwary to resort to self medication with harmful drugs and appliances, or to resort to quacks who indulge in such advertisements for treatment which cause great harm. The Act deems it necessary, in public interest, to put a stop to such undesirable advertisements. It controls drug advertisements and also publicity advertisements; advertisements of remedies stated to possess magic remedies. An advertisement includes any notice, circular, label, wrapper, or other documents and announcement made orally or by any means of producing or transmitting light, sound or smoke.

*The Emblems and Names (Prevention of Improper Use) Act*, 1950 prohibited list (1) Name, emblem or official seal of the United Nations Organization, World Health Organization, International Civil Aviation Organization, World Meteorological Organization, UNESCO, International Atomic Energy; (2) The Indian National Flag. The name, emblem or official seal of Government of India, Govt. of State, Parliament, the Legislature of a State, Supreme Court, High Court, Secretariat of Central or State Government, President of India, Governor of a State or Republic of India; (3) Name and pictorial representation of Rashtrapati Bhavan, Raj Bhavan, Chatrapati Shivaji Maharaj, Mahatma Gandhi, Jawaharlal Nehru or the Prime Minister of India, except the pictorial use thereof on calendars where only the name of manufacturer and printers of the calendars are given and the calendars are not used for advertising goods. Ashok Chakra, medals, badges or decorations instituted by the Government of India from time to time. The emblem of St. John Ambulance Association (India), St. John Ambulance Brigade (India), Tuberculosis Association of India. Any name which may suggest or be calculated to suggest the patronage of the Government of India or of the State Government.

*Essential Commodities Act, 1955* provides in the interest of general public, for control of the production, supply and distribution of trade and commerce in certain commodities. The commodities include inter alia paper, including newsprint, paper board and straw board. *Indian Contract Act, 1872* governs the rights and duties of the advertising agencies.

*Indian* Official *Secrets Act, 1963* consolidates the law relating to official secrets. The Act makes it an offence if any person for any purpose prejudicial to the safety or interest of the State-(a) approaches, inspects, passes over or is in the vicinity of or enters any prohibited place; or (b) makes any sketch, plan, model or note which is calculated to be or might be or intended to be directly useful to enemy; or (c) obtains, collects records or publishes or communicates to any other person any sketch, model, plan, article or note or other document or information which is calculated to be or might be or intended to be directly or indirectly useful to enemy.

*Indian Penal Code, 1868* prohibits anything that brings or intended to bring into hatred, to contempt, or excites disaffection towards Government, promotes or attempts to promote feeling of enmity or hatred between different classes of citizens of India. It provides that a book, pamphlet, paper, writing, drawing, painting, representations, figures or any other object shall be deemed to be obscene if it is lascivious or appeals to the purient interest or if its effect is such as to tend to deprive and corrupt persons who are likely, having regard to all relevant circumstances, to read, see or hear the matter contained or embodied in it.

*Indian Post Office Act, 1898* prohibits transmission by post of tickets, proposals, etc. relating to unauthorized lotteries. It also prohibits transmission by post any indecent or obscene painting, photograph, lithograph, engraving book or card, or any other indecent or obscene article or any postal article having thereon, or on the cover thereof, any words, marks or designs of an indecent, obscene, seditious, scurrilous, threatening or grossly offensive character. It prohibits transmission by post of newspapers which are printed and published contrary to the Press and Registration of Books Act, 1867. It empowers its officers to detain in the course of transmission any newspaper, book or document containing any seditious matter.

*Indian Telegraph Act, 1885* enables the Government, or any officer specially authorized by the Government, on the occurrence of any public emergency or in the interest of public safety (a) to take temporary possession of any telegraph established, maintained or worked by any person, licensed under the Act; and (b) to order that any message or class of messages from any person or class of persons or relating to any subject brought for transmission or transmitted or received by any telegraph shall not be transmitted or shall be intercepted or detained or shall be disclosed to the Government or the officers specially authorized.

*Indian Telegraph (Amendment) Rule, 1984:* Telegram means written or printed matter intended to be transmitted by telegraph and includes radio telegram or photo telegram.

*Newspaper (Price and Page) Act, 1956* is an Act in pursuance of the Press Commission's recommendations that legislation be enacted empowering Government to issue from time to time a price page schedule fixing minimum price at which papers of a particular size can be sold.

*Newspaper (Price Control) Act, 1972* provides for the control, in the interest of general public, of the prices of newspapers with a view to ensuring that newspapers continue to function, in the prevailing conditions, as effective mass communication media and for securing their availability at fair prices. The Act extends to the whole of India and was to cease after the expiry of two years.

*Newsprint Control (Amendment) Order, 1982* provides that (1) every consumer of newsprint who is a printer or publisher or both of a daily newspaper shall print prominently on the front page of each copy of the newspaper every day-the total number of copies actually printed; (2) every consumer of newsprint who is a printer or publisher or both of a periodical other than a daily newspaper shall print prominently in each copy of the periodical-the total number of copies actually printed.

*The Press Council Act, 1978* is an Act to establish a 29-member Press Council for the purpose of preserving the freedom of the Press, and of maintaining and improving the standards of newspapers and news agencies in India.

*Prevention of Insults to National Honour Act, 1971* provides for punishment for disrespect of National Flag, the Constitution of India, or the National Anthem. It prevents overt acts of insults on the national symbols by burning, trampling, defiling or mutilating in public. The Act extends to the whole of India.

*Prevention of Publication of Objectionable Matter (Repeal) Act, 1977.* Freedom of the Press is necessary for the successful functioning of democratic institutions. The Prevention of Publication of Objectionable Matter Act, 1976 has been repealed to safeguard the Press freedom.

*Prevention of Seditious Meeting Act, 1911* is to consolidate and amend the law relating to prevention of public meeting likely to promote seditions or to cause disturbance of public tranquillity.

*Prize Competition Act, 1955* provides for control and regulation of prize competitions. It prohibits the prize competition where the prize offered exceeds one thousand rupees a month. It also provides for licensing of prize competitions where the prize offered does not exceed one thousand rupees a month. The Act states where any newspaper or other publications contain any prize competition promoted or conducted in contravention of the provisions of this Act or except in accordance with the provisions of a licence under this Act or any advertisement thereto, the State Government may, by notification in the Official Gazette, declare every copy of publication containing the prize competition or the advertisement, to be forfeited to the Government.

*Sea Customs Act, 1978* enables the Central Government from time to time to prohibit or restrict the bringing or taking by sea or by land of goods of any specified description into, or out of, India across any customs frontiers. The Act also prohibits dissemination of news relating to an emergency and public safety.

*Standard of Weights and Measures Act, 1976* requires that all units and measurements be given in metric units. Any advertisement or public notice in non-metric units is prohibited.

*Trade and Merchandise Marks Act, 1958:* With the increase in trade and commerce, commercial advertising has also increased. This Act effectively protects the trade marks and trade descriptions. A trade mark is a mark used or proposed to be used in relation to goods for the purposes of indicating, or so as to indicate, a connection in the course of trade between the goods and some person having the right as either a proprietor or as registered user to use mark, whether with or without indication of the identity of that person, and the mark includes a device brand, heading, label, ticket name, signature, work, letter, numeral or any combination thereof. Trade description means any description, statement of other indication, direct or indirect, concerning trade. This description or statement may be regarding number, quality measure gauge, or weight of any goods. Any use or application or use of false trade mark or description is punishable under the Act.

*Working Journalists (Fixation of Rates of Wages) Act, 1958* provides for the fixation of rates of wages in respect of working journalists. It provides inter alia for the payment of gratuity and provident fund to working journalists. The Act regulates hours of work, holidays with pay, notice period for termination of service, etc.

*Working Journalists (Conditions of Service) and Miscellaneous Provisions (Amendment) Act, 1974* extends the application of Working Journalists (Condition of Service) and Miscellaneous Provisions Act, 1955 to other newspaper employees also, i.e., non-journalist newspaper employees.

*Working Journalists and Other Newspaper Employees (Conditions of Service) and Miscellaneous Provisions (Amendment) Act,* 1981 provides that no employer in relation to a newspaper establishment shall, by reason of his liability for payment of wages to newspaper employees at the rates specified in an order of the Central Government under sections 12,13AA or 13DD, dismiss, discharge or retrench any newspaper employee. Further, the Act extends protection to even part-time employees.

*Young Persons (Harmful Publication) Act, 1956* provides penalty for a person who sells, lets to hire, distribute publicly, exhibits or in any manner puts into circulation any harmful publication, or for purposes of sale, hire, distribution, public exhibition or circulation, prints, makes or produces or has in possession any harmful publication; or advertises or makes known by any means whatsoever, that any harmful publication can be procured from or through any person. The Act extends to the whole of India.

*Maps: By* a notification issued under Criminal Law (Amendment) Act, publication of maps in which the boundaries of India with neighbouring countries are deleted requires the approval of the Surveyor-General of India.

**Press Council**

The Press Commission (1954) recommended the setting up of a statutory Press Council to look after the editorial independence, objectivity of news presentation, and fairness of comments, etc. on the part of newspapers. The Council, according to the Commission, was also to foster the development of press, protecting it from external pressure, and regulate its conduct in matters of such objectionable writing as was not legally punishable. In pursuance of this recommendation, the Press Council of India was constituted by the Government of India in 1966 under the Press Council Act, 1965, which was later amended on 31 March 1970. The Council's term, which expired in December 1975, was not extended during the Emergency.

The Council, prior to its termination, consisted of a chairman and 26 members. A committee consisting of the Chairman of the Rajya Sabha, the Chief Justice of India, and the Speaker of the Lok Sabha nominated six editors, seven journalists other than editors, six persons either owning or in the management of newspapers, and one person representing the management of news agencies. A member each was nominated by the University Grants Commission, Sahitya Akademi, and Bar Council of India. Two members were nominated by the Speaker of the Lok Sabha, and one by the Chairman of the Rajya Sabha.

The Press Council was an autonomous body. Its object, broadly, was to preserve freedom of the press and to improve the standard of newspapers and news agencies in India. The Council could warn, admonish, or censure a newspaper or a news agency for any professional misconduct, or breach of the code of journalistic ethics, or an offence against public taste. It could also condemn the government or other organizations for interfering with the freedom of the press. It enjoyed the same powers, while holding an enquiry under the Press Council Act, as are vested in a civil court while trying a suit under the Code of Civil Procedure. The Council could also ask a defaulting newspaper to publish the Council's findings or observations against it.

***Revived Council :*** The objectives of the revived Press Council of India, according to the Press Council Act, 1978, are "to preserve the freedom of the press and to improve standards of newspapers and news agencies in the country". The Act is more or less on the same lines as the Press Council Act, 1965. (During the Emergency, the Press Council was dissolved with effect from 1 January 1976.)

The functions of the revived Council include, among other things, 'building up' (not to formulate) a code of conduct for newspapers, news agencies, and journalists in accordance with high professional standards, and to encourage the growth of sense of responsibility and public service among all those who are engaged in the profession of journalism. The code is to be evolved through case law and conventions over a period of time.

The Council is empowered to hold enquiries on complaints, made to it or otherwise, against offending newspapers and news agencies. For the purpose of performing its functions or holding any enquiry, the Council has the same powers throughout India as are vested in a civil court, while trying a suit under the Code of Civil Procedure in certain respects. These powers include summoning and enforcing the attendance of persons and examining them on oath, requiring discovery and inspection of the documents, receiving evidence on affidavits, requisitioning any public record and issuing commissions for the examination of witnesses or documents.

The Press Council of India is to be a body corporate having perpetual succession and consists of a Chairman and 28 members. The Chairman of the Council is to be nominated by a panel comprising the Chairman, Rajya Sabha; Speaker, Lok Sabha and a person elected by the members of the Council. Thirteen of the members are to be nominated, in accordance with such procedures as may be prescribed, from among the working journalists including six editors. The number of working journalists, representing newspapers published in Indian languages, has been raised from 3 to 4.

Six of the 28 members are to be nominated from among those persons who own or carry on the business of management of newspapers. Five MPs are also to be nominated on the Council.

Besides, one representative from among persons who manage news agencies, and three other members from the field of education and science, law, and literature and culture are to be nominated by the University Grants Commission, the Bar Council of India, and the Sahitya Akademi. No member on the Council is to be nominated by the government.

The power to appoint the chairman and a member of the Press and Registration Appellate Board, under the Press and Registration of Books Act, 1867, has been given to the Press Council of India.

The Act also contains an enabling provision empowering the Council to levy graded fees on newspapers with over 5000 circulation and news agencies for the services it proposes to render.

Like the former Press Council, the revived Council is also a statutory, quasi judicial, and self-regulating body without 'teeth' (power to impose legal penalties). However, it differs with the earlier body in three important respects, namely, in regard to the procedure of appointment of its chairman and its composition; the power to consider complaints against the government and criticize the governmental action; and to levy fee on the newspapers and others for its work.

The enabling provision empowering the Council to levy fees on newspapers and news agencies reduces its dependence on government's financial support, and provides scope for inculcating a sense of participation of newspapers in the affairs of the Council.

In the revived Press Council, English newspapers as also the newspaper chains would not be able to dominate, since there is now no distinction between languages in so far as the representation of owners or managers on the Council is concerned.

The Press Council has residual powers to undertake any studies suo moto relevant to the discharge of its functions. The Press Council's reports are to be placed in Parliament, and as such members of Parliament are in a position to criticize the government on the basis of Council's observations.

It is expected that the Council, in course of time, would be not only a mechanism for 'self-regulation' for the press but also a `bulwark' against any attack, pressure or encroachment on the freedom of the press from any source-government, proprietors, advertisers, political parties, trade unions and other interested groups. It has also been empowered to look into ownership pattern of newspapers or news agencies, which may impinge on the independence of the press, and to help them to maintain their independence.

Under the Press Council Act, 1978, the first Press Council of India was constituted in 1979, the second in February, 1982, the third in July, 1985, and the fourth in 1988. The term of the Council is for three years.

The Press Council safeguards freedom of the press, maintains and improves the standard of newspapers and news agencies. It is comprised mainly of representatives from the newspapers, who are charged with the responsibility of regulating the conduct of their brethren. The Council has thus come to assume the role of a self-regulating body of the newspapers themselves.

The Council has the power to consider complaints suo moto, in addition to inquiring into complaints brought before it. It has also been empowered to make observations against any authority, including government, if it considers it necessary for the performance of its functions.

The Press Council of India is a body with powers which, though wide, are not unlimited. Its powers are conferred upon it by its constituent organizations and are embodied in its constitution. It cannot exceed them. One of its objects is "to maintain and improve the standards of newspapers and news agencies in India," and it is in relation to this object that it is empowered to consider complaints about the conduct of the press. What it is empowered to criticize or condemn is a downward slide in professional standards.

The Indian Press Council which is a statutory body is unique in nature from its parallel institutions, in that while most of the other similar bodies are voluntary in nature, the Indian Council is a creation of an Act of Parliament. It, however, functions independent of any government control. Under Section 15(4) of the Press Council Act, 1978, the Council has been empowered if it considers it necessary for the purpose of carrying out its objects or for the performance of any of its functions under this Act, to make such observations, as it may think fit, in any of its decisions or reports, respecting the conduct of any authority, including government.

Simultaneously, the statute casts a duty on the Council to maintain and improve the standards of newspapers and news agencies in the country and to encourage the growth of a sense of responsibility and public service among all those engaged in the profession of journalism. Through diligent efforts, the Council has rendered adjudications on cases filed before it and has pronounced views and opinion in regard to matters of vital importance to the free and unhampered working of the print media. Out of proportion increase in the number of complaints received by the Council both against the press and the authorities is a matter of concern to everyone.

The effectiveness of a self-regulatory body such as the Press Council has been recognized in several countries. In UK, the Council came into existence in 1953. The Japanese body-Nihon Shimbum Kyokoi-came into being as early as 1946. In West Germany and Israel, similar institutions were set up in 1956 and 1963 respectively.

# Appendices

## Code of Conduct

*Preamble :* The First Amendment, protecting freedom of expression from abridgment by any law, guarantees to the people through their press a constitutional right, and thereby places on newspaper people a particular responsibility.

Thus journalism demands of its practitioners not only industry and knowledge but also the pursuit of a standardise integrity proportionate to the journalist's singular obligation. To this end the American Society of Newspaper Editors sets forth this Statement of Principles as a standard encouraging the highest ethical and professional performance.

***ARTICLE 1. Responsibility***

The primary purpose of gathering and distributing news and opinion is to serve the general welfare by informing the people and enabling them to make judgments on the issues of the time. Newspapermen and women who abuse the power of their profession role for selfish motives or unworthy purposes are faithless to that public trust.

The American press was made free not just to form or just to serve as a forum for debate but also to bring an independent scrutiny to bear on the forces of power in the society, including the conduct of official power at all levels of government.

***ARTICLE II. Freedom of the Press***

Freedom of the press belongs to the people. It must be defended against encroachment or assault from any quarter, public or private.

Journalist must be constantly alert to see that the public's business is conducted in public. They must be vigilant against all who would exploit the press for selfish purposes.

***ARTICLE III. Independence***

Journalists must avoid impropriety and the appearance of impropriety as well as any conflict of interstellar the appearance of conflict. They should neither accept anything nor pursue any activity that might compromise or seem to compromise their integrity.

***ARTICLE IV. Truth and Accuracy***

Good faith with the reader is the foundation of good journalism. Every effort must be made to assure that the news content is accurate, free from bias and in context and that all sides are presented fairly. Editorials, analytical articles and commentary should be held to the same standards of accuracy with respect to facts as news reports.

Significant errors of fact, as well as errors of omission, should be corrected promptly and prominently.

***ARTICLE V. Impartiality***

To be impartial does not require the press to be unquestioning or to retrain from editorial expression. Sound practice, however, demands a clear distinction for the reader between news reports and opinion. Articles that contain opinions or personal interpretation should be clearly identified.

***ARTICLE VI. Fair Play***

Journalists should respect the rights or people involved in the news, observe the common standards of decency and stand accountable to the public for the fairness and accuracy of their news reports.

Persons publicly accused should be given the earliest opportunity to respond.

Pledges of confidentiality to news sources must be honored all costs, and therefore should not be given lightly. Unless there is clear and pressing need to maintain confidences, sources of information should be identified.

These principles are intended to preserve, protect and strengthen the bond of trust and respect between American journalists and the American people, a bond that is essential to sustain the grant of freedom entrusted to both by the nation's founders.

***Principal Ethical Guidelines :*** These are the principal ethical considerations that a newcomer to journalism should remember on initial reporting assignments:

* Play it straight. Don't try any tricks. Ask all the necessary questions and write a factual story about a sensitive issue straight down the middle.
* Protect your sources wherever necessary and respect confidences that are freely offered.
* Respect the law and the rights of privacy of people in the news.
* The instructions given to you by your editor or news director and your own loyalty to the pubic interest should be the only considerations that will influence you on assignment.
* When in doubt, always ask the editor who gave you the assignment to clarify any problem that arises.
* Do not represent yourself to be thing other than a reporter unless you have specific instructions from your news organization.
* Beware of accepting free trip, free tickets, free dinners or other freedom in connection with an assignment; even when you are not on duty, you should never accept any gift that will have the appearance of impropriety.

* Remember that a "composite figure" in a story is a made-up figure with mythical characteristics. The "composite figure"if used in a news story-is bound to create misunderstanding, and reporters should avoid creating this type of journalistic monster.

* All reporters should keep a decent distance between themselves and even the best of news sources. If does not pay to be too chummy with people who are in a position to influence the shaping of the news.

* If there is a strong reason to withhold a name or an address in connection with a news break, such as a kidnapping or a terrorist who is holding hostages, clear the position you want to take with the editor in charge and make sure that you both have the same understanding about what should be done.

* When it becomes necessary to work with law enforcement authorities, you should ask for guidelines from your news organization on how much cooperation is to be expected of you. Remember that news people should not be under the control of any source outside their own news organization.

* Always try to avoid becoming a part of the news. It is not your hob to create news. Your assignments is to cover it, write or photograph it and explain it.

* Always try to go in the front door and don't look for short cuts.

* The same ethical considerations apply to all journalists.

# Calcutt Code (U.K.)

*Accuracy*

(i) Newspapers and periodicals should take care not to publish inaccurate or distorted material.

(ii) Whenever it is recognised that a significant misleading statement or distorted report has been published, it should be corrected promptly and with due prominence.

(iii) An apology should be published whenever appropriate.

(iv) A newspaper or periodical should always report fairly and accurately the outcome of an action for defamation to which it has been a party.

*Right to Reply :* Individuals or organisations should be given a proportionate and reasonable opportunity to reply to criticisms or alleged inaccuracies, which are published about them.

*Comment Conjecture and Fact :* Newspapers should distinguish clearly between comment, conjecture and fact.

*Privacy*

(i) Making enquiries about the personal lives of individuals without their consent is not generally acceptable.

(ii) Publishing material about the personal lives of individuals without their consent is not generally acceptable.

(iii) An intrusion into an individual's personal life can be justified only for the purpose of detecting or exposing crime or seriously antisocial conduct protecting public health or safety, or preventing the public from being misled by some public statement or action of that individual.

(iv) An individual's personal life includes matters of health, home, personal relationships, correspondence and documents but does not include his trade or business.

*Hospitals*

(i) Journalists or photographers making enquiries at hospitals or similar institutions should identify themselves to a responsible official and obtain permission before entering.

(ii) The restrictions on intruding into privacy are particularly relevant to enquiries about individuals in hospitals or similar institutions.

*Misrepresentation*

(i) Journalists should not generally obtain or seek to obtain information or pictures through misrepresentation or subterfuge.

(ii) Documents or photographs should be removed only with the express consent of the owner and only with an indication that they might be published.

(iii) Subterfuge (including the use of concealed cameras or recording devices) can be justified only for the purpose of detecting or exposing crime or seriously antisocial conduct, protecting public health or safety, or preventing the public being misled by some public statement or action of an individual and which could not be obtained by other means.

*Harassment*

(i) Journalists should neither obtain nor seek to obtain infirmation or pictures through intimidation, harassment or trespass.

(ii) They should not persist in telephoning or questioning individuals after having been asked to desist and should not remain on their property after having been asked to leave.

(iii) They should not follow individuals unless this is necessary for the purpose of detecting or exposing crime or seriously antisocial conduct, protecting public health or safety, or preventing the public from being misled by some public statement or action of an individual.

(iv) They should not photograph individuals on private property without their consent unless it is necessary for one of these purposes.

***Payment for Article***

(i) Payments or offers of payment for stories, pictures of information should not be made to witnesses or potential witnesses in current criminal proceedings or to people engaged in crime or to their associates.

(ii) Associates includes family, friends, neighbours and colleagues.

(iii) Payments should not be made either directly or indirectly through agents.

(iv) Editors should not publish such material if there is reason to believe payment has been made for it.

(v) Payment may exceptionally be justified if information cannot be obtained by any other means for the purpose of detecting or exposing crime or seriously antisocial conduct, protecting public health or safety or preventing the public from being misled by some public statement or action of an individual.

***Intrusion into Grief or Shock***

(i) The Press should not intrude into personal grief or shock, in particular in the aftermath of accidents and tragedies.

(ii) Unsolicited approaches to the recently bereaved can be justified only to obtain material which cannot be obtained by other means for the purpose of exposing crime or seriously antisocial conduct, protecting public health or safety or preventing the public from being seriously misled by some public statement or action of an individual.

(iii) In these instances, enquiries should be carried out and approaches made with sympathy and discretion.

(iv) The Press should take care not to publish pictures which are likely to exacerbate grief or cause distress.

*Innocent Relatives and Friends :* The Press should not identify relatives or friends of persons convicted or accused of crime unless the reference to them is necessary for the fair and accurate reporting of the crime or legal proceedings.

*Interviewing or Photographing Children*

(i) Journalists should not normally interview or photograph a child under the age of 16 in the absence or without the consent of a parent or other adult who is responsible for the child.

(ii) Children should not be approached or photographed while at school without the permission of the school authorities.

*Children in Sex Cases :* The Press should not, even where the law does not prohibit it, identify children under the age of 16 who are involved in cases concerning sexual offences whether as victims or as witnesses or defendants.

*Victims of Crime*

(i) The Press should not, even where the law does not prohibit it, identify victims of sexual assaults or publish material likely to contribute to such identification.

(ii) The Press should not identify victims of any crime when identification is likely to put at risk the physical or mental health or security of the victim or that of his home.

*Criminal Convictions :* Even where the law does not prohibit it, an individual's criminal convictions should not be published unless the reference to them is directly relevant to the matter reported.

*Discrimination*

(i) The Press should avoid prejudicial or perjurative references to a person's race, colour, religion, sex or sexual orientation or to any physical or mental illness or handicap.

(ii) It should not publish details of a person's race, colour, religion, sex or sexual orientation, unless these are directly relevant to the story.

***Stories About the Recently-Dead :*** Newspapers should apply the same principles of accuracy, respect for privacy and nondiscrimination to stories about the recently dead as to stories about living.

***Financial Journalism***

(i) Even where the law does not prohibit it, journalists should not use for their own profit financial information they receive in advance of its general publication nor should they pass such information to others.

(ii) They should not write about shares or securities in whose performance they know that they or their close families have a significant financial interest without disclosing the interest to the editor or financial editor.

(iii) They should not buy or sell either directly or through nominees or agents, shares or securities about which they have written recently or about which they intent to write in the near future.

***Confidential Sources :*** Journalists have a moral obligation to protect confidential sources of information.

# A Publisher's Contract

**1. Memorandum of Agreement**

made this day of One thousand Nine Hundred and Seventy between millhouse Press, of 13 Stable Road, London WCI 5XX, hereinafter refereed to as 'the Publishers' of the one part, and of hereinafter called 'the Editor' of the other part.

B. The Publishers shall publish at their own risk and expense a work consisting of essays by various contributors edited by the Editor and provisionally entitled (hereinafter referred to as 'the Work')

C. Copyright in individual essays shall be assigned to the Publishers by individual contributors. Copyright in the Work is hereby assigned by the Editor(s) to the Publishers on consideration of its publication and on the terms hereinafter expressed.

D. Two copies of the final typescript of the Work shall be delivered to the Publishers in good order ready for Press on or before the said final typescript consisting of not more than approximately words on the line of the attached synopsis.

E. If in the opinion of the Publishers an index is required it shall be supplied by the editor or at his or her expense.

F. The Editor undertakes to obtain and deliver to the Publishers upon delivery under clause hereof (or, with the agreement of the Publishers at some late date) written permissions for any textual or illustrative material which is to be included in any part of the Work written by the Editor and of which the copyright is not the Editor's and the Publishers undertake to assist and advise the Editor in this task. All relevant permission and reproduction fees shall be paid by the Editor. The Editor further undertakes to secure with the Publishers' assistance and advice such further permissions as the Publishers may from time to time require for the purpose of exercising their rights under this Agreement and to pay all relevant permission and reproduction fees. The Publishers shall themselves be entitled but not required to obtain all or any of such permissions and to deduct from any moneys due-to the Editor such sums as may have been paid by them but are by virtue of this clause the responsibility of the Editor.

G. The proof sheets of the Work shall be read by the Editor and by the relevant contributor(s) but the final typescript of the Work shall be deemed to constitute the final version of the Work and corrections of substance (i.e. corrections other than those of printers' and publishers, errors) at proof stage by individual contributors or by the Editors shall be allowed only under exceptional circumstances. If the total alterations in proof (corrections of printers' and publishers' errors excepted) exceed 10% of the cost of composition then the excess shall be paid for by the Editor.

H. During the legal period of copyright the publishers shall pay the following royalties, such royalties being divided ax follows-20% to the Editor and 80% equally divided between the contributors to the Work.

(a) a royalty of 10% on the English published price of all copies sold of the hardcover edition rising to 15% after the sales of the first 5000 copies (except as hereafter provided);

(b) a royalty of 71/2% on the English published price of any paper-back edition sold (except as hereafter provided);

(c) a royalty at the appropriate rate as specific in (a) or (b) above on the net receipts from all copies sold at a discount of 45% or greater discount.

J. The Publishers shall use their best endeavours to obtain revenue from the sale of volume and subsidiary rights and shall undertake all necessary negotiations.

(b) In the even of the Publishers leasing translation or reprint rights in the volume as a whole (as distinct from the leasing rights in a part or parts of the Work) then the Publishers shall pay the Editor 50% of the net proceeds.

K. The Publishers shall not be responsible for any accidental loss of or damage to the Work (including illustrations or other material) by fire or otherwise while it is in their custody or in course of production.

L. No royalties shall be paid in respect of the following:

(a) Copies of the Work presented to the Editor, or to others, or to the press.

(b) Copies of the work destroyed by fire, water, enemy action, in transit or otherwise.

(c) Copies of the Work sold at or below cost of production.

M. (1) An account shall be taken annually of all sums due to the Editor hereunder in each year up to 31 December and the amount due accordingly shall be paid to the Editor (less any contra account) in the April next following.

(2) The Editor warrants to the Publishers that the Work is in no way whatever a violation of any existing copyright that it contains nothing libellous and that he or she will indemnify the Publishers from and against all claims proceedings damages losses and costs which may be taken suffered or incurred on the ground that the Work or any part thereof infringes copyright or contains anything libellous.

N. The Editor shall receive two free copies of the Work. Other contributors shall receive one free copy each of the Work.

Further copies for personal use (not for resale) may be obtained at a discount of 30% off the English published price.

O. (a) The Publishers shall have the power at their discretion too dispose of by sale (at the best obtainable price) or otherwise the residue or part of the residue of any edition after not less than two years from first publication. (In respect of copies disposed of by sale at a price greater than cost the Editor shall be entitled to receive a royalty on the net receipts of 10% in respect of the hard cover edition of the work and 71/2% in respect of a paper-back- edition of the Work.)

(b) Where the said residue or part of the residue of any edition is to be disposed of by sale the publishers shall give the Editor the option of purchasing some or all of such stock at the said best obtainable price, such option to be deemed to have been complied with by the Publishers four weeks after they shall have given notice in writing to the Editor containing an offer of said stock and to have been refused by the Editor in the absence of notice in writing by the Publishers within the said period accepting such offer.

P. If any difference shall arise between the Editor and the Publishers touching the meaning of this agreement or the rights or liabilities of the parties hereunder the same shall be referred to the arbitration of two persons (one to be named by each party) or their umpire, in accordance with the provisions of the Arbitration Act 1950 or any statutory modification or re-enactment thereof.

## FORM OF ASSIGNMENT OF COPYRIGHT

Continuing developments in international legislation make it essential for copyright in [the publisher/journal] to be controlled by a central organization this will both ensure maximum protection against unlawful use and enable [the publisher/journal benefit from cooperative licensing arrangements, which are already being established.

Authors are therefore asked to sign and return the statement below, keeping the duplicate copy for their records.

Please note:

1. Authors may reuse minor parts (such as some of the tables or illustrations) of their own material after publication without seeking further permission, subject only to full acknowledgement to [the book/journal] as the original source.
2. For commercial use by third party the author's approval will be sought (to be assumed one month after notice has been sent to last known address).
3. Where the copyright rests with the author's employers their consent should (if possible) be obtained to [the publisher/journal] handling copyright matters for the article with third parties and in particular to include it in any lengthening arrangements made for [the book/journal] as a whole.

Copyright assignment:

In consideration of the publication in by of my chapter/article/comment(s) entitled

I hereby assign to the copyright throughout the world in the chapter/article/comment(s) on the conditions mentioned above:

Signed ......................

Date ......................

Name ......................

Address ......................

If the copyright belongs to your employers, please given their name: and indicate whether [the publisher/journal] may register the article and part of the complete issue and handle copyright matters on their behalf with third practices: Yes/No

Please return to :

The Editor ......................

......................

......................

## LETTER TO POTENTIAL CONTRIBUTORS TO A MULTI-AUTHOR BOOK

Sample letter to a potential contributor to a book on lung liquids

14 September 1979

Dear

As you may know, I am planning to compile a book on Lung liquids, and I am writing to ask if you would like to contribute a chapter.

The book will deal with water and solute exchanges across capillary and alveolar epithelia-a subject less familiar than gas transfer across these membranes. Its purpose will be to show how basic research can contribute to the understanding of clinical problems, and it is directed to post-graduate research workers and clinicians in respiratory physiology, membranology and fetology. The idea is to describe basic physiological research on the properties of epithelial membranes and to point out how that work applies to what happens in the lung, particularly the fetal lung, fin both normal and normal conditions. I hope to include recent work on other respiratory epithelia such as the fish gill.

The present plan is for the book to open with a section on some aspects of lung structure. The water and solute permeability of lung capillaries and epithelium in fetal and postnatal life and their function in controlling bulk water movements will then be considered. Next, some aspects of epithelia function and ion transport across the fish gill, amphibian lung and mammalian lung will be compared, special attention being paid to the fetus. Finally, the pathogens is and pathophysiology of lung oedema will be discussed.

What I should very much like from you, if you are interested in contributing, is a chapter on the clinical disorders associated with lung liquids, to close the book. The chapter should be between 6000 and 8000 words, plus tables and figures as necessary.

The time table for the book is as follows:

Manuscripts to reach me by 15 January 1980

Final revision of manuscripts to be completed not later than I April 1980.

Proofs to reach you by about 15 June 1980

Your corrected proofs to be returned to me by I July 1980

Book to be published by mid-September 1980

It will be essential for everyone to keep strictly to these deadlines. If typescripts do not reach me in time, I may have to revise the plan of the book with the omission of certain chapters, or write those chapters myself-which won't be nearly as satisfactory as if they were written be others! My own part in the book, apart from the editing and an introducer review of the present state of research on lung liquids, will be a chapter on ion transport across amphibian lung-

I am inviting as other contributors. J. Brown, H. Schmidt, (etc.). ' D. Horn and L. Cavalli have already undertaken to provide the chapters on.

The book will be published by the Millhouse Press, which will hold the copyright. Those who accept the invitation to contribute will be asked to assign the copyright in their chapters to the publisher. In recognition of this, you will receive 8% of the royalties payable. Secretarial and postage costs will both be paid. Contributors will receive one copy of the book and 50 free reprints of their own chapter. Contributors will also able to obtain further copies of the book at a discount.

I look forward to having a response from you within the next week or two, and I hope it will be positive. I should also be glad to have your comments on the general plan for the book as outlined here.

Yours sincerely,

**GUIDELINES FOR AUTHORS**

Example (with comments in italics) of guidelines for authors contributing to a multi-author monograph entitled Lung liquids'.

*Aims and Scope :* The book will deal with water and solute, exchanges across capillary and alveolar epithelium. Its purpose is to show how basic research can contribute to the understanding of clinical problems. The readers will be research-oriented clinicians working in paediatrics or general medicine and postgraduate research workers. Basic physiological research on the properties of epithelial membranous will be described, and its application to normal and abnormal conditions in the lung-particularly the fetal lung-will be discussed. Recent work on other respiratory epithelia such as the fish gill will be included.

***Typescripts of Chapters :*** Length: 6000-8000 words (20-30 typescript pages; types double-spaced).

Submission: By 15 January 1980 (ribbon copy plus one other) to [address]

***Publisher, Copyright and Fee :*** The book will be published by Millhouse Press Ltd, London. Your acceptance of the invitation to contribute to the book will be taken to mean (a) that your chapter will be an original review of your own and others' research, not previously published elsewhere, and (b) that you agree to assign copyright to the publishers, in return for which your will receive a copy of the book and 50 free reprint of your chapter. You will also receive 8% of the royalties paid by the publisher.

***Reproduction of Previously Published Material :*** If you use any previously published tables or illustrations, or cite lengthy passages of text, it is your responsibility to obtain the copyright-holder's written permission for the material to be reproduced in this book. If the copyright-holder is not the author, please obtain the author's permission too. The written permission(s) should accompany the typescript.

Many authors think that obtaining permission to reproduce material is the responsibility of the editor or publisher. It is not. Authors should be asked to obtain such permissions themselves. Strictly speaking, they need obtain only the permission of the copyright-holder-sometimes a journal, a learned society or a publishing house rather than the original author-but the original author should be asked as well. This often leads to an unexpected bonus in the form of new information.

In the USA, publications based on work supported by public funds and which carry no copyright notice can be used freely.

***Ethics :*** Where relevant, please provide proof that your own experiments have been conducted in accordance with named ethical guidelines, and send a copy of the approval of any relevant ethics committee. Try not to include references to ethically dubious work published by others, unless you add a comment about your reservations.

Authors are primarily responsible for considering all ethical matters before they begin work that will affect any living person or creature. In most countries there are mechanisms to ensure that they do so. The editor must assume secondary responsibility, and insert comments when appropriate (e.g. when authors discuss work, not their own, which has been published even though its ethical justification was questionable). Every time ethically dubious work is published or referred to, it acquires some degree of respectability which may encourage other investigators to follow a bad example.

***Form and Style :*** Write simply and concisely, remembering that the book will be read by people from other disciplines. Use short words rather than long ones, and concrete rather than abstract terms; where appropriate, prefer the first person singular or plural to the third person, and the active to the passive voice. Avoid vague statements, jargon and laboratory slang, and words not defined in dictionaries. Give references in the text by name and date, not by numbers (see below, under References). Avoid footnotes and abbreviations; when these are essential, place all footnotes together on a separate page or pages, and define abbreviations in the text at first mention. Acceptable abbreviations for this book are given on the last page of these guidelines, but please use even acceptable abbreviations sparingly and with discretion. A recommended guide to form and style is Writing Scientific Papers in English: an Else-Ciba foundation guide for Authors (O'connor & Woodford 1975 Elsevier/Excerpta Medica/ North-Holland, Amsterdam, Paper-back 1978 Pitman Medical, Tunbridge Wells.)

***Avoidance of Footnotes :*** For the reader, footnotes are distracting; for the print they may be difficult and expensive to keep track of and to insert on the right page. Their content can usually either be worked into the text, deferred to an appendix or omitted altogether; but occasionally for example, when an editor's comment, elucidation or cross-reference to another article is called for) a footnote can be invaluable to the reader and should not be transformed in any of these ways.

The request to the author to type footnotes on a separate page is appropriate only if hot-metal typesetting is being used, in which the printer uses different machines to set type of different sizes (since footnotes are usually set in smaller type than the main text). When this is so, the printer must be able to give the page on which the footnote is typed to a different machine operator. The type set up elsewhere has to be reunited with the main text, on the correct page; hence the extra cost.

*Avoidance of Abbreviations :* An excess of abbreviations irritates and confuses readers, especially those who are not familiar with the subject or the language.

When a cumbersome name, or phrase must be used frequently in a text, and cannot always be replaced by a pronoun or shortened version, abbreviation, are useful; but readers must be able to look up the meaning of any abbreviation easily. Some readers consult only part of a chapter or journal article, and therefore see abbreviations long after these have been first mentioned and defined. A page of abbreviations and their explanations can usefully be placed at the beginning of a book as well as to the beginning of each chapter, and a list is sometimes placed at the beginning of journal articles. The editor must also, of course, ensure consistency in use of abbreviations. For a book, it helps if the guidelines for authors include a list of permitted abbreviations, culled from the leading journals in the discipline, or (in the life sciences) from O'Connor & Woodford or such guides as the CBE Style manual or the European Journal of Biochemistry; this is preferable to a simple reference to these sources, since authors may not have easy access to them.

*Title Page :* Make the title accurate and informative, but not too long (up to 100 characters and spaces). Provide a short title also, if necessary (up to 45 characters), for running headlines in the book. Write your own name, with given name(s) or initials(s), and those of your coauthors, if any, in the way that you and they usually write names for by-lines. Given the name and address to which correspondence should be sent.

*Names of Authors :* Many authors seem to enjoy publishing under different names at different times-or at least to specialize in including or omitting one or other initial or other part of their names on different occasions. Ibis confuses computers (and even human indexers) terribly and is to be discouraged, as authors will end up being indexed separately under every possible version of their names.

***Abstract :*** An abstract in English of preferably no more than 200 words, should precede the text. It should convey the scope of the paper and given as much information as possible. It will normally outline the purpose and methods of the work, and detail important findings and conclusions. (For further information on writing the abstract see Landau & Weiss.) The abstract is not an intrinsic part of the paper it must be intelligible on its own, without reference to the main text. It should enable a reader to decide whether or not to read the paper; it should be suitable for filling and for use by abstracting journals. A good title and abstract help information services to publicize work rapidly and facilitate future retrieval. Title and abstract are the keys to your work-write them accordingly.

*Index Entries :* On a separate page, please list about a dozen items suitable for the subject index of the book.

The indexer, who aims for constancy, may not actually use the author's terms as main entries, since different authors may choose different synonyms for the same object or concept. However, if authors bring terms they consider important to the indexer's attention these items will at least be cross-referenced.

Index entries should not be (but frequently are) confused with keywords, which have a different function.

*Text :* Please ensure that the chapter can be understood by readers from other disciplines. Say how your chapter relates to the subject of the book.

***Headings In Text :*** Please make ranking of headings and sub-headings clear by marking them (in pencil) A,B or C in the margin. Please do not use more than three orders of headings in the text.

***Style of Headings :*** It is useless to explain to authors that (for example) 'bold face caps, centred' will be used for first-order headings, 'bold face, initial cap only, flush left', for second-order headings, and so on Whatever rules are ıaid down, typists and authors mostly insist on underlining capitalized headings (which mean to a printer italic capitals, please-a headland rarely, if ever, used). Authors can, however, easily rank-order headings, though the editor has to check that this has been down properly, and that the various chapters or articles are consistent in this respect, as in others.

***Acknowledgement :*** Group these in a paragraph at the end of the text. Please obtain permission to make the acknowledgement, and approval of the wording, from the person thanked.

It may seem strange to ask authors to obtain permission to make acknowledgements, but it is surprising how often this is refused, or a request made to re-phrase the acknowledgement.

***Tables :*** Tables should be intelligible without reference to the text. Please keep their number and size to a minimum. Large tables are difficult to read and often impossible to print. The tables double-spaced, on separate pages, and number the with Arabic numerals in the order they are referred to in the text. Give each table a brief descriptive title, avoiding abbreviations if possible. Do not rule vertical lines or use ditto signs.

***Illustrations :*** Keep illustrates to a minimum (not more than 10). If previously published illustrations are essential, please obtain the copyright holder's written permission. Please supply glossy photographs in black and white only, unmounted, and of the highest possible quality (a line drawing or a written- description is often preferable to a poor electro-phoretogram or similar photograph). Line drawings, diagrams. Graphs and formulae should be in black ink on heavy white paper or card not larger than 210 x 297 mm (i.e. A4 paper). (Good glossy photographic prints, unmounted and correctly lettered, are also acceptable instead of the original.) Keep lettering on illustrations to a minimum, and have it done professionally (or in pencil on an overlay), making sure that lettering is unbroken and that symbols and abbreviations correspond with those in legend and text. Lettering, axes and curves must be large and clear enough to stand any necessary reduction. Do not use lettering go greatly differing sizes, as all sizes will have to undergo the same percentage reduction. The maximum size of illustrations in the book is 115 x 165 urn, provided that the legend does not exceed 20 words; smaller if the legend is longer. Please keep these proportions in mind when you design the originals. Include scale bars where necessary, or (less desirable) state magnifications of material submitted. Trim off or mask redundant areas of prints and indicate 'Top' in soft pencil on the back. Number illustrations with Arabic numerals in the order they are referred to in the text (and, in the margin of the text, indicate the approximate positions at which you would like to see them inserted eventually). Write your name on the back of every illustration. Type legends consecutively, double-spaced, on a separate page or pages. Please do not place legends on the illustrations themselves. Do not use paperclips on any illustrations.

***References :*** A carefully selected list of references, not an exhaustive one, is desired. Please make sure that all citations in the text appear in the reference list, and vice versa. Names and dates should be used in the text, not numbers, and the reference list should be arranged alphabetically. Do not include unpublished work in the list unless the paper describing it has been accepted for publication; instead, put '(A. B. Smith, personal communications, 1978)' or '(K.S. Jorgensen, unpublished work)' in the text. Please consult Smith or Jorgensen as to the appropriateness, accuracy and acceptability of giving such a citation in the relevant passage.

Form of references. The instructions for references given here are based on the suggestions given in full in Appendix 6.

Unpublished work. The citation of unpublished work which has not been through the fire of refereeing and editing can be misleading. Readers should therefore be alerted as they read the text that an argument using such a citation may rest on shaky ground; they are simultaneously warned that they will be unable to examine the evidence for themselves. Further, when authors are requested to consult the originator of the unpublished work (the, personal communicator') before citing it, they often find that they have mis-numbered or misinterpreted the information or that in has in the meantime proved to be incorrect

Note that the accuracy of references is the author's responsibility. Please check, with the original source if possible, that details are correct and complete, as in the examples given below.

***Citations in the text :*** Use 'Jack & Smith (1977) and Braun et al (1978)' if the authors' names form part of the sentence; otherwise put (Jack & Smith 1977, Braun et al 1978), When there are three or more authors, use the form Braun et al every time. If several papers by the same author(s) published in the same year are cited, put a,b,c, etc. after the year of publication, e.g. smith (1971b).

***The list of reference***

Form

Type double-spaced throughout

order of names

Arrange alphabetically; but arrange papers by three or more authors chronologically (earliest paper first) after all papers by the same first author alone or with one co-author. List all authors of a paper, up to and including six names; if there are seven or more authors, write et al' after giving the first three names, Add a, b, etc. to the date when there are two or more papers by the same author(s) in the same year. List names beginning with 'De', 'Van', etc. under or 'V/v'. etc.

***Order of items :*** Please note punctuation and order of items in these examples:

Abel B C, Cain A D, Adam E. Eve A 1976, Bark thickness in apple trees Tree J 12:90-99.

Bull F, Friend A 1975 Jumping over the moon. In: Jones M, Lloyd P (eds) vol 3:1-24 edn.

Space travel. Galaxy Press, Houston (Soc Space Sci Symp 21)

Zorba A, Quinn A 1976 Bone structure of early Creatans 3rd Elsevier/Excerpta Medica/North-Holland, Amsterdam

That is, give names and initials of up to six authors, year of publication, title of paper or chapter, title of book or abbreviated journal title, volume number (if any), and first and last pages of papers of chapters. For books, add edition number if second or more, editor's name and initials (if there are three or more editors, give the first name and 'et al'), publisher and place of publication, and information (if any) about the series. For journal, omit the issue or part number unless each issue, rather than each volume. Abbreviate journal titles as in the International List of Periodical Title Word Abbreviations (the system used by Chemical Abstracts, Biological Abstracts and Index Medicus).

*Proofs :* You will receive two sets of proofs of our chapter by about 15 June 1980. Further sets of proofs cannot be supplied. Please write essential corrections clearly in ink in the marins of the proofs, with corresponding marks in the body of the text. Answer any queries written in the margins of proofs, if only by writing 'OK as set'. Keep corrections to a minimum and do not add new material. Please make sure that your coauthors (if any) approve of any changes. Please return one set of corrected proofs by I July 1980 to: [name and address]. Failure to do so will result in the chapter being printed without your corrections.

*Reprints :* The publisher will send the principal authors of each chapter 50 free offprints of the chapter when the book is ready. Extra reprints can be ordered from the publisher before the book is printed; an order form with prices will be sent with the proofs.

*Books :* The principal author of one or more chapters (but not the coauthors, if any) will receive a copy of the book as soon as it is published (about mid-September 1980). Contributors may order further copies from the publisher [name and address of Sales Department] at 30% discount on the list price.

*Abbreviations :* Please use abbreviations sparingly, if at all. Abbreviations acceptable in this book are as follows:

(Give the list, in alphabetical order.)

These guidelines can be adapted for conference proceedings and journal articles.

## CHECKLIST FOR MANUSCRIPTS: QUESTIONS AND ACTION ON RECEIPT IN EDITORIAL OFFICE

1. Does the title page include:

   title

   keywords (if requested)

   names of all authors and third affiliations

   running title

   address for correspondence and reprint requests?

2. Is an abstract provided? Is it

   Informative

   intelligible without reference to the text

   suitable for direct use by abstracting services of suitable form and length?

3. Are the pages numbered consecutively? Are they all present?
4. Are all table numbered and present? Are they complete with titles and footnotes to make them intelligible without reference to the text? Are Any of them too large for the format of the book or journal?
5. Are legends for illustrations separately listed?- Are they typed in the correct form?
6. Are all diagrams, graphs and photographs of good quality? Are they all identified in pencil? Do they correspond to the legends?
7. Is there a separate page of references, typed double-spaced in correct form and complete with titles and inclusive pagination?
8. If a second copy of the manuscript has been requested, is it present and complete with respect to items 1-7?

9. If the paper was solicited, does the abstract indicate that the author has dealt with the subjects requested, and does the text—quickly perused—confirm this? Are any ethical problems likely to arise?

10. If anything is missing, or does not follow the guidelines, the paper is best returned to the author immediately with a request for rectification. A copy of the guidelines for authors, marked appropriately, may help to clarify the request.

Note: At the end of the first round of refereeing and editing, items 2, 4, 5 and 6 will have to be reconsidered in the light of the editor's greater familiarity with he manuscript's contents. All the above questions can, however, be adequately judged when a manuscript first arrives, and should be checked before the manuscript is sent to the referees.

## GUIDELINES AND REVIEW FORM FOR REFEREES

Dear

The enclosed manuscript has been submitted for publication in the Journal of Botanical Geology. I would very much appreciate you advice as to its suitability for publication. The enclosed form may be helpful in indicating the kind of advice we are seeking. If you consider the article good, excellent, or outstanding I would appreciate your comments on both major and minor aspects of the paper; otherwise, on major aspects only.

If for any reasons you find yourself unable to review the manuscript within the next two weeks, please return it to me immediately using the return envelope provided. Alternatively, if you can suggest another referee-perhaps a colleague in your department please discuss the possibility with me (by telephone if convenient). Refereeing by a junior colleague must be supervised, and subject to the usually constraints of confidentiality.

Please type any comments you think would be useful to the author(s) on the page provided with the enclosed for and on any continuation sheets as necessary. Harsh phraseology should be avoided. The comments may be singed or unsigned, as you prefer.

Any comments intended for the editor but not for the author(s) should be sent in a covering letter when your reply. Please do not communicate with the author(s) in any way.

The referee's form asks for your assessments of various aspects of the paper. Please tick the appropriate comment—or N/A (not appropriate)—under each number. Use of the form is not obligatory, but the categories listed do indicate criteria the editorial board considers important for acceptance of papers for publication. Please note that we are concerned solely with whether the article is suitable for this journal, not with whether it deserves publication at all. Consequently, journal, policy may dictate that I act contrary to your advice when it comes to a decision. If this happens, I hope you will not be offended; I shall try to given reasons for my decision.

For acceptable papers, we are anxious to improve clarity, succinctness and quality of presentation generally. Your suggestions to this and will be welcome if you have time to offer them in your comments. Please do not write on the manuscript itself, but on a photocopy of it if you wish to go into this degree of detail. Tables and illustrations areas important as text in the quality or presentation. Please also examine the title and abstract critically, with the needs of information retrieval in mind.

We are most grateful for your help.

Yours sincerely,

The Editor

Enc.

The enclosed referee's form might look something like the following sample (drawn up by K. Faegri as the outcome of the Else Working Group on refereeing practices).

***Refereeing Form***

Journal:

Manuscript:

Author(s):

1. Paper
   of general importance
   important in the field of...
   very specialized
   outside m competence-should be submitted to...
2. Information contained
   new
   valuable confirmation
   repetition of known results
3. Technical and experimental methods
   new
   adequate, well controlled
   inadequate, controls insufficient
4. Amount of experimental material and data
   large
   adequate
   small
   insufficient
5. Calculations
   adequate
   erroneous
6. Statistical treatment
   adequate
   erroneous
7. Interpretation
   adequate
   not warranted by data
   suffers from important omission
   suffers from loose generalizing
8. Title
   adequately descriptive
   should be changed (to...)
9. Abstract
   clear and adequate

should be rewritten
missing

10. Language
grammatically good
needs revision

11. Presentation and style
adequate
too brief for clarity
too comprehensive, must be shortened
contain irrelevant material
may cause offence
arrangement unsuitable, should be better sub-divided
do not follow Instructions to authors

12. Illustrations
number and quality adequate
Fig .... may be left out
A figure is desirable to illustrate...
Fig... Need not be in half-tone/a separate plate
Quality of prints/drawings inadequate

13. Tables
adequate
should be rearranged to represent data more clearly
table ... may be left out

14. Abbreviations, formulas, units
conform with accepted standards
do not conform with accepted standards, should be changed
should be explained

15. Literature references
adequate
inadequate
to ... cannot be located

16. The paper is graded as
excellent

good acceptable

sound, but dull

confirmatory

significance not obvious

weak

too speculative

too preliminary

outside the scope of the periodical, might tube suitable for... and

deserves urgent publication

is acceptable with minor/extensive revisions as indicated

is not acceptable (conditional/unconditional)

17. Further information necessary before decision
18. Comments

# Bibliography

Akbar S. Khan, *Media Ethics,* Peacock Publication, Singapore, 2004

Altschull, J.H.: *Agents of Power: the Role of the News Media in Human Affairs,* Longman, New York, 1984.

Berelson, B.: *Content Analysis in Communication Research,* Free Press, Glencoe, Illinois, 1952.

Blumer, J.G. and McQuail, D.: *Television in Politics: Its Uses and Influence,* Fabes, London, 1968.

Chaney, D.: *Processes of Mass Communication,* Macmillan, London, 1972.

Cohen, S. and Young, J. : *The Manufacture of News,* Constable, London, 1973.

Davison, W. Phillips : *Mass Communication Research: Major Issues and Future Directions,* Praeger, New York, 1974.

Deutsch, K.V.: *Nationalism and Social Communication,* MIT Press, Cambridge, 1966.

Eaman, Ross A.: *The Media Society: Basic Issues and Controversies,* Butterworths, Toronto and Vancouver, 1987.

Fiske, J.: *Introduction to Communication Studies,* Methuen, London, 1982.

Gurvitch, M., Bennet, T. and Woollacott, J. : *Culture, Society and Mass Media,* Methuen, London, 1982.

Hovland, C.I., Lunsdane, A. and Sheffield, F.: *Experiments in Mass Communication,* Princeton University Press, Princeton, 1950.

Innis, Harold Adams: *Empire and Communication* : University of Toronto Press, Toronto, 1972.

Katz, E. and Szecsko, T. : *Mass Media and Social Change,* Sage Publications, Beverly Hills and London, 1981.

Lang, K. and Lang, G.E.: *Collective Dynamics,* Cornwell, New York, 1961.

McQuail, D.: *Towards a Sociology of Mass Communication,* Collier Macmillan, London, 1969.

Mendelbaum, S.J.: *Community and Communicating,* Norton, New York, 1972.

Nettle, J.P.: *Political Mobilization—A Sociological Analysis of Methods and Concepts,* Faber and Faber, London, 1967.

Peterson, R.C. et al.: *The Mass Media and Modern Society,* Holt, Rnehart and Winston, New York, 1965.

Schramm, Wilbur: *Mass Media and National Development,* Stanford University Press, Paris: UNESCO, 1964.

Singh, Yogendra: *Modernization of Indian Tradition,* Rawat, Jaipur, 1988.

Szalai, A. : *The United Nations and the News Media,* UNITAR, New York, 1972.

Trenaman, J.S.M.: *Communication and Comprehension,* Longman, London, 1967.

Verma, M.M.: *Gandhi's Technique of Mass Mobilization,* R.K. Gupta and Company, New Delhi, 1990.

Wilkinson, T.S. and Bhandarkar, P.L.: *Methodology and Techniques of Social Research,* Himalaya, Bombay, 1987.

Zaina, A. Michael : *Codes for Media,* Rashmi Publications, Chennai, 2002.